"An informative, funny and provocative analysis of one of the most elusive and prized qualities of human sexuality . . . Blank has no shortage of fascinating facts . . . Blank also has a pleasing, highly readable style that allows her to convey large amounts of information with wit and agility . . . Thoroughly researched, carefully argued and written with a sly sense of humor, this is a bright addition to the popular literature of women's and cultural studies."

—*Publishers Weekly* (starred review)

"Hanne Blank's *Virgin* is a magisterial work of impeccable scholarship and an absolutely riveting read. Blank's assured command of a range of diverse materials ranging over centuries never fails as she weaves these into a compelling narrative demonstrating the historical and contemporary significance of ideas about virginity, in contrast to the elusiveness of its reliable physical identification. This book is an important event in the history of gender, sexuality and the body, as well as having remarkable relevance to current issues."

—Dr. Lesley A. Hall, senior archivist, Wellcome Library for the
History and Understanding of Medicine, London

"Her survey is engrossing and informative . . . she's willing to do research both in the stacks of law libraries and in the back shelves of video stores."

—*New York Observer*

"Blank's revealing history of virginity begins with discoveries related to women's bodies over time, then quickly moves on to a fascinating analysis of the roles economics, religion, and urbanization have played in the changing attitudes toward virginity. From the Roman Empire to the Jazz Age and beyond, with appearances by Jesus, Elizabeth I, Samuel Pepys, and Alfred Kinsey, this is a rich history indeed."

—*Booklist*

continued . . .

VIRGIN

The Untouched History

HANNE BLANK

BLOOMSBURY

Published by Bloomsbury USA, New York
Distributed to the trade by Macmillan

All papers used by Bloomsbury USA are natural, recyclable products made from wood grown in well-managed forests. The manufacturing processes conform to the environmental regulations of the country of origin.

THE LIBRARY OF CONGRESS HAS CATALOGED THE HARDCOVER EDITION AS FOLLOWS:

Blank, Hanne.
Virgin : the untouched history / Hanne Blank.—1st U.S. ed.
p.   cm.
Includes bibliographical references and index.
ISBN-13: 978-1-59691-010-2 (alk. paper) (hardcover)
ISBN-10: 1-59691-010-0 (alk. paper) (hardcover)
1. Virginity—Social aspects.   2. Virginity—History.   I. Title.

GN484.47B53   2007
306.4—dc22
2006017172

First published by Bloomsbury USA in 2007
This paperback edition published in 2008

Paperback ISBN-10: 1-59691-011-9
ISBN-13: 978-1-59691-011-9

1 3 5 7 9 10 8 6 4 2

Typeset by Westchester Book Group
Printed in the United States of America by Quebecor World Fairfield

For my mother Shanna Spalding,
my mother's mother Ruth West Spalding,
Elizabeth Tamny, Heather Corinna, Leigh Ann Craig,
and for each and every virgin, everywhere.

CONTENTS

EXTRA VIRGIN: A NOTE TO READERS

As I worked on this book, I joked with friends that I was going to give it the subtitle Everything You Think You Know About Virginity Is Wrong. Like many people, and perhaps like you yourself, I blithely believed when I began this work that I already knew what there was to know about what I then considered to be a trivial topic. Surely, I thought, my academic and professional work in women's and gender studies and in the field of human sexuality had already told me everything one might need to know about virginity.

How very wrong I was. From the day that I first wandered into Harvard's Countway Medical Library—spurred by the questions of some adolescents with whom I was working as a sex educator—to look up medical definitions of virginity, my assumptions have been repeatedly uprooted, my expectations confounded, and my prejudices smashed to smithereens. I was vexed to discover that most of the medical textbooks I was looking through didn't even bother to discuss virginity, and those that did rarely seemed to define it. I was also astonished and utterly enthralled by the idea that I had stumbled across a subject clearly related to the human body, one whose existence and importance has been asserted for thousands of years, and yet it appeared, somehow, to have left virtually no trace in the modern medical literature.

I continued to search. A few months later, I conjectured that it was possible there simply was not much to be known about virginity and virgins. I was finding little enough that was relevant, and nothing at all remotely like the comprehensive overview of the subject I was hoping to find. Even though my interests were limited to virginity and virgins in the Western world, it was rapidly becoming obvious to me that if I wanted to read a comprehensive survey of virginity, I was going to have to write it. Given the slim pickings on the library shelves in my initial research, I figured the job wouldn't be too difficult.

On this score, too, I was proven laughably wrong. I began to read the work of a lonely handful of scholars, primarily literary and religious historians, who had looked at questions of virginity during the medieval and Renaissance eras. Their books and articles, without which this book could never have come to be, instantly became my beacons and touchstones. But every time I turned a page of this slender pile of scholarship, I seemed to have several dozen new questions. I rapidly realized that the reason the book I wanted didn't exist wasn't that there wasn't enough information to fill it, but rather that the topic has long been neglected. The information is scattered across numerous fields and disciplines, completely disorganized, and often tricky to find. Virginity's very nature—socially, religiously, physically, and otherwise—means that it has often been a taboo, uncertain, and sometimes deliberately obscured subject.

Answering my questions about the history and nature of virginity became a task that occupied the better part of four years of my life. It led me on a wildly interdisciplinary scavenger hunt that encompassed specialty libraries in law, medicine, and art; humanities research collections; archives; interviews; museum collections; Internet Web sites; and mountainous piles of government documents from several different countries. I found myself visiting "adult" bookstores to scrutinize their virginity porn offerings and standing in grimy inner-city parking lots taking pictures of pro-virginity billboards. In hot pursuit of information I couldn't find elsewhere, I learned to negotiate (sometimes torturously) sources written not only in foreign languages that I knew how to read, but also in others—Greek, Portuguese, Swedish—that I did not. Swiftly I learned that regardless of the source or when it was written, information relating to virginity is rarely presented in such a way that it is free of bias, superstition, or simply the kind of inaccuracies that often sneak into even academic books under the guise of "things everybody knows." Separating the data from the digressions added its own complications to my work.

My problem, in the end, was not that there was too little information available on virgins and virginity, but too much. To make navigating these sometimes overwhelmingly dense waters a little easier for the reader, I have divided this book into two parts. The first, Virginology, centers on the medical and scientific sides of virginity, while Virgin Culture, the second part, deals with virginity in society and culture. Although I have worked hard to make *Virgin: The Untouched History* as inclusive as possible, no single book on the subject can provide a completely comprehensive treatment of this vast subject. Each chapter of this book could easily be a complete book on its own . . . and, in some cases, several books. If a favorite bit of virginity trivia fails to appear in these pages, or if specific questions about virgins and virginity are not answered here, it's likely not because I haven't encountered said trivia or looked into the same questions myself, but rather because neither I nor my hardworking editors could find a way to make everything fit. Exponentially more information on virginity and virgins exists than I have been able to detail, and much more remains to be found. For the reader who would like to expand his or her experience of this book, however, some of the excerpted material is available on the Internet at VirginBook.org.

What you read there, and between these covers as well, may confuse, distress, and surprise you. Indeed, I hope that it does. Numerous times during my research I found myself cackling at some ridiculous bit of virginity trivia or other, but I was just as likely to end up recoiling in horror, weeping with sorrow and sympathy, or outraged at yet another example of misogynist cruelty justified in the name of virginity. Even more frequently than that, however, I found myself surprised: at the things that hadn't changed in millennia; at the things that had only changed during my own lifetime; at the unsubstantiated projection that often passes for truth where virginity is concerned; and most of all at the things that I'd been told were true that turned out to be demonstrably false. As I mentioned at the beginning of this preface, the subtitle really should, in many ways, have been Everything You Thought You Knew About Virginity Is Wrong.

This book is about much more than cocktail party virginity trivia. It is about something that is ancient and abstract at the same time as it is absolutely contemporary and utterly intimate. Virginity has been, and continues to be, a matter of life and death around the world, very much including within the first world. Virginity is the butt of innumerable jokes, the subject of timeless art, the center of spiritual mysteries, a locus of teenage angst, a popular genre for pornography, and the nucleus around which one of the world's most powerful governments has created unprecedented policy. For all these reasons, and many more, I am honored to be at the helm for this maiden voyage into a fascinating untouched history.

PART I

Virginology

This idol which you term virginity
Is neither essence subject to the eye,
No, nor to any one exterior sense,
Nor hath it any place of residence,
Nor is't of earth or mould celestial,
Or capable of any form at all.
Of that which hath no being, do not boast;
Things that are not at all, are never lost.

—Christopher Marlowe,
Hero and Leander (1598)

CHAPTER 1

Like a Virgin?

It is easy enough to be certain. One has only to be sufficiently vague.
—Charles Sanders Peirce

B Y ANY MATERIAL RECKONING, virginity does not exist. It can't be weighed on a scale, sniffed out like a truffle or a smuggled bundle of cocaine, retrieved from the lost-and-found, or photographed for posterity. Like justice or mercy, we can only determine that it exists at all because of the presence of its effects—or its side effects. Unlike many of our habits and practices, virginity reflects no known biological imperative and grants no demonstrable evolutionary advantage, nor has being able to recognize it in others been shown to increase anyone's chances of reproduction or survival. Perhaps this is why even our nearest animal relatives, whose sexual behavior and social structures are often startlingly similar to our own in other respects, show no signs at all of knowing what virginity is.

Virginity is as distinctively human a notion as philanthropy. We invented it. We developed it. We disseminated the idea throughout our cultures, religions, legal systems, bodies of art, and works of scientific knowledge. We have fixed it as an integral part of how we experience our own bodies and selves. And we have done all this without actually being able to define it consistently, identify it accurately, or explain how or why it works.

How *do* we define virginity? How have we defined it in the past? How do we tell who is and isn't a virgin? How do we know what virginity is and does and means? These questions, so basic to a book like this one, tempt even the most thoughtful of us in the direction of snap judgments and pat answers. We live in a culture that does not appreciate ambiguity when it comes to either sexuality or morality, after all, and virginity is inextricably twined with both.

As adolescents, we learn that there is a right answer and a wrong answer to the question, "are you a virgin?" What the right answer *is* might well depend on who asks us and under what circumstances. The reputations we want to achieve for ourselves often trump literal truth when we talk about sex, and the realm of virginity is no exception. No matter the circumstances, though, we never really conceive of there being more than two possible answers to the virginity question. It is, we are taught, a solid-state thing, on or off, yes or no. We operate under the assumption that those two options are not only adequate to the task of identifying this particular status, but that everyone who uses them means the same thing. But as many of us have discovered, this is far from the case. Real life is too full of messy and confusing variables. Exceptions are inevitable: What if he only put it in a little bit? What if she didn't bleed? The gray area is vast, yet when the question is *are you a virgin?* "maybe" isn't usually an option. Any uncertainty is your own private problem and frequently your own private hell. After all, as virtually all of us learn growing up, "everyone knows" what virginity is.

In truth, however, everyone most assuredly does not know what makes one person a virgin and another person not one. Virtually no one does, as a matter of fact. And this state of affairs is nothing new.

For as long as we have had a notion of virginity at all, its parameters have been controversial and, as often as not, vague. Even in pre-Christian Greek writings, there is already a tendency to talk about virginity metaphorically and in imprecise, gestural terms. Depending on the context and the writer, Greek virginity might have been described as an object that is subject to seizure (*lambanein*), a value that must be respected (*terein*), or a covered or wrapped thing that must be unwrapped or unbound (*lyein*). Depending on circumstances and on what an author had to say about it, virginity could be metaphorical, abstract, or physical, imposed from without or inspired from within, guarded or stolen, covered or unbound.

Christianity, despite what people often assume, failed to provide much in the way of clarification. Even the most august of the Doctors of the Church have not quite agreed on just how virginity should be defined or how virgins should be treated, and their virginity debates have smoldered for millennia. For thirteenth-century theologian Thomas Aquinas, for example, virginity was a particular quality of the virtue of temperance and a subset of the class of behaviors that bore the label of "chastity." But Aquinas also said that chastity had both a specific and a metaphorical meaning, one relating specifically to the pleasures of sex and the other much broader, a *spiritualis castitas*, or spiritual chastity, that dealt with the refusal to enjoy things that were judged to be against God's design. It hardly seems a realm in which yes-or-no answers would suffice.

Neither have literature or medicine simplified things. Three hundred years after Aquinas, sixteenth-century writer Thomas Bentley's *The Monument of Matrones, conteining seven severall Laumps of Virginitie* defined virginity with a laundry list of behaviors, including "sobernes, silence, shamefastnes, and chasti-tie, both of bodie & mind." And although physician Helkiah Crooke, writing less than fifty years after Bentley, argued vehemently that "the only sure note of unsteyned virginity" was the newly discovered vaginal hymen, even he was un-sure. In almost the same breath as he lauds the diagnostic value of the hymen, he offers an alternate test for virginity that involves measuring the head with a piece of string.

Things haven't gotten any simpler since then. In 1992 legendary syndicated advice column "Dear Abby" was asked to pass judgment on the virginity of a young woman who gave birth, as a host mother, to a baby conceived through in vitro fertilization. (Abby's verdict: since the host mother had never experienced intercourse, she was entitled to call herself a virgin.) Recently, several studies completed in the 1990s and early 2000s indicated that young people are deeply divided over whether oral sex or anal intercourse constitute "having sex," calling into question just who might be qualified to call himself or herself a virgin.

Virginity has a long and distinguished heritage in Western culture, but it has no single hallowed and unassailable standard. "Everybody" most certainly does *not* know what it is and how it works. No one ever truly has. Anyone who claims otherwise simply hasn't done enough reading.

What we mean when we say "virginity" is as ephemeral, as relative, and as socially determined as what we mean when we say "freedom." Like love or misery, virginity has its trappings. We associate particular physical phenomena with it, we have a set of conditions and sensations that we expect from it, both in others and in ourselves. We tend to feel gratified when these things happen and confused, even betrayed, when they don't. As with piety and sensuality, we often believe that virginity tells us something about a person's morality, character, and spirituality. We claim that virginity is tangible, part of the physical body, just like a beautiful face or a powerful muscle, but just as we acknowledge inner strength and beauty that cannot be seen with the eye, we also accept that virginity transcends mere flesh.

The broadest and most general way to define virginity—since a book on the topic does raise the question—would be to say that virginity is a human sexual status that is characterized by a lack of any current or prior sexual interaction with others. But this raises its own questions in turn. What counts as "sexual interaction"? Whose standards do we apply, and do we apply them identically to every person and in every circumstance? Do we judge women's virginity by the same standards as men's, children's by the same standards as adults', a Christian's by the same standards as an atheist's, a Jew's, a modern-day Pagan's, a Muslim's, a Buddhist's?

Those of us who consider ourselves to be nonvirgins can usually explain why. Those of us who consider ourselves still-virgin can typically articulate what would have to happen to change that status. We usually know what criteria we would employ if asked to determine whether someone else's virginal status had changed. But the criteria we might apply to someone else are not necessarily identical to the ones we apply to ourselves. Moreover, we do not necessarily know that our next-door neighbors' criteria, or even those of our partners or parents, would be identical to our own.

This isn't to say that virginity is relative and therefore irrelevant. To the contrary, we have more than two and a half millennia of written history that make it abundantly clear that virginity is relative and therefore *immensely* relevant. It is precisely its relativity that makes virginity so troublesome and so fascinating.

Virginity has not always served the same purposes in society, been experienced in the same ways, or been predicated on the same understandings of sexuality, sexual activity, or sexual identity. It hasn't even always had to do with the same body parts: the hymen, which we often think of as synonymous with virginity today and assume must have been so for our ancestors, too, wasn't even confirmed to exist until the sixteenth century. From law to religion to medicine to art and beyond, the variety of ways we have understood, defined, and used virginity over the course of Western history reflects the shapes and motions of the giant, constantly changing entity that is our common culture.

This helps explain why we're so bad at defining it. As one of the large-scale background conditions of human life and human sexuality, our ideals in regard to virginity, like those in regard to gender and class and race, have always depended on historical circumstance. As cultural circumstances have shifted, our thinking about virginity has shifted, too, changing slowly and often subtly over time to reflect changes in demographics, economics, technologies, religious dogmas, political philosophies, scientific discoveries, and attitudes about the roles of women, children, and the family. Because these things tend to change so slowly, it is common for people to see them as unchanging, monolithic givens, things that existed before they were born and which will continue to exist, substantially unchanged, long after their deaths. Frequently this is even true, since large-scale cultural change tends to happen at a pace that, by comparison to human life spans, seems downright glacial. But even the largest and slowest-moving glacier cuts grooves into the earth as it goes, leaving a trail behind it.

To trace the changing ideologies and operations of virginity, then, we follow the tracks of cultural glaciers. The secrets of virginity are not coded into our DNA or even etched in stone. Insofar as they exist at all, they exist in novels and plays, religious writings and works of art, medical texts and philosophical tomes, courtship patterns, wedding traditions, the oral literature of old wives' tales and barroom ballads, and even the syndicated columns of daily newspapers. It is an enormous, dazzling, confusing array.

Perhaps the easiest way to demonstrate this is to take a historical overview of a few of virginity's many varieties. In everyday early-twenty-first-century conversation we tend to think of virginity in one way only: a matter of sexual activity. Either one has "done it" or not. While the nature of that critical "it" may come under considerable debate, it is not controversial to view virginity and its loss as being a matter of having done "it" or not, whatever "it" is construed to be. But this is only one way to think about virginity.

In his fourth-century *De civitate Dei* (*The City of God*), Saint Augustine argued that being raped did not constitute a loss of virginity, providing one had resisted with all one's heart and soul. Augustine's reasoning? If virginity could be said to be irrevocably lost by forcible physical action, then it could hardly be claimed to be an attribute of the soul. Augustine's solution was to define virginity as existing in two valid forms, a physical virginity based in the body and a spiritual one based in the soul. Depending on circumstances, these two forms might coexist or not. As for Thomas Aquinas later on, there was not a single virginity for Augustine, but more than one.

The idea of multiple virginities has been quite popular. Thirteenth-century philosopher and scientist Albertus Magnus, who wrote a treatise on chastity around 1240, discussed four distinct types of virginity. Infants who had not yet reached the age of reason possessed innate virginity. Once a person was old enough to know what they were doing, however, a virgin had to choose virginity. One could choose virginity as part of a religious vow, or a less formal virginity that was not vowed. Finally, Albertus noted with disapproval, there were virgins who didn't look or act like virgins. Virgins might, he wrote, even act like prostitutes. For Albertus, then, virginity *might* be an inborn quality, or it could be a rather wide range of other things. It certainly wasn't something one could tell at a glance.

Far from being a monolithic, universal, ahistorical given of the human condition, virginity is a profoundly changeable and malleable cultural idea with an enormous, vital, and mostly hidden history. If we are to attempt to understand virginity, we have to understand not only what it seems to be to us today, but what it has been to our ancestors. We have to understand not just the meanings we might want it to have for our children but the meanings it has had for us, for our grandparents, and for their great-great-great-grandparents. Most of all, we have to understand that these meanings have not always been the same. With virginity as with so much else that pertains to the human condition, the only real constant is change.

Lines in the Sand

We have long recognized that virginities and virgins come in a range of modes and types. We distinguish between them not only by what they've done or haven't in sexual terms, but also on the basis of age, developmental stage, sex, motivations, prior behavior, religious affiliation, and even physical appearance. But not all of these aspects matter equally, and not all of them matter in the same way or to the same degree at any given time in history, place in the world, or subculture within the vast and complicated framework of what we loosely call the West.

Because of this, the question of who gets to define what virgins are and what virginity is matters enormously. Defining virginity means directly affecting the lives of nearly all women, and many men as well. Despite what some people appear to think, defining virginity is not merely a philosophical exercise. It is an exercise in controlling how people behave, feel, and think, and in some cases, whether they live or die.

Virginity has been used as an organizing principle of human cultures for millennia. In the present as well as the past, any woman who trespasses against what her era, religion, community, or family holds as constituting virginity might be teased, harassed, shamed, ostracized, prohibited from marrying, or disowned. In some places and at some times her family might have been fined or punished because of it, or the woman herself might have been sold into slavery. She could be imprisoned, maimed, mutilated, flogged, raped, or even killed as punishment for losing her virginity . . . or even if it was merely believed that she had done so. And lest such humiliations and so-called honor crimes seem the province only of faraway countries with oppressive or backward religious views about women, or insular immigrant communities that adhere to outdated traditions, it bears remembering that twelve-year-old Birmingham, Alabama, schoolgirl Jasmine Archie was murdered by her mother in November 2004—forced to drink bleach, then asphyxiated—because Jasmine's mother believed that the girl had lost her virginity.

Because the stakes can be so high, it is doubly important to recognize that virginity does not truly have any single ironclad definition and never has. In practical terms, virginity is usually defined through a complicated kaleidoscope of partial definitions, and almost always backward and by exclusion: we define virginity by deciding what terminates it, what virginity is not. No matter how we try, though, it seems that there is always some lingering question, exception, or circumstance that renders even the best definition less than watertight.

Straight White Female

One of the things we learn from looking at history's multiple virginities is that virginity is not necessarily about not having sex. At the same time, across history and cultures, the lowest common denominator of virginity—or rather *loss* of virginity—has, for countless centuries, been the insertion of a penis into a vagina.

This particular juxtaposition of body parts certainly may occur in the context of what we call "having sex." But so may a lot of other anatomical arrangements. Many different body parts—fingers, lips, breasts, tongues, anuses, etc.—might be involved in activities we consider to be "sex." Works of art and literature dating back centuries before the dawn of Christianity attest that none of these variegated techniques, whether they be performed between men, between women, or between a woman and a man, can be remotely construed as modern innovations. Sexual activity has always encompassed a great deal more than just penises and vaginas.

Why, then, we might wonder, is it the particular combination of a penis and a vagina that has for so long been considered the definitive sex act, the act that terminates virginity? There are several reasons. For one, the only form of sexual activity that renders women pregnant is that which involves inserting a penis into a vagina. Second, penis-in-vagina intercourse is the single uniquely heterosexual act of which human beings are capable. The other common sexual permutations of body parts of which humans are capable are essentially gender-neutral. Kisses and caresses know no gender, to say nothing of oral sex. For a penis to be inserted into a vagina, on the other hand, there can be only one man and one woman, and furthermore they must be performing the single specific action that cannot be performed by a man on another man or by a woman on another woman. What this means is that virginity, at least in the classical, canonical form, is exclusively heterosexual.

Virginity is also female. The male body has never commonly been labeled as being virginal even when it is, but rather as "continent" or "celibate"; even within the Catholic church, male renunciation of sex has been characterized as a matter of continence, not virginity. Additionally, virginity has never mattered in regard to the way men are valued, or whether they were considered fit to marry or, indeed, to be permitted to survive. As a result, virgins are, and always have been, almost uniformly female. The very word "virgin" comes from the Latin *virgo*, meaning a girl or never-married woman (the two were basically synonymous in the culture of ancient Rome, where girls were commonly married off in early puberty), as opposed to *uxor*, a woman or wife. Similar linguistic shorthand exists in many other languages: *parthenos* (girl/virgin) and *gyne* (woman/wife) in Greek, *betulah* and *almah* in Hebrew, "maid" and "wife" in a slightly antiquated English. Even today, "virgin" tends to mean female unless stated otherwise.

In the West, virginity not only has a sexual orientation and a gender, it has a color. Christian symbology traditionally uses light and lightness of color to indicate purity and holiness, while darkness and darker colors are associated with sin and corruption. When European white Christians began to colonize parts of the world where people had darker skins, they often took this light-equals-good/dark-equals-bad mentality with them. Because the sexual rules of these darker-skinned people's supposedly "primitive" cultures failed to map neatly onto what European Christians had come to expect as normal, natural, and indeed God-given laws regarding gender, sex, and the organization of families, European whites often assumed that the indigenous peoples of Africa, the Americas, and elsewhere were simply wicked and lacking any sense of sexual morality. From such encounters, Europeans frequently derived the belief that virginity was an attribute of being civilized, which was to say Christian, European, and white.

All these things are part of how we in the West understand virginity to exist and function even today. They are part of our virgin heritage. Our way of thinking about virginity and virgins has been changing quite a bit in the past century or so, but much of the age-old ideological paradigm we have inherited in regard to virgins and virginity remains sturdy and strong. The case of Rosie Reid provides an excellent demonstration of the slow and mixed ways that change comes to the ideology of virginity. When the eighteen-year-old University of Bristol student created a scandal in 2004 by deciding to sell her virginity to the highest bidder in an online auction to help pay her educational expenses, neither she, the men who rushed to place bids, nor the numerous news organizations that covered the story seemed to find it at all incongruous that Ms. Reid billed herself as a virgin while simultaneously making it clear that she was a lesbian involved in a long-term sexual and romantic relationship with another woman.

It did not seem to occur to anyone reporting on Reid's story that perhaps her virginity was already a thing of the past. There was no discussion of whether Reid and her lover might have engaged in vaginally penetrative sex using fingers or sex toys, as hundreds of thousands of women who have sex with women have done throughout history. The condition of Reid's hymen, so often considered a definitive parameter of virginity in our materialist and medically oriented age, was never brought under question in news reports. Whether her body had ever been "opened" did not seem to be on anyone's mind at all, although it would have been very much on the minds of the Greeks. Nor did anyone care whether Reid had ever experienced either sexual desire or orgasm, both of which would have mattered greatly to medieval theologians and physicians.

Instead, an authoritative silence told the world that Reid's lesbian sexual experience was not considered valid. All that mattered to either the journalists or the many men who placed bids in the hopes of gaining one-time sexual access to Reid was that she had never been penetrated by a penis. The sum total of what defined virginity in Rosie Reid's story was the insertion of a penis into a vagina, an exclusively heterosexual action performed by a biological male on a biological female. What Reid sold, and the ultimate winner of the auction purchased, was nothing more or less than a tangible confirmation of the ideology that a woman is not sexually "real" in her own right, and that it takes a man and his penis to make her so.

Virginal Variety

Rosie Reid's case raises many fascinating questions, not the least of which is how we might characterize the variety of virginity she, as a sexually active lesbian, might have represented. If we accept that Ms. Reid was in fact a virgin prior to the successful sale of her virginity (having paid €12,000—roughly $14,500—for her maidenhead, we can at least assume that the man in question believed she had one to sell), what kind of virgin was she?

To paraphrase P. T. Barnum, there's a virgin born every minute. But not all virgins are alike. No matter how much stock we put in the whole canonical penis-in-vagina factor, we are extremely unlikely to perceive Rosie Reid's virginity as being the same as the virginity of a nun, an eleven-year-old girl, a thirty-year-old career woman, or an elderly maiden aunt. Just as Albertus Magnus did in the thirteenth century, we also notice and acknowledge that virginities and virgins come in different types and modes. Strangely, though, although we have been recognizing different types of virginity and virgins since at least the second century C.E., we have developed precious little terminology with which to describe the variety we perceive.

The only phrase the West generally uses in this capacity is the nineteenth-century French term *demi-vierge*, which roughly translates to "half-virgin." Currently we might, at least in the United States, use the term "technical virgin" to mean more or less the same thing, someone whose life has not been entirely devoid of sexual experience, but who retains some claim to the virgin title by virtue of not having yet crossed some particular experiential threshold, typically the penis-in-vagina one. The *demi-vierge* or technical virgin, though, accounts for only one of the possible types of virginity. For many others, we have no words at all.

This odd lack of vocabulary speaks volumes. We no longer live in a society in which the most important thing one could know about a woman was whether or not she was owned by her father—unmarried and presumably virginal—or by a husband, and thus presumably nonvirgin. But our culture has been profoundly concerned with just those things for most of its history, and it shows. The minimalist vocabulary we've inherited in regard to virginity, and the limits it puts on our ability to discuss virginity and virgins, is a legacy of past priorities.

This does not stop us, however, from recognizing that different sorts of virgins and virginities exist. At a minimum, Western culture today recognizes four major modes of virginity, with every individual example of a given mode constituting inevitable variations on the theme. The first, default virginity, parallels the first class given by the estimable Albertus Magnus: we are all born virgins. Children's lack of active sexuality is expected and taken for granted, so much so that we find it odd to refer to children as specifically being virgins. They are, as Carl Jung put it, presexual. Despite evidence that some aspects of active genital behavior begin quite early (many children self-stimulate their genitals; fetuses have even been observed stimulating their own genitals while still in utero, thanks to ultrasound technology), we still think of prepubescent children as not yet being sexual beings.

But eventually adolescence hits, and with it come flash floods of sex hormones, the fast-growing shrubbery of facial and pubic hair, the dangerous curves of breasts and hips, and the unmistakably messy evidence of fertility signaled by first ejaculations and menstrual periods. When the body becomes physiologically sexually mature, we lose the luxury of imagining that the individual is not a sexual entity. This is the point where virginity really begins to count for something.

The most common postadolescent form virginity takes rests on the assumption that eventually, people will become players in the game of sex, and specifically that they will take part in the enormous generational work of creating new families and bearing children. For if this is to happen, virginity cannot be perpetual, but only transitional. This is precisely what virginity is for most people, a transitional state that bridges the end of childhood and the assumption of full social adulthood, a passage that has often been embodied by marriage.

Transitional virginity has not always been the most highly regarded form of virginity in the West—under Christianity, in fact, it took a distant backseat to the vowed virginity of nuns and monks until after the Protestant Reformation—but it has always been the commonest one. The average ages at which people have married have varied widely over the course of human history. Although there have been certain periods of time over the last 2,500 years during which it has been common for at least some women not to marry until they were over twenty, it has been more common for women to be married off as adolescents, often very close to the time they begin to menstruate.

Child betrothals and adolescent marriages are a source for scandal in the West today—an Associated Press report of the tumultuous 2003 wedding of twelve-year-old Ana Maria Cioaba, daughter of the self-proclaimed king of the Romanian branch of the Roma people, generated shocked responses in the news media—but were quite normal for much of our history. Catherine of Aragon was betrothed at age three to Arthur, son of Henry VII of England, and married to him when she was fifteen. Shakespeare's Juliet, all of thirteen years old, is advised by her mother to "think of marriage now; younger than you, here in Verona, ladies of esteem are made already mothers: by my count, I was your mother much upon these years that you are now a maid." Even today, when average ages at first marriage hover in the mid to late twenties,* matches where a premium is placed on the bride's virginity, like the first marriage of the heir to a throne, often feature a relatively youthful bride. The late

---

*The 2001 U.S. Census indicated that the average first-time American bride was twenty-five years old and her groom twenty-six; in the United Kingdom, the average ages were higher, twenty-eight and thirty respectively. Throughout the West, first marriages taking place in the second half of the twenties are increasingly the rule.

Lady Diana Spencer was a fresh-faced nineteen-year-old in 1981 when she became engaged to marry thirty-two-year-old Prince Charles of England; by the time they married and she became Princess of Wales, she had been twenty for all of twenty-eight days.

As average ages of first marriage for women have varied, the lengths of time that the average woman would have been expected to maintain her transitional virginity have varied, too. Today, with women's ages at first marriages greater than they have ever been, a Western woman who maintains her virginity until she marries can probably, if she marries at the average age for her peer group, expect to sustain anywhere from ten to twenty years of transitional virginity between the time she reaches puberty and the time she marries. When we consider that even the vestal virgins were only expected to maintain their virginity for thirty years, from the time they were consecrated at age six until they finished their term of service at the age of thirty-six, it puts such modern-day commitments to premarital virginity into a most intriguing perspective.

Then again, a modern Western woman may choose not to maintain her virginity until marriage at all. This option has only quite recently—within the last thirty years or so—become widely acceptable. Even so, nonmarital and premarital sex has still by no means received a universal seal of approval, and many socially conservative groups and religious bodies continue to condemn it. Even the U.S. federal government, despite a long history of not having national policies concerning sexuality (sex-related law is formulated and enforced primarily at the state level in the United States), has in recent years come down forcefully and paternalistically in favor of the old-fashioned ideology of transitional virginity, which holds that any premarital sexual activity is wrong. Beginning in 1996 big-budget federal initiatives to promote and enforce the teaching of what is euphemistically called "abstinence-based sex education"—curricula that teach that virginity is the only appropriate sexual status for unmarried people—have inserted a vociferously pro-transitional-virginity agenda into the curricula of U.S. public schools. This stunning backlash against changing virginity expectations, and the odd and telling isolation in which the United States pursues it, is proof positive that a culture's approaches to virginity may be more emotional and political than anything else.

Because transitional virginity's end has long been linked with social adulthood, and social adulthood has long been linked to marriage, we have developed an abbreviated ideology of virginity that equates virginity with childhood and loss of virginity with adulthood. But it is, of course, possible to be both an adult and a virgin. Indeed, for roughly the last seventeen centuries, countless thousands of adult women and men have maintained lifelong virginity within the burgeoning monastic institutions of the Roman Catholic Church. Although the Reformation permanently destroyed monasticism's ubiquity and prestige, and even though the numbers of those pursuing monastic vocations have dwindled precipitously over the last century, the abstract and the reality of vowed virginity is still with us today.

Perhaps ironically, most of the vows we think of as being vows of virginity in the context of Roman Catholicism are actually vows of celibacy. Priests, nuns, and monks need not necessarily be virgins in order to be admitted to vows of celibacy, although traditionally nuns have been referred to both as "vowed virgins" and as "brides of the Church," and entering the convent has, until relatively recently, been the only means by which a woman could be guaranteed permission to preserve her virginity in perpetuity. However, it remains true that while celibacy is a required element of maintaining virginity, virginity is not a required element of maintaining celibacy.

The Church does have a vocation for women who are specifically and exclusively virgins. It is not a common or well-known office, and it is not part of any monastic order. The Rite for the Consecration of Virgins Living in the World has been available to Catholic women only since May 31, 1970, although it has precedents dating from the earliest years of the Church. The few thousand women worldwide who have consecrated their virginity to God through this rite do not take vows. Instead, they are understood to have already promised their virginity to God privately, as a personal commitment. They wear no habit, follow no holy orders or monastic rule, live on their own, and practice whatever secular professions they please. These vowed virgins of the contemporary Church, in other words, are likely to fly well under the radar of most of the people they encounter in their daily lives. Aside from being single and devotedly Catholic, there is little to distinguish them from any other woman on the street.

Considered from a historical perspective it is startling that any woman can, in effect, be a "stealth" consecrated virgin. In the past the exemption from the roles of wife and mother always made vowed virgins extremely visible exceptions to a nearly universal rule. The ideology of spiritualized virginity holds that a body that is closed to the demands of sexuality and reproduction is more open to the demands of the Divine. Vowed virgins have historically been viewed as members of a rarefied class who sacrifice a "normal" life trajectory—marriage and motherhood—in exchange for an existence as a living emanation of Divine priorities. It represents an extraordinary change in the way our culture is organized that, at least in some cases, women choosing such a path find that the singlehood and virginity that define their religious commitment do not make them appear terribly unusual in the context of the culture at large. A life-long commitment to remaining uncoupled once forced a woman completely out of the cultural or social mainstream. But our culture has been transformed politically, economically, legally, and socially to the extent that uncoupled adult women are now relatively commonplace. A woman's sexual choices now include, in ways that have not historically been the case, the option to decline.

The ability to refuse sexual activity simply because it is unwanted is the core of the fourth major type of virginity we recognize today: avoidant virginity. Avoidance of sexual activity plays a role in any form of ongoing virginity, of course. What is distinctive about avoidant virginity as I characterize it here is that it does not necessarily require a larger agenda. An avoidant virgin doesn't have to be saving herself for marriage or planning to enter a convent. Avoidance of sex may simply be a matter of personal preference. But only quite recently has it become possible for women to be economically and socially viable and remain unattached to either husband or church: pre-1970s spinsterhood generally meant penury and ostracism. Independent singlehood today need mean neither.

In another light, avoidance is frequently enlisted in the service of promoting virginity. The potential consequences of sexual activity, from pregnancy and childbirth to venereal disease to the demands of a spouse, have for centuries been invoked as reasons one might consider prolonging one's virginity. For women, on whom the burdens of pregnancy, childbearing, and childrearing fall unequally, these arguments can be particularly compelling. Contemporary sex education pamphlets often spin unappealing tales of prematurely ended education, dead-end jobs, and endless, friendless nights of screaming babies and smelly diapers. Avoid sex, they explain, and you also avoid these unpleasant outcomes. But such scare tactics are hardly new. Indeed, they've scarcely changed in at least the last eight hundred years. The thirteenth-century middle English text *Hali Meiðhad*, intended to awaken readers to the various benefits of the "holy maidenhead" (religiously vowed virginity) of the title, holds some remarkably similar descriptions:

> And what if I ask you: isn't it odious what a wife is faced with when she walks in and her baby is screaming, the cat nibbling at the bacon and the dog gnawing at the hides, her cakes burning on the hearth and the calf drinking up all the milk, the pot boiling over and putting out the fire, and even her hired hands complaining about it all.

In the interests of getting people to avoid sex and stay virgins, the consequences of a sexual life, then and now, are often depicted as messy, unpleasant, dead-end mundanity and humiliation. Different eras and different lives, to be sure, but the message is identical.

The specter of sexually transmitted disease has a similarly lengthy history as a sex-avoidance motivator. "Beware of chance acquaintances," a Jazz Age advertisement produced by the United States Public Health Service warned young female urbanites, "as disease or childbirth may follow. Believe no one who says it is necessary to indulge sex desire." Since the early twentieth century, when increasing urbanization, industrialization, and mobility contributed to the rise of a sexually volatile youth culture, efforts to curb the sexual impulses of young adults have been considered an appropriate goal for public policy. In the eyes of public health and morality crusaders, avoidant virginity is just as good as any other kind.

When Is Sex Not Sex?

The relationship between culture and sexuality has always been fraught. Not all sex is the same. Not all sexual activities are identically meaningful. When we talk about sexual acts, we do so within complicated frameworks of understanding that prioritize and value some kinds of sex, demonize others, and may even ignore a few. In codes like law codes, for instance, different sexual misdeeds are understood to warrant different penalties. In the codes of the Catholic Church, masturbation is a misdeed even if it is done in private, and a penance is exacted for it. In the eyes of civil law, on the other hand, private masturbation doesn't even warrant a mention: anyone attempting to bring a case against someone for masturbating privately would be laughed out of court. In the Catholic, Canon law scheme of things, masturbation is taken more seriously than it is in civil law. It mandates a real penalty. It is more "real" in Catholic thought than it is in civil law.

The validity or realness of any given aspect of sexuality is a slippery, tricky thing to talk about and an even more problematic thing to gauge. It is to some degree abstract, it is profoundly cultural, and to a great degree, it is personal. Yet we somehow expect that everyone knows what kind of sexual experience is sufficiently real or valid to be the kind of sex that constitutes the end of virginity. (We don't.) In recent years, however, we have begun to be able to understand from statistical research just how unintuitive and nonuniform distinctions between "real" and "not-real" sex can be.

Thanks to the ongoing fascination with adolescent sexuality, which continues to be such a source of concern to much of the West and particularly the United States, researchers have begun to look directly at the question of what kinds of sex are currently being construed as "real" in the sexual ideologies of contemporary teenagers. The *Seventeen*/Kaiser Family Foundation survey *Sex Smarts: Virginity and the First Time*, released in October 2003, for example, indicated that in the population they surveyed there was a roughly fifty-fifty split between teens who perceived oral sex to be "real" sex and those who said that if they had had oral sex, they would not describe it as "having had sex."

This is, many would say, mere adolescent casuistry. But on a number of levels it makes perfect sense. Penis-in-vagina intercourse has for millennia been considered the sexual act of record in our culture. It is the sexual act capable of producing pregnancy, and thus the sexual act with the most far-reaching consequences. Particularly for teens, in whose lives the consequence of pregnancy is perpetually held up as a horrible thing that will poison their lives permanently, potentially reproductive sex is "real" in a way that nonreproductive sexual acts cannot be.

Those parents and grandparents who have the honesty to look unflinchingly at their own sexual histories may recognize a certain similarity between the tendency to think of oral sex as "not real sex" and some of the contextual redefining of sexual acts they themselves might have done at a similar age. In the forties and fifties, for instance, non-intercourse sexual activities that were utterly unthinkable if one were not "going steady" might well have become a permissible extension of making out if one were. Some sort of progressive scale of sexual "realness" was in play in these attempts to help young people find answers to complex equations of fear, desire, and potential negative consequences. Across history, it has been a tremendously useful calculus.

It is, of course, also a tremendously situational one. The fundamental problem of sexual realness is perhaps the single fundamental problem with defining virginity. Both sex and virginity are maddeningly abstract and largely social things, mercurial mixtures of custom, consensus, experience, and ideology. They are important to us personally and culturally. The stakes can be murderously high. We desperately want these volatile aspects of our lives to be knowable and dependable. But like notions of what constitutes real sex, they can only be as unchanging and as definitive as the human beings in whose lives they play a part, which is to say not very, not often, and not for long. Where we do achieve a sense of certainty, it is often at the expense of looking honestly at what the historical record has to show us.

The more we look and the deeper we see, the more we realize that over the course of the millennia we have recognized virginity to exist, it has never been static or unitary. Answering the question of what exactly virginity is, for once and for all, is probably an impossibility. Even if we could, we would still be left with an even deeper problem: the question of why we care about virginity in the first place.

CHAPTER 2

The Importance of Being Virgin

The high value set upon her virginity by a man wooing a woman
seems to be so deeply planted and self-evident that we become almost
perplexed if called upon to give reasons for it.
—Sigmund Freud

I'M BEING PUNISHED," angsty teen overachiever Paris wails, melting
down horribly halfway through a televised high school speech. "I had sex,
so now I don't get to go to Harvard." "She's never had sex," Paris continues,
referring to her friend and fellow speechmaker Rory, "she'll probably go to
Harvard. She's a shoo-in!" By the end of this spring 2003 episode of the WB
network's award-winning sitcom *Gilmore Girls*, the virginal Rory does indeed
end up wallowing in acceptance letters from Harvard, Princeton, and Yale, as
her mother warbles her glee at having "the good kid" not so much because of
her daughter's enviable college prospects as because she is still a virgin. These
scenes alarmed many feminist *Gilmore Girls* fans who questioned, in forums like
Bitch: Feminist Response to Pop Culture, *Gilmore Girls* creator Amy Sherman-
Palladino's decision to make an equation between virginity and Ivy League
college acceptance.

More curious than Sherman-Palladino's decision to use virginity this way,
though, and far more curious than the feminist response to it, is why the plot

device worked at all. Why, indeed, would such a conceit make dramatic sense to viewers who know full well that even the choosiest Harvard admissions officer would neither know nor likely care about any given applicant's virginity or lack thereof?

The gambit makes sense on the level of social expectation, long-standing philosophical beliefs, and emotion. The equation of virginity with virtue and virtue with success makes emotional sense not just to Paris and to Rory's mom within the context of the show, but to the audience. For good or ill, we live in a culture that cares deeply about female virginity and has a long history of punishing those who lose it under the "wrong" circumstances and praising those who retain it until the "right" ones are at hand.

Whether or not we agree with the values and meanings our culture attaches to virginity, we cannot escape them. We participate in a larger culture that circulates and recirculates its virginity ideologies in various forms and guises— for instance, in episodes of *Gilmore Girls*. We tell stories about virginity in part to remind ourselves what we as a culture think and feel about it, to help explain how it functions in our culture, and to teach people about the ramifications virginity might have in our lives . . . even if, as in this case, those ramifications are more symbolic than real. The long history of virginity narratives in art and literature stretches back thousands of years—one of the earliest pieces of ancient Greek fiction, *Daphnis and Chloë*, revolves around virginity—and remains a constant today. Looking at the historical record, it certainly seems as if our concern with virginity has simply always been with us.

But why? What drove us to begin to identify virginity as a special status? What factors came into play that it should become so fraught with meaning that in the twenty-first century, there is still some level on which we can believe that being a virgin might make a difference to a university admissions decision? Why do we care so much? Why do we care at all?

On certain levels, our fascination with virginity seems very strange. No other animals, so far as we can tell, perceive the existence of virginity. Human beings have no monopoly on physical virginity. But we have cornered the market on it, both in terms of recognizing that it exists and in making it useful in the ways we organize our cultures and our relationships with one another. There is no question that virginity means a great deal to human beings. Taking a look at how much it *doesn't* mean to other species helps give us clearer perspective on why this may be so.

Sealed for Your Protection

Occasionally one comes across the claim that the reason humans are the only creatures who recognize the existence of virginity is that we are the only creatures who possess hymens. Alas, this is not so. Humans are emphatically not the only animals with hymens. A diverse spectrum of mammal types, including female llamas, guinea pigs, bush babies, manatees, moles, toothed whales, chimpanzees, elephants, rats, ruffed lemurs, and seals all have them.

Compared to some of the others that exist, the human hymen is nothing special. Imagine the grand proportions of the elephant hymen, or the eye-popping durability of the fin whale's, which is so resilient that it usually is not ruptured until the animal gives birth. A rat hymen may not be particularly impressive in size or persistence, but when one pauses to realize that the average nubile lady rat is as well-equipped as the average teenaged girl insofar as having a hymen is concerned, it does put that particular scrap of tissue into a bit of perspective.

Neither are human hymens functional. Unlike those of whales, seals, and manatees, they are not capable of keeping water or waterborne foreign substances out of the vagina, as evolutionary biologist Elaine Morgan argues is the case for marine mammals. Human hymens also do not seal the vagina against sexual intrusion. Guinea pigs and bush babies, so far away from us on the evolutionary scale, have hymens that completely seal the vaginal opening when the animals are not fertile. When the animals ovulate and go into heat, the hymen dissolves. When the animals are no longer in estrus, their hymens grow back until next time. Thanks to their resealing hymens, these animals can only be vaginally penetrated when they are actually capable of conceiving.

For a few animals, then, the hymen may serve a demonstrable function. For human beings, however, and for most other hymen-bearing species as well, the hymen is nothing more or less than a functionless leftover, a tiny idle remnant of flesh that remains when the opening of the vagina forms.

What is most fascinating about human hymens is that we have become aware of them at all. No other species seems to know or care. Zoologist Bettyann Kevles, in her book *Female of the Species*, writes that from the perspective of natural selection, hymens "are explicable only if the male of the species finds it to his advantage to seek a virgin. But there is no evidence that mammal males seek inexperienced females, and no evidence that females with this particular anatomical feature remain monogamous." A gentleman lemur is, in other words, no more or less likely to try to mate with a lady lemur whose hymen is intact; a female elephant who has no hymen left to speak of after having borne young is every bit as sexually attractive in the eyes of males.

There is no evidence that animal males are the slightest bit aware of when females have hymens and when they don't. Furthermore, there is no evidence that the females are automatically aware of it either, including when they have sex for the first time. So much for Desmond Morris's wishful thinking that the hymen's function was to produce pain if penetration were attempted, thus making it more likely that virgins will postpone penetrative sex, or his corresponding theory that this pain was what made early humans aware of virginity. Not so. Humans are not alone in having hymens, and humans are far from alone in not being innately aware of them. Women are generally not aware of having hymens at all unless these small scraps of tissue create some sort of problem. This may or may not ever happen. It is rare for the hymen to present a problem on its own. As for problems associated with penetration, a given woman's vagina may or may not ever be penetrated, and even if it is, hymens and vaginas vary considerably, as do reactions to vaginal penetration.

There simply are no symptoms occasioned by virginity loss that are uniform enough to point directly and unequivocally to the existence of the hymen. One would in any case reason that if there were, or if human beings did possess some innate awareness of the existence of hymens—an awareness, again, that all other hymen-bearing animals appear to lack—it would not have taken us until 1544 to figure out exactly what the hymen was and where it was located in the body. Truly, human beings are not so different from all the other animals that have hymens. We too very rarely have any inkling that our hymens exist.

It seems much more probable, given the importance human beings attach to virginity, that our awareness of the hymen came into existence the other way around. In other words, we became aware of hymens because we are aware of something we call virginity. We found the hymen because we found reasons to search women's bodies for some bit of flesh that embodied this quality we call "virginity," some physical proof that it existed. Humans are not alone in having hymens. We're merely alone in knowing it, and in having given ourselves a reason to care.

Big Daddy and the K-Strategist

There is no purely biological argument that explains human interest in virginity, so we are forced to begin considering the possibility that awareness of virginity may have stemmed from social factors instead. Indeed, the leading hypothesis concerning how and why human beings became aware of virginity posits that the concept of virginity arose as a social bargaining chip in negotiations involving a father's investment in his offspring. The so-called paternity/property hypothesis places virginity squarely in the middle of the tangled web of human social organization, arguing that it filled a broadly pragmatic role in mediating the conflicting interests of pregnancy, childrearing, access to material goods, and the creation and maintenance of kinship groups and social hierarchies.

When it comes to reproduction, human beings are what anthropologists and biologists call "K-strategists." We have relatively few offspring over the course of our lives, and we have to devote enormous energy, time, and resources to the gestation, birth, and upbringing of those children in order to maximize their success in the world. Pregnancy is a lengthy, intense process fraught with dangers to both mother and fetus. Human childbirth is almost ridiculously difficult and long. Only with relatively recent specialized obstetric techniques and technologies has childbirth—at least in the first world—become a process that mothers and infants are expected to survive as a matter of course. Childbirth is just the beginning. As any parent can attest, childrearing is a long, resource-intensive process with tremendous demands.

These demands fall almost exclusively on the shoulders of mothers. Fathers, after all, have no biological compulsion to stick around long enough even to find out whether a particular act of intercourse has produced a pregnancy, let alone long enough to care for their offspring. This, the hypothesis holds, is the problem at the root of the idea of virginity: how can mothers most efficiently encourage fathers to invest in the children they have sired?

Archaeologists do not know precisely when the ideas forming the backbone of the social organizational principle known as patriarchy (from the Greek *patria*, father, and *arché*, meaning rule or basis) emerged. Nor do they know precisely when the idea of private property became popular. We know only that they did so, and that they were deeply rooted in a vast number of cultures around the globe long before written history began. Based on the historical record derived from burial objects, preserved settlements, and so forth, archaeologists estimate that the twin developments of patriarchy and property arose as elements in human social structures sometime during what is known as the Neolithic era, a period that lasted from roughly 8500 to 2600 B.C.E.

Another notable development in human civilization, the development of agriculture and the domestication of plants and animals, took place in the same general time period, probably more or less simultaneously in numerous locations around the world. As humans exchanged nomadic life for farming, they began, researchers theorize, to think in terms of property as a way to articulate the things that they had put effort into creating or making useful: *my* land, *my* field, *my* cow. From there it would have been a short leap to think of human beings as belonging to other human beings in similar ways: *my* woman, *my* child. Combining the ideas of ownership and patriarchy, or the organization of social groups based on members' relationships to a head male, would have provided the origins for the idea of patrimony, or the inheritance of a father's property by his children. This is where virginity fits in. Garden-variety self-interest encourages healthy investment in ensuring the survival and success of one's offspring. It also makes it an object of concern that one's hard-won resources not be squandered or given away to unworthy recipients.

Virginity became a key to both because virginity can render paternity knowable. Maternity is rarely in doubt: childbirth makes it pretty easy to know who has given birth and to whom. Paternity, on the other hand, is a lot trickier to prove. Human women do not go into heat the way some animals do. Because we are stealthy ovulators, it is nearly impossible to know for sure when a woman is and is not fertile; even with modern medical technology, predicting fertility is a matter of educated guesses, not certainties. Because there's no easy way to know whether a given incidence of sexual intercourse is likely to prove fertile, the simplest way to determine the identity of the father of a given child, and thus to know that the child "belongs to" a particular male, is to limit who has sexual access to individual women.

The scenario that has the highest potential for producing offspring whose fathers are known is a marriage system that most severely limits women's prerogatives in regard to sex, a system in which sexual access to a woman is reserved for a single man. Female premarital virginity ensures that a woman's first child is of guaranteed paternity. Her post-marital monogamy assures that future children will be of similarly reliable lineage.

This raises the question of what women stand to gain from limiting their options so severely. Human women, like other female animals of other species, are not necessarily given to such a system by nature. Primates do not often behave monogamously. This common tendency toward nonmonogamous sexual behavior is partially explained by the desire to have the most genetically superlative offspring possible. It is to the biological advantage of a species when females are at liberty to choose to mate with genetically superior males wherever those females might find them. The myth of the naturally monogamous female and the corresponding myth of the naturally promiscuous male have been trotted out for centuries to help reinforce the double standard that has been so pervasive in Western culture. But as numerous scientists have now proven (Bettyann Kevles's *Females of the Species* provides a reader-friendly, soundly researched introduction), it simply isn't so. Women are no more inherently monogamous than men. If a woman is to behave consistently in a way that runs counter to the biological imperative of maximizing genetic potential—that is, if she is to voluntarily participate in a scheme where she will remain a virgin until she mates with one man, and never mate with any other man thereafter—the incentive has to be a strong one indeed.

The incentive is indeed strong: K-strategist females need a lot of help if their babies are going to survive. In a burgeoning patriarchy, where property and the distribution of goods are controlled primarily or exclusively by men, this means inducing men to feel that they have an investment in helping to provide food, shelter, clothing, social affiliations and protections, and physical care for women and babies. One of the best ways a woman historically has had of doing this is to convince a man to publicly acknowledge his paternity of her child.

The stakes in the bid for paternal recognition are high. Not for nothing is it considered a curse to call someone a bastard. In a patriarchy, it is hard to survive without the sponsorship of a patriarch. To this day, being disowned by one's parents is considered serious business. In the distant past, being disowned or not acknowledged by a parent generally meant death, particularly if the child was an infant. Many legal systems still use the terms "legitimate" and "illegitimate" to indicate whether a child was born within the confines of a heterosexual marriage. It is a telling sign of the deep and lasting power of patriarchy that in so many places it remains the prerogative of men to determine whether children are, in the eyes of their society and its institutions, legitimate, and therefore fully real.

For the K-strategist female in a patriarchy, securing a future for her children means trading on monogamy generally and on virginity specifically. The trade is not necessarily either equal or fair, and the male side of the bargain is easily withdrawn. Nor does a woman who grants exclusive sexual access to her body to just one man always receive, in return, a guaranteed supply of resources to meet her needs and those of her child or children. But for a K-strategist living in a patriarchy, it has historically been her best bet.

Pure Goods

The process by which this quid pro quo transaction evolved into an institution invested with enormous religious and moral significance is lost to us. As it did, however, men and women alike became profoundly invested in perpetuating the ideology that holds that female virginity is singular and valuable.

This ethos has formed a huge part of the bedrock on which our sexual, social, and familial relationships rest, but its prominence does not mean that valuing virginity is something that is inborn or inherent to human beings. Anthropologists have found examples of too many other cultures that do not value virginity or which value it very differently than we do, including cultures in which both private property and virginity are essentially nonexistent concepts, for us to claim that the way our culture does it is either the way that humans are "supposed to" do things, or the only way they can be done. The way we do it may be a popular, even dominant paradigm among human cultures worldwide, but it is hardly the only basis on which human beings might organize their sexual lives.

The same thing holds true of our tendency to regard virginity as a commodity. Again, we must return to our Neolithic grandparents to imagine the roots of this practice, but the reigning theory runs that as it became increasingly popular for men to bring only virginal women into their households for purposes of having greater control over the paternity of the children they supported, they and their women alike began to pay more attention to controlling the sexuality of their daughters in turn. Their daughters would then be more appealing to the men of other households or clans, bait for attracting useful allies.

Raising daughters of quality became another mode of production, as valuable as breeding healthy sheep, weaving sturdy cloth, or bringing in a good harvest. As the head of his household or clan, the patriarch took ultimate responsibility for its productivity and performance. A clan's standing or honor could be affected by its ability to compete economically. Status could similarly be affected by whether the clan brought properly virginal daughters to the marriage market. The gesture is now generally symbolic in the first world, but we nonetheless still observe the custom of a father "giving" his daughter in marriage. Up until the last century or so, however, when laws were liberalized to allow women to stand as full citizens in their own right, this represented a literal transfer of property from a father's household to a husband's.

If an inopportune loss of virginity jeopardized this system, it could be catastrophic. It undermined the father's and the clan's status. But far more than mere loss of face hung in the balance. Virginity lost before marriage often rendered the woman unmarriageable, useless on the marriage market. When a valuable commodity is destroyed, the owners seek recompense from the person who destroyed it, or at least the nearest person to whom blame can be made to stick. Thus the unmarried woman found to be (or merely reputed to be) no longer a virgin might be disowned, sold into slavery, beaten, mutilated, or killed in order to redress the loss of property and face.

An excellent and well-known example of how this worked in practical terms comes from the second half of the twenty-second chapter of the Old Testament book of Deuteronomy, written down around the seventh century B.C.E.

[13]If a man takes a wife, and goes in to her [to consummate the marriage], and hates her, [14] and speaks libelous words against her, and calls her by evil names, and says, "I took this woman [as a wife], and when I went to her [as a husband], I found her not a virgin," [15] then shall the girl's father and mother bring forth the tokens of the girl's virginity unto the elders of the city, at the city gate. [16] The girl's father shall say unto the elders "I gave my daughter to this man as his wife, and now he hates her [17] and has libeled her, saying 'I did not find your daughter to be a virgin,' yet these here are the tokens of her virginity." And the parents shall spread the cloth before the city elders. [18] Then the elders of the city should take the man and flog him, [19] and fine him a hundred shekels of silver to be given to the girl's father, because he [the accuser] has cast an evil name upon a virgin of Israel. She will be his wife [the marriage will be upheld as valid] and he may not divorce her. [20] But if this thing [accusation] is true, and the tokens of the girl's virginity were not found, [21] then they will bring

the girl to the gate of her father's household and the men of her city will stone her to death because she has done an obscene thing among her people Israel by committing whoredom in her father's house. So you will cast evil away from you.

In the Deuteronomist's formulation, wrongfully accusing the father of the bride of having presented "damaged goods" constitutes a crime against the bride's father. Slander is a civil crime, not a religious one, as indicated not only by the language used to describe the offense but also by how it is remedied. The father who is slandered by having his daughter falsely accused of having not been a virgin at marriage is paid damages for the damage to his reputation, and whatever social or material gains he had achieved through the marriage of his daughter are solidified because the marriage is upheld. Despite the fact that it was her virginity and her honesty that were impugned, however, his daughter is not perceived as having been slandered by a false accusation. She is never compensated for any damage done to *her* reputation. Because her marriage is valid, she is considered to have nothing to worry about.

Should the accusation be upheld, however, the nature of the crime is suddenly and horribly transformed into a capital offense not just against man but against God. Moreover, there is no question of who is to blame. The woman alone—and not her father, her mother, or the man who was involved in deflowering her (if indeed she had been deflowered at all)—bears all the responsibility.

Never mind that a woman does not, even in the long-ago Judaean imagination, lose her virginity all by herself. And never mind that the standard of proof—most likely blood on a cloth—was sufficiently fallible that even the rabbis of the Talmud argue about whether it constituted valid evidence for a decision by a religious court. The woman who was judged to have lost her virginity prior to her wedding was presumed to have committed whoredom, a crime against her father's household, in other words, a crime against her father's patriarchal right to control the women under his roof.

For this crime, which was not merely the destruction of a useful commodity but also the destruction of patriarchal control, the daughter was put to death. But she was not killed by her father, the man whom she had ostensibly wronged. She was put to death by all the men of her city, symbolically allowing every man to join in reaffirming the right of men as a class to determine the fate of women as a class, and to reinforce the principle that men were not only permitted but obligated to punish women who evaded their control. Such an evasion, after all, constituted "evil" and had to be repaid with a human life crushed under a bloody pile of stones . . . even though lying about whether a woman had managed such an evasion of male control earned no such epithet and could be repaid with a pile of shiny silver.

By the time the Deuteronomist was writing, verifiable paternity had already become a subsidiary concern to the existence or nonexistence of virginity itself. Virginity had come to carry the symbolic weight not just of a husband's desire to control the ancestry of children born under his roof but of male desire to control the behavior of women and children. It had become a symbol of successful patriarchy as a whole.

Long before the birth of Christianity, then, there was already a strict framework of social law in which virginity kept was good and valuable and virginity lost was bad and worthless. The stakes were high and the consequences were extreme. As a result virtually every member of the culture, male or female, old or young, could be counted upon to participate in one way or another in the practices of policing and commodifying virginity. To do otherwise was to invite disaster.

CHAPTER 3

Hymenology

Given the pronounced variations in size and shape from woman to woman, perhaps it would be more accurate to identify the hymen as a site than as an anatomical part. To make an analogy: we all have insteps, but to identify precisely where the "top" of the instep is would be very difficult. However, if identifying the exact location of the top of the instep were, in some Swiftian fashion, crucial to social identity, then insteps would become the subject of much controversy indeed.
—Kathleen Coyne Kelly

PUT IN THE SIMPLEST TERMS POSSIBLE, a hymen is what's left over when you dig a hole.

Hidden from view in the warm, wet dark of her mother's womb, a female fetus develops genitalia and reproductive organs, including the uterus, fallopian tubes, ovaries, vagina, and the external folds, flaps, and openings we collectively call the vulva. She doesn't intend to, nor does she know she's doing it. It just happens, triggered and guided by the complicated coded instructions of her uniquely female DNA. At some point during the process, the exact instant of its formation unbeknownst to her or anyone, she also develops a hymen.

The hymen forms not on its own, as a stand-alone structure, but rather as a by-product of the complex creation of the female genitalia. At the beginning of the fourth month of pregnancy, the female fetus does not even have a vagina, let alone a hymen. But by the time this fetus reaches the end of her sixth month of gestation, she will have both. The hymen forms because the vagina does. It is the lone physical reminder of the time when the interior portions of a female's genitalia were completely separated from the external ones.

The female genitals develop in separate internal and external sections. Until their development is all but complete, they do not connect up to form a single contiguous system. In the early stages of the reproductive system development of a female fetus, a space or hollow called the urogenital sinus forms close to the surface of the body. This space will gradually become the vulva, developing the various folds and ridges of labia minora, clitoral hood, and so on.

Inside the fetus's abdomen, meanwhile, within the space enclosed by the bones of the pelvis, a pair of structures called the müllerian tubercles (also known as paramesonephric ducts) enlarge and form what is called the vaginal cord. One end of this cord is anchored to the inside surface of the body wall. The other end is anchored to the uterus. The body wall end will ultimately become the opening of the vagina. The other end will become the cervix, the gate between the vagina and the uterus.

As the vaginal cord matures, it hollows out. This process is called canalization, and it is exactly what it sounds like: the process in which a solid cord turns into a canal or tube. The last step of canalization is when the canal forms an opening, right through the body wall, giving the vagina its outlet.

This is what creates the hymen. At the threshold between the external urogenital space and the internal vagina, a small, flexible flange of what used to be body wall tissue remains around the rim of the newly formed opening. This remnant is the hymen. Although some people imagine that the hymen is like the head of a drum, a skin that is stretched across the opening of the vagina, normal hymens are anything but. The reason the hymen exists at all is that the vagina cannot function without an opening to the outside of the body. This tiny leftover of the process of genital development is the piece of flesh by which the reputations, futures, and in some cases, lives of millions of women have hung in the balance.

Generally speaking, where you find a vagina you also find a hymen. Contrary to currently popular belief, virtually every woman is in fact born with one, with the estimated frequency of women being born without discernible hymens given at less than 0.03 percent. Yet for most of us, and that includes the lion's share of the medical profession, the vaginal hymen is a mystery. Very few of us have ever knowingly seen one, or would be able to identify one if we saw it in a photograph. Most women report no awareness of their hymens as a separate structure or part of their bodies, which makes perfect sense since it isn't one. The hymen is part and parcel of the vagina, no more separate from its surroundings than the nostrils are separate from the nose. Like the top of the instep of the foot, as Kathleen Coyne Kelly's remark quoted in the chapter epigraph suggests, it is more a landmark than it is an entirely separate entity. The only time that most women become aware of what they perceive to be the hymen—although the hymen, as we'll discover later, may not in fact turn out to be what they're perceiving at all—is during their initial experiences with vaginal penetration.

We know very little about the hymen. Medical science has paid it only scant attention. The hymen is not medically compelling. It is physically tiny, and it serves no known function. Aside from the one or two potentially problem-causing hymenal deformities that sometimes occur, it's one of the more law-abiding bits of the human anatomy. No one has ever suffered from cancer of the hymen, sclerosis of the hymen, or hymen dystrophy, died of a sudden hy-men attack, or been plagued by paralysis of the hymen. In human beings it simply doesn't do much, for good or ill. Aside from its social role as a supposed determiner of a woman's virginity, the human hymen is really awfully dull.

The only thing truly noteworthy about human hymens is the significance we've attached to them. In humans and most other animals that have them, they do not appear to have any significance to mating, pregnancy, or successful reproduction. If hymens don't appear to have a role to play in the lives of the animals that have them, though, we might well ask why they ever developed in the first place. British historian of the vagina Catherine Blackledge suggests, based on what we know about animals like guinea pigs, that perhaps the hu-man hymen once also had a directly reproductive function. Or perhaps, as evolutionary theorist Elaine Morgan suggests in her book *The Aquatic Ape*, in which she advances a marine-mammal background for the human species, it once had a protective barrier role to play in keeping water and foreign objects out of the vagina while our proto-human ancestors paddled their way through prehistoric seas. It would be difficult, if not impossible, to test these hypothe-ses. Whether the hymen is a leftover from some distant evolutionary past where it had a concrete function or, as it now appears to medical science, it is merely a vestige of a particular prenatal developmental process remains an open question. We don't know, and, given the fact that soft tissues like the hymen generally don't leave a fossil record behind them, it is entirely possible that we never will.

What information we do have about the human hymen is likewise dramatically incomplete. Unlike so much of the rest of our bodies, hymens do not have a long and extensive history of being examined, dissected, surveyed, and documented by medical science. There is more extant medical writing on the subject of athlete's foot than there is regarding the hymen. The hymen simply hasn't been the subject of much scientific study. To be fair, it has also not been an easily available subject for researchers, since moral objections having to do with virginity and modesty have often precluded the study of women's hymens. Much of what we know about the hymen's specifics is of very recent vintage. All of the fairly small quantity of serious research that has been done concerning the human hymen has been done since the turn of the twentieth century, and most of it has been done since the 1970s.

What we have learned about the hymen, scanty and recent as it is, is nonetheless useful. We can compare what science has to tell us about the hymen to the old wives' tales and folk wisdom that have accumulated on the topic, and see where what we've assumed to be true about the hymen turned out actually to *be* true, and where what we've assumed to be true turned out to be very false indeed.

Hymen 101

The location of the hymen is obvious once one knows how it forms. But for those who don't, figuring out just where the hymen is supposed to be can prove a source of consternation. It is not too unusual, for example, to find virginity loss scenes in modern novels that include descriptions of a man's penis penetrating a woman's vagina by several inches before he abruptly hits the ironlike barricade of her hymen, implying that it is some sort of buried treasure wedged halfway up the vagina. The hymen is in fact found at the very entrance of the vagina. It is part of what is known as the vaginal vestibule: one cannot enter the vagina at all without passing through the portion where the hymen is found. The floor and walls of the vaginal vestibule are the base of the hymen, which extends upward and inward toward the center of the vaginal opening from there. The hymen is nothing more than a ridge or flange of the very same tissue.

This tissue is the same stuff that forms the inner layer of the rest of the vagina. It is a thin, flexible, smooth, hairless mucous membrane. Just like the inside of the mouth or nose or the side of the eyelid that touches the eyeball, it is moist and very soft. Unlike the rest of the vagina, however, the hymen has no muscular tissue underneath that thin, smooth upper layer, because that thin upper layer is all it is. Also unlike the rest of the vagina, the hymen typically possesses either few nerves or none at all. Whatever nerves the hymen does have, if it has any, are likely to be nearer the base of the hymen than the rim. The same pattern is true of blood supply. This is one of the numerous reasons that while some women bleed when their vaginas are sexually penetrated for the first time (or the first several times, in some cases) others don't bleed a bit: there may not be blood vessels in places where they are traumatized by such things.

Hymens offer a wide and colorful variety of configuration and shape. There seems to be a sense among many people that, insofar as they have any idea what a hymen looks like to begin with, all hymens must look alike. Nothing could be further from the truth.

The hymen type that seems most common in the popular imagination is actually one of the least common types of hymens in terms of what actually occurs in women's bodies. Many people imagine that the hymen actually covers the entirety of the vaginal opening with an unbroken expanse of skin, like the paper-covered hoop through which the circus lion tamer makes his charges leap. Hymens like this do exist. The condition is called imperforate hymen, and it is considered to be a minor birth defect. It is caused when the canalization of the vagina does not quite finish going all the way through the body wall, and instead of having a vaginal opening, a layer of skin remains over the place where the opening should be. Imperforation of the hymen is the most common malformation of the female reproductive tract, but estimates of frequency range widely, from one in twelve hundred to one in ten thousand. Because it makes menstruation impossible, imperforate hymen is corrected surgically. A hymen with no opening is a bug, not a feature.

The diameter of the opening of the hymen, like most other parts of the human body, starts out small and grows as the child does. It typically starts out at two to three millimeters in diameter and increases at a rate of one to two millimeters a year until the child reaches puberty, so older children are more likely to have larger hymenal openings than younger ones. Lest it be thought that all virginal hymenal openings are minuscule, a study published in 2000 showed that 93 percent of the virginal girls examined by Dr. Astrid Heger and her team had hymenal openings large enough to permit the doctors to view part of the interior of the vagina without using a speculum or any other tool.

The size of the hymen's aperture is only the beginning of a veritable cornucopia of variety. Hymenal tissue itself appears in a number of forms. It might be fragile and barely there, or resilient and rubbery. It might be so scanty as to be overlooked, or appear in plentiful, tender, flowerlike folds that double over on themselves. The American Professional Society on the Abuse of Children, in line with many medical textbooks, identifies five primary hymen shapes: annular, crescentic, redundant, fimbriated, and septate.

The most common hymen shape is annular—a word derived from the Latin *annulum*, meaning "circle" or "ring." A ring of tissue is precisely what the annular hymen is, outlining the vaginal opening all the way around. Similarly named for its shape, and almost as common, is the crescentic hymen. This crescentlike hymen is roughly U-shaped. According to a comparison of hymen research studies done by Astrid Heger and Lynne Ticson, annular and crescentic hymens together account for over half of all hymens, and may account for as many as four-fifths. It is difficult, however, to get an accurate statistic in terms of precisely how common each one is, because some annular hymens appear to have some propensity to change shape as girls grow older, turning into crescentic hymens.

The least common hymen shape, by contrast, is septate. A septate hymen can be thought of in two different ways, either as a hymen whose opening is divided by a bridge, or septum, of tissue, or as a hymen with more than one opening, each opening divided from the next by a thin strip of tissue. Rarely, septate hymens that have more than two openings are seen. They can in fact have multiple openings, each separated from the other by a thin strip of membrane, creating a hymen that bears a certain visual resemblance to a kitchen colander. Because of this, they are also sometimes called cribiform or cribriform—from the Latin *cribrum*, meaning sieve—hymens.

Less common than annular or crescentic hymens but more common than septate hymens are the redundant hymen and its relative, the fimbriated hymen. The redundant hymen is a particularly extravagant variety, formed of sufficient flesh that it folds back on itself not unlike the folded-over cuff of a sock or shirtsleeve. Fimbriated hymens are less fleshy but may have multiple projections or indentations along the rim that give the hymen a ruffled appearance. Redundant hymens tend to become less so with time, however: University of Texas researcher Dr. Abby Berenson has discovered that redundant hymenal tissue often recedes during the first three years of life, so much so that a hymen that was redundant at birth might change to become fimbriated or even annular by the time the child turned three.

It seems strange, since we think of them as being static unless they are "torn" or "broken," but hymens change shape all by themselves. Between birth and age three, and in some cases again between ages three and five, hymens can go through quite a bit of alteration in shape and size. These changes take place painlessly, silently, and virtually unnoticeably, without the girl in question (or anyone else, in all likelihood) being any the wiser or noticing any change. We don't know why the hymen changes shape, and we don't know how it happens, but the phenomenon has been observed many times. The best way to think of it is that like other body parts, the hymen continues to develop after birth, and this means that sexual penetration is absolutely not required for a hymen to be different or look different from one day, one week, or one month to the next. This calls into question the very notion of the "intact" hymen: if the hymen can change all by itself, can we ever accurately call it "intact" or "unaltered"?

In addition to appearing in different shapes, hymens vary in other ways. Hymenal tags, elongated protrusions of tissue that extend from the surface of the hymen, are a fairly common accessory. Hymens can also have bumps, mounds, notches, concavities, and depressions. Although seventeenth-century English midwife and medical writer Jane Sharp described the hymen as looking like a "clove-gilliflower" (a pink, or carnation), in reality hymens are observed in a range of colors along the purple/red spectrum. Likewise, the inner rim of the hymen can be smooth or scalloped, or show evidence of past tearing or stretching in the form of clefts. These can be superficial notches or complete transections. It is less common for women who have not experienced some sort of vaginal penetration to have complete transections in the most substantial portions of their hymens, so in examinations, for instance exams conducted after allegations of child abuse, these are considered a red flag that penetration might have taken place. But not all hymens with complete transections have been penetrated, not all vaginal penetration is sexual, and not all sexual penetration causes a complete transection of the hymen—or indeed any at all.

Resistance and Resilience

The physical appearance and general form of the human hymen runs a wide gamut and is prone to change without either external cause or warning. Much the same is true of the nature of the hymenal tissue itself. Just as we all have different qualities of hair and skin, with some being fine and delicate and others being robust and resilient, the thickness, strength, flexibility, durability, and sturdiness of hymenal tissue varies, too.

Part of this, like the characteristics of any of the other tissues in our bodies, is genetic. We inherit our hair color, eye color, propensity toward certain diseases, and a million other things from our parents—so why not the characteristics of our genital tissues? There is some evidence that imperforate hymens may be inherited matrilineally, so it would make sense if similar things were true of other aspects of the hymen as well.

Hymen tissue is also affected by hormones. Estrogen, to which a female fetus is exposed in utero and which her body will manufacture in increasingly large quantities as she heads into puberty, both thickens the genital mucous membranes and makes them more elastic. Because of their prenatal estrogen bath in the mother's womb, the hymens of very young girls (approximately under the age of two) can in some cases be more elastic than those of girls just a few years older. As the effects of the fetal hormone bath wear off, the elasticity of the vagina can correspondingly decrease and its tissues become more fragile. Then, as puberty arrives, a girl's own estrogen increases enormously and with it, so does the elasticity of her genital tissues.

Thickness and resilience of hymen tissue also varies. In general, the hymen is thinner than an eyelid. Many are described as being translucent. Some are so thin and fragile that it is impossible for doctors to examine them without damaging them in the process. Others are thicker, even rubbery. Researchers have found that some hymens remain fairly thick, others remain fairly thin, and still other hymens may become thinner over time.

The thickness, thinness, and relative fragility of different hymens often complicate attempts to make virginity diagnoses based on what the hymen looks like. Some more or less disintegrate on their own. Others are quite robust and can be shoved around rather roughly without looking any worse for wear. Nineteenth- and early-twentieth-century gynecologists sometimes explained away women who did not bleed the first time they had intercourse as having "complacent" hymens, meaning that the hymen was so elastic as to simply bend or fold on impact. The knowledge that the female genitalia could simply "give in" to penetration without struggle or damage was itself sometimes used to cast aspersions upon a woman's chastity, on the assumption that any woman who could disguise her sexual indiscretions probably had already done so. Some women who believe that they never had hymens because they did not bleed or feel pain the first time they had sex may simply have hymens that are sufficiently sturdy to bend instead of breaking.

Because we're taught to think of hymens as inherently fragile, the notion of a resilient hymen is especially intriguing. Some hymens are so resilient that they endure years of sexual intercourse quite handily, only to be discovered during prenatal gynecological exams or even in childbirth. In the January 2002 edition of *Midwifery Today E-News,* midwife Brenda Capps reported her attendance of the labor of a young first-time mother who had a thick, very resilient septate hymen that had apparently survived intercourse with no sign of damage and had to be cut to allow the baby to be born.

An even more impressive case is the topic of a 2002 *Australian and New Zealand Journal of Gynecology* report about a Taiwanese woman in her early thirties. Diagnosed with an imperforate hymen at thirteen, this patient had surgery to correct it. Despite the surgery, the hymen grew back, and she underwent a second hymenotomy when she was eighteen. Everything seemed fine for some time, and the woman married and became pregnant, delivering by caesarean section. At the time that she gave birth, doctors noted that her hymenal orifice was quite narrow. The patient admitted that her husband had a problem with premature ejaculation and that she rarely, if ever, felt penetration during their sexual encounters. (The underappreciated fact that lack of penetration is no barrier to pregnancy is certainly one of the morals to this story.) Whatever the nature of this woman's sex life, it must have been sufficient to the task, for the patient soon became pregnant a second time. When she arrived at the hospital to give birth, however, the doctors discovered that her hymen had once again resealed. The baby was delivered successfully by caesarean, and the patient was given a third hymenotomy. One hopes that the old maxim "third time's the charm" held true, and that this woman and her incredible re-sealing hymen have required no further run-ins with the scalpel.

At the far opposite end of the spectrum are the fragile hymens. Not a lot is known about fragile hymens for the simple reason that they fall apart too easily to ever be noticed. It is probable that some of the women who, due to lack of any evidence to suggest the contrary, thought they must have been born without a hymen have in reality merely had very fragile ones, so slight as to be negligible.

Far from being a uniform bit of female anatomy, hymens prove to be a motley crew indeed. From a practical perspective, this means that merely saying that someone has a hymen is, all by itself, a bit like saying someone has skin: knowing that they have it doesn't tell us what it looks like, whether it is rough or soft, scarred or smooth. Certainly knowing that someone has a hymen, as all but a very small percentage of women do, does not tell us whether or not she has had any sexual experiences. All we know, when we know that someone has a hymen, is that it exists . . . although this itself was for centuries a matter of hot debate.

CHAPTER 4

A Desperate and Conflicted Search

In som virgins or maidens in the orifice of the neck of the womb
there is found a certain tunicle or membrane called of antient writers Hymen . . .
But I could never find it in anie, seeking of all ages from three to twelv,
of all that I had under my hands in the Hospital of Paris.
—Ambroise Paré, 1573

IT IS EASY TO ASSUME that our ancestors understood things sexual in the
same way we do today. After all, human sex organs and the range of sexual
acts we have at our disposal have been roughly the same since the time the human species began. It simply doesn't occur to us to think that while our predecessors may have had all the same bits and pieces we do, and may have put
them to use in substantially identical ways, they may well have thought—and
indeed often did think—of them very differently indeed. Sometimes historical
conceptions of the body and its parts can be so different from ours as to seem
bizarre. To wit: the saga of the hymen.

Various ancient writings from Egypt, Greece, the Middle East, and Asia Minor make reference to virgins and virginity, yet none of them mention the
hymen. We can read what the Talmud has to say about the signs of virginity,
consult the Old Testament about virgin brides, and survey the myths and
legends of Artemis, Cybele, Athena, and other virgins both earthly and

supernatural and find no mention of the hymen anywhere, nor any suggestion of such an anatomical tidbit. Why not?

The answer is so simple that most historians have missed it: for our ancestors in the ancient world, the hymen did not exist. This doesn't mean that women of that era weren't born with hymens as part of their bodies, but rather that neither they nor anyone else knew that they were there.

We might wonder how the physicians of the ancient world could have possibly missed such a thing. In part the answer is that they literally weren't looking. At that time it was strongly taboo for male doctors to examine women's bodies directly. Occasional exceptions did occur, but in all the medical texts attributed to the school of Hippocrates there are only two examples of a physician carrying out a vaginal examination, which gives the impression that these instances were rare indeed. Examinations on women were done by midwives, not physicians.

Even if doctors had performed gynecological exams every day, though, they still probably wouldn't have found a special thing called a hymen inside anyone's vagina. For one thing, they wouldn't have been looking for it. Having no concept that such a thing should be expected, they would have been unlikely to notice it as anything but just another of the various ridges and folds of the female genitals. The second-century physician Galen's exhaustive anatomical treatise *De usu partium*, for example, makes no mention of it, and this from a meticulous observer who identified and explained the foreskin, buttocks, labia, and clitoris—something that a startling number of later anatomists managed somehow to forget was there. But never once does Galen mention anything like the structure many people believe constitutes the physical presence of a woman's virginity.

In the Beginning Was the Word

The other major reason ancient physicians wouldn't have found hymens in women's bodies even had they looked for them is that, for them, at that time, the word "hymen" meant something altogether different than it does today. In the literature of early Greek medicine, the word "hymen" comes up constantly. Aristotle, particularly, is full of them. There is a hymen of the brain, a hymen of the heart, a hymen of the intestines. You can hardly go three pages without a hymen popping up somewhere, because to Aristotle and the rest of the Greek world of his time, the hymen was nothing more or less than a membrane. Any membrane. The thick membrane around the brain that we call the dura was one such hymen. The mesentery, which anchors all of our intestines in place inside the abdominal cavity, was another. So too with the sac around the heart we call the pericardium, the muscular wall between the chest and abdomen that we call the diaphragm, the sac around the lungs that we call the pleura, and virtually every other structure that divides or separates one anatomical feature from another.

Hymens, hymens everywhere, but not the kind you'd think. How, then, did this catch-all term for "membrane" come to mean something so specific? Not every twist and turn of the tale is known—many texts of this period have been lost to us—but virginity researchers including medieval history scholar Kathleen Coyne Kelly and historian of ancient Greece Giulia Sissa have been able to trace the outlines of the transformation.

After Aristotle and the writers of the school of the so-called father of medicine, Hippocrates of Cos, the next major Western writers on medicine are two Greeks, the second-century Galen and the third-century Soranus of Ephesus. Galen uses the term "hymen" to mean "membrane," just as his predecessors did. Soranus does so, too, but interestingly enough, he defines the vagina itself as a hymen, saying that in his eyes it resembles an intestine with an ample interior. The vaginal canal, to him, was a membrane that formed part of the larger structure of the uterus, or matrix, which to Soranus and everyone else of his era was the female genital par excellence. The rest of the female genital anatomy, in texts of this period, is rarely discussed in terms of specific parts. Only the uterus, with its miraculous capacity to turn sperm and blood into babies, was considered truly relevant.

After Soranus, there are a few examples of the Latin word *himen* (again meaning "membrane") in reference to matters gynecological. Often it is used, as in the tenth-century *De viribus herbarum,* to refer to the amniotic sac, the membrane that encloses the fetus while it grows in the womb. Occasionally *himen* is used in ways that seem to allude to a "virginal membrane," but not in ways that identify any particular part of the body. In the medieval era the *himen* of virginity, when the term is even used that way, seems to be more metaphorical—a symbolic boundary between virgin and nonvirgin—than it is something that anyone could point to in a dissection, or a patient's body. For centuries, though physicians clearly understood that there had to be some reason that women often bled when their vaginas were sexually penetrated for the first time, they saw no reason that such bleeding necessarily had to be associated with any specific bit of the genital anatomy.

Kathleen Coyne Kelly has found that usage of the word "hymen" to refer to the same thing we mean when we use the term today did not occur until the fifteenth century, when physician Michael Savonarola used the word in his *Practica maior*. "The cervix is covered by a subtle membrane called the hymen," Savonarola wrote, "which is broken at the time of deflowering, so that the blood flows." Savonarola's vague placement of the hymen somewhere "in front of the cervix" can perhaps be excused by the tendency, even in the 1400s, to view the uterus as the true womanly genital, and the vagina merely as an accessory passageway. In any case, he seems to have an understanding that this bit of tissue—it is technically something of a misnomer, although a common one, to call it a membrane—is inconspicuous and often not noticed unless it is damaged.

Savonarola's usage of "hymen" to mean the vaginal hymen was rapidly followed by the first such usage in English. The 1538 dictionary produced by Londoner Thomas Elyot cites it thus: "a skinne in the secrete place of a maiden, which whanne she is defloured is broken." From this point on, "hymen" becomes more and more commonly the vaginal hymen and less and less commonly anything else. By the seventeenth century, physicians and midwives writing in the vernacular use the term "hymen" in their discussions with the expectation that readers will automatically know which, out of the many parts of the body that could be called the hymen, they mean.

This chronology leaves no evidence to support the idea that there is a direct connection between Hymenaeus, the Greek god of marriage, and the name we've ended up using for the small bit of genital tissue that bears the name "hymen." While it does indeed seem like a fine bit of poetic justice that the story of Hymenaeus, a tragedy involving the death of a young groom on his wedding night, would come to be associated with a piece of anatomy that traditionally doesn't survive the wedding, the etymological timing simply doesn't make a causal relationship plausible. Had the ancient Greeks used the word "hymen" to mean something more anatomically specific, even if only in the specific sense of meaning a membrane whose functional destiny lay in its being broken (the amniotic sac, for instance), the argument that Hymenaeus lent his name to the hymen might hold a bit more water. As it stands, Greeks of the era during which Hymenaeus was actively worshipped did not, as we've seen, acknowledge the existence of a specific vaginal membrane, much less name it after their patron god of weddings. Just as the hymen itself is vestigial, a remnant of the time in the formation of the female body when the vaginal canal did not yet open into the vulva, so is the term we use to identify it, a throwback to an era where anatomical knowledge was so generalized that every membrane in the body could carry the same name.

Virginity Before the Hymen

The story of the anatomical hymen begins in earnest with the Greek Soranus, practicing and writing in third-century Rome. Soranus's claim to fame is his *Gynecology*, one of the earliest works on the topic that has survived in its entirety, and what Soranus has to say about the physical nature of virginity is very interesting indeed.

> In virgins the vagina is depressed and narrower, because it contains ridges that are held down by vessels originating in the uterus; when defloration occurs, these ridges unfold, causing pain; they burst, resulting in the excretion of blood that ordinarily flows. In fact, the belief that a thin membrane grows in the middle of the vagina and that it is this membrane that tears in defloration or when menstruation comes on too quickly, and that this same membrane, by persisting and becoming thicker, causes the malady known as "imperforation," is an error.

This description of the vagina as an expanding vessel with corrugated walls was considered authoritative for centuries due to its combination of intelligent observation and meticulous logic. Soranus refused to believe in the rumors he had heard about some strange membrane in the vagina because, as he wrote in *Gynecology*, he had no evidence that proved it existed. He had never been able to find it in dissection. He had never experienced any barriers to the insertion of probes into the vaginas of virgin patients. It also seemed, to Soranus, that if "the breaking of the membrane during defloration were the cause of pain, there would also have to be pain before defloration, at the time of the menstrual period. During defloration there should no longer be any." Last but not least, he opined that if a vaginal membrane were the cause of the malady of vaginal imperforation, doctors would always find the obstruction in the same place in every patient who suffered from that malady, and this was not the case.

And indeed Soranus is completely correct about all of this. One can insert a slender probe into a virgin's vagina and not encounter an obstacle until the end of the probe hits the cervix. Women do indeed menstruate when they are still virgins without any barrier in the vagina needing to be removed or altered before the flow can begin, and furthermore, virgin women can menstruate without the menstrual flow causing them pain. It is also true that occlusions of the female reproductive tract, what Soranus is calling "imperforations," may occur in a number of locations within the complex of vagina, uterus, and fallopian tubes.

In hindsight, the flaw in Soranus's reasoning is obvious. He is not imagining a membrane that normally has a hole in it, as we now know the typical hymen to be. Soranus is thinking of the hymen as a solid, contiguous, unbroken thing, like the lid of a jar or an oiled bladder stretched tight over the mouth of a wine jug. There was every reason he should have thought of it this way. In the ancient world, the predominant image of the womb, that most important of the female organs, was that of a vessel. Some described it as an upside-down jug with a long neck, others as a bowl in which male and female fluids were mixed and blood added to produce a child, giving the womb a functional resemblance to a *krater*, the cup or jar in which wine was mixed with water before being drunk. A jug without a stopper easily spills. A lid with a hole in its middle is hardly a lid at all. All of which is to say that what we might be tempted to view as a misconception is not ill-conceived at all. Soranus was being rigorously logical.

Not believing in the existence of a vaginal membrane, however, does not mean that Soranus did not believe in virginity. On the contrary, Soranus was, in contrast to Hippocrates and other Greek doctors before him, a proponent of virginity for both men and women. *Gynecology* is unique in the ancient world in that it actually takes seriously the notion of preserving virginity, and discusses the question of how long a girl could remain healthy as a virgin and what sort of lifestyle would best maintain her health. Soranus was a man of his time in this respect. This odd notion of a woman remaining a virgin rather than being married off at puberty was beginning to become a very charged and public issue in the Rome in which Soranus lived and wrote—a place in which a new faith, Christianity, was gradually gaining its feet.

But what of this idea of a membrane inside the vagina? Where did it come from, and if Soranus believed it wasn't true, who believed it was? Unfortunately, Soranus neglected to mention where he heard the concept. We have no idea if the idea came from some now-lost medical tract, from some unusual report given by a woman or midwife, or from some other source entirely. Classicist Aline Rousselle offers the idea that the "sealing membrane" hypothesis may have been a Roman notion that evolved out of the Roman practice of frequently marrying girls off even before they had had their first menstrual periods, a practice the Greeks did not follow and to which Soranus was opposed. The Romans would have observed, on multiple occasions, young women beginning menstruation only after they had been physically "opened" by intercourse, and they might then have conjectured that this opening of the passages by a penis removed some obstruction, making it possible for the menstrual blood to flow out.*

We don't know whether Rousselle is correct in her speculation about the Romans, and it is possible that we never will. Given the circumstances under which Soranus worked, a Roman source is certainly one of the most likely. Unfortunately, though, we have no documentary evidence, and so Soranus's mention remains merely a tantalizing hint of an alternate theory.

In any event, Soranus and his contemporaries did not need the hymen in order to have a concept of virginity. Nor did they need it to explain the symptoms commonly associated with virginity loss. Greek physicians believed that the uterus itself changed size when a girl began to menstruate, showing her readiness to conceive, and changed again when she left off being a *parthenos*

---

*Although it is beyond the scope of this book to discuss the many variants of this belief in depth, this is not as far-fetched an idea as it may seem. Similar notions have arisen in many cultures around the world. Even in the twentieth century, among indigenous Central and South Americans like the Cubeo of the Colombian Amazon, the Kayapo and Bororo of Brazil, and various rural Mexican populations, menstruation is often explained as the moon having sex with a woman, deflowering her so that she bleeds. Unlike a man, the moon only opens a woman partway, so that the moon must return to her and reopen her body each month until she marries. In these cultures it is believed that while the moon only opens the woman temporarily, a man opens her for good.

("girl" or "virgin" depending on context) and became a *gyne* ("woman" or "wife"). In a *parthenos*, the uterus was significantly smaller than it was in a *gyne*, and perhaps a little bit firmer, hotter, or drier as well. The humoral system by which ancient medicine was organized characterized heat, hardness, and dryness as qualities related to youth and maleness; coolness, sponginess, and moistness were associated with femaleness and age. According to this system, a fertile, childbearing uterus would be large, spongy, and moist. At least theoretically, virginity could be diagnosed with little more than a glance.

Such theories lived on long after Soranus, and were repeated more or less verbatim from one text to the next. It is not until the brilliant early-eleventh-century Persian scientist and physician known to the Western World as Avicenna (Avicenna is a Latinization of ibn Sina; his full name was Abu Ali al-Husain ibn Abdullah ibn Sina) that we acquire a vision of the vagina that is substantially different from Soranus's. At the end of his chapter on the anatomy of the womb, Avicenna states that prior to the defloration of a virgin girl, there are membranes in the mouth of the womb woven from veins and extremely delicate ligaments. These are, he claims, destroyed by the man who "violates" her, and the blood that is in them runs out. Translated into Latin by Gerard of Cremona sometime around the mid–twelfth century, Avicenna's description became the second influential model of the physical aspects of female virginity.

Throughout the medieval era, physicians employed a range of visual metaphors for this "virginal seal." The most common were the images of a woven web, as we find in Avicenna and later in the *De animalibus* of Albertus Magnus, and the image of a "knot of virginity" or *nodus virginalis* or *virginitatis*. William of Saliceto was a fan of the knot image, and his *Summa conservationis et curationis* of 1285 describes the *nodus virginitatis* as "tightly tied and wrinkled with veins and arteries that stand out like creases on a chickpea." The images of a veil that hung within the vagina and that of a flap or sheet of skin were also popular. An anonymous commentator on the fourteenth-century *De secretis mulierum* refers to a *pellicula*, a skin, in the vagina and bladder that is broken when a virgin first consorts with men. As we can infer from certain of the more unusual claims, like the creased and ridged surface William of Saliceto claims for his "knot" and the odd location of the *pellicula* claimed by the commentator on the *De secretis*, it is unlikely that any of these writers was, so to speak, sketching from an original model. That did not happen until 1544, when the internationally famous Flemish anatomist Andreas Vesalius finally found the hymen in dissection . . . although ironically, he too failed to sketch what he saw.

Vesalius Finds the Hymen

Given how many people were interested in the nature and identity of the hymen, it is certainly strange that it was never isolated in an actual dissection until the middle of the sixteenth century. Why was the hymen not physically isolated until so late in the game? Certainly the relative infrequency of dissections of female bodies accounts for part of it. In most places, the only bodies legally available for medical dissection were the corpses of criminals who had been executed, which would make legal dissections of female bodies a rare event indeed. Another factor was almost certainly that virginity, as fascinating a topic as it is, has never been as medically important as pregnancy. Most premodern anatomies of women's bodies exist to detail the uterus, the fetus, and the stages of pregnancy. Given how many women have died in childbirth, as compared to the relatively infinitesimal number who have ever suffered more than temporary physical complications from being deflowered, we can excuse our progenitors for thinking that the search for the hymen was perhaps a legitimately lesser priority.

Finally, however, in early 1544 in the university town of Pisa, Italy, Vesalius deliberately undertook dissections of the bodies of two women whom he believed to be virgins, intending that they serve a documentary, scientific purpose. The results of the dissections themselves remained unpublished until 1546, when Vesalius published a report of them as part of a tract he wrote about the use of ginseng in the treatment of venereal diseases, his *Epistola rationem modumque propinandi radicis Chynae decocti* (*Letter on the China Root*).

We do not know the names of the women whose bodies Vesalius dissected, and we know little about their lives. One was a nun of middle years (Vesalius gives her age as "at least thirty-six years old") who had died of pleurisy, her corpse acquired from Florence. Scholars believe the nun's body came from the Hospital of Santa Maria Nuova in Florence, where Duke Cosimo de'Medici, one of Renaissance Italy's great patrons of the arts and sciences, had sufficient influence to arrange such a thing as an illegal body snatching without anyone asking too many questions (he had done so in the past for Leonardo da Vinci).

A letter from a secretary of the University of Pisa, dated 22 January 1544, survives in the Florence city archives, detailing Cosimo de'Medici's assistance in secretly acquiring bodies and having them shipped, at night and by barge, down the River Arno to Pisa where the celebrated visiting anatomist would dissect them.

The second woman in whom Vesalius, during his Pisan sojourn, located a hymen was a seventeen-year-old hunchbacked girl. Vesalius said that he "examined the uterus [meaning the genitals overall] of the girl since I expected her to be a virgin because very likely no one had ever wanted her." The hunchbacked girl's body was stolen from the Camposanto, Pisa's medieval cemetery, to which, by well-established medical school tradition, enterprising students had arranged to find themselves in possession of gate keys. Among medical men of the time, body snatching and grave robbing were both commonplace and illegal. In his *De humani corporis fabrica* (1543), Vesalius himself quietly acknowledged that grave robbing was of unfortunate necessity to the medical man.

On the dissections themselves, Vesalius said:

When the flesh had been removed from the bones of the nun and the girl for the preparation of the skeleton, in the presence of a few students I examined the uterus of the girl since I expected her to be a virgin because very likely nobody had ever wanted her. I found a hymen in her as well as in the nun, at least thirty-six years old, whose ovaries, however, were shrunken as happens to organs that are not used.

Vesalius's *Epistola* and the dissections he discusses within it do indeed represent something of a watershed in the medical history of the hymen. Finally, an anatomist with sufficient credibility to be taken seriously (and an audience of medical students to boot) had found the elusive hymen, allowing it to be inscribed in the record books once and for all as a duly verified anatomical entity. At the same time, Vesalius's confirmation of the physical existence of the vaginal hymen was not exactly a gynecological "shot heard 'round the world," transforming medical science and attitudes toward women's bodies and virginity overnight. It would be more accurate to say that Vesalius's discovery began to apply the brakes to what was, at that point, a twelve-hundred-year-long debate about what the hymen was and what it looked like.

Even after Vesalius, as a matter of fact, medical science *still* didn't know what the hymen looked like. Vesalius never drew the hymen. This omission, in the work of an anatomical artist of Vesalius's caliber, is extremely curious, the more so since he knew full well that no one else had done it. We cannot expect that he would have included the hymen in the first edition of his 1543 *De humani corporis fabrica* (*On the Formation of the Human Body*). But it is genuinely odd that the hymen was also not included in the 1555 *De humani corporis fabrica epitome*, the edition of the *Fabrica* he created for use as a teaching text. Given Vesalius's self-proclaimed emphasis on correcting the errors made by the ancients, it would seem to have been precisely in his bailiwick to include it, but it is nowhere to be found.

Why did Vesalius not detail the hymen? He himself left no clue. Some apologists for Vesalius, like the English physician Helkiah Crooke in his *Microcosmographia: a Description of the Body of Man* (1615), explained it away by saying that the female drawings in the *Fabrica* were based on the body of a pregnant woman, and thus the hymen would not have been present. But perhaps—and this is merely conjecture—there is another reason that Vesalius did not diagram the hymen. It may very well be that despite having located it physically, Vesalius, as would prove to become the case with many other estimable medical men, was not entirely convinced that the humble-looking bit of flesh that is the hymen was all it was cracked up to be.

Dueling Hymens

It didn't seem to matter that Vesalius had neglected—we can only assume intentionally—to include the hymen in his highly thorough and scientific diagrams of the human body, and buried his testimony of discovering it in the depths of another treatise. The hymen was too much of an obsession for too many people for Vesalius's findings to go unnoticed. Other physicians leapt upon Vesalius's record of finding the hymen like the proverbial starving dogs, loudly proclaiming that they had seen the hymen, too, or if they hadn't seen it themselves, that they knew someone who had.

James Guillemeau, author of a major treatise on midwifery, Helkiah Crooke, Johannes Vesling, and Séverin Pineau were among the European doctors only too happy to take up the hymenal ball and run with it. Of these, Pineau was probably the most influential. His 1597 *De virginitatis et corruptionis virginum notis* (*On Virginity and the Signs of Corrupted Virginity*) is a discussion of virginity from the medical perspective, a self-proclaimed "true history" of the hymen. It includes full descriptions of the size, function, and anatomical makeup of the hymen and enthusiastic instructions on how to detect ruined virgins.

Pineau's fans expanded upon his assertions willy-nilly: Crooke states that the hymen is not a single membrane but is really made up of eight parts, "caruncles" and membranes, and says that "all these particles together make the form of the cup of a little rose half blowne." Vesling confuses the issue further. He claims both "caruncles," after Crooke, but also a "fleshy skin that covers the passage" and is guarded by the aforementioned caruncles. Confusingly, Crooke additionally points to a membrane "vulgarly taken for the Hymen," explaining that there is yet *another* "thin skin" in the female genitals that is "stretched across the chink like a zone." Marie Loughlin, who chronicles this astounding proliferation of Renaissance hymens in the first chapter of her 1997 book *Hymeneutics: Interpreting Virginity on the Early Modern Stage*, aptly characterizes it as a "desperate and conflicted search."

Just how conflicted these writers really were, and how anxious they were to confirm an irrefutable physical proof of virginity, can be seen in Crooke's utter failure to maintain the courage of his own vociferous convictions. Proclaiming first that the hymen is the "onley sure note of unsteyned virginity," he proceeds directly to make reference to an alternate virginity test. Essentially a parlor game, this test involves measuring a thread from the tip of a woman's nose to the base of the skull, then wrapping it around her neck. If the woman is a virgin, the thread should precisely encompass her neck, but if it is too short or too long, she is not. The test is a bizarre offering, coming from a man who clearly wants to believe that the hymen alone can prove or disprove virginity.

French surgeon Ambroise Paré, a late-sixteenth-century pioneer of military surgery and the study of birth defects, would have answered Crooke's angsty self-contradiction with a derisive Gallic snort. Paré, a highly experienced surgeon and actively dissecting anatomist, was medicine's most vocal opponent of the hymen. He knew about the anatomical discovery of it, and was well aware of descriptions claiming it to be a membrane stretched across the vaginal opening.

Like Soranus, though, Paré preferred to trust the testimony of his own observations. What he observed was that the hymen, as it had been described to him, simply didn't exist.

> In som virgins or maidens in the orifice of the neck of the womb there is found a certain tunicle or membrane called of antient writers Hymen, which prohibiteth the copulation of a man, and causseth a woman to be barren; this tunicle is supposed by manie, and they not of the common sort onley, but also learned Physicians, to bee, as it were, the enclosure of the virginite or maiden-head. But I could never finde it in anie, seeking of all ages from three to twelv, of all that I had under my hands in the Hospital of Paris.

At the same time, Paré understands that imperforate hymens do exist. His text cites a rather gruesome case study of a girl whose imperforate hymen, prior to surgery, led to such an extreme case of hematocolpos (backed-up menstrual blood that cannot exit the body) that it was "as if she had beene in travail with child." Later, in his *Des monstres et prodigues*, a 1573 compendium on monstrous births and birth defects, Paré would cite the hymen, along with extra fingers or toes and similar malformations, as an example of a malformation of the body that maims the person unlucky enough to be born with it, but that is not truly monstrous. As if this were not sufficient to clarify Paré's feelings on the matter, he furthermore made it clear in his *De la Generation de l'Homme* (Concerning the Generation of Man) that the unsupportable myth of the virginal hymen could interfere with the workings of legal justice:

> Midwives will certainly affirm that they know a virgin from one that is deflowered by the breach or soundness of that membrane. But by their report credulous Judges are soon brought to commit an error, for that Midwives can speak nothing certainly of this membrane may be proved by this, because that one saith that the situation thereof is in the very entrance of the privy parts, others say it is in the midst of the neck of the womb, and others say it is within at the inner orifice thereof, and some are of the opinion that they say or suppose that it cannot be seen or perceived before

the first birth. But truly of a thing so rare, and which is contrary to nature, there cannot be anything spoken for certainty.

For Paré, a hymen was a membrane that sealed the vagina, and nothing else. When he did not find such a thing in the normal women and girls he examined, it was sufficient for him to state that the hymen did not normally exist, and that in cases where it did, it was a serious defect. Anyone who thought otherwise was a fool.

Then and Now

In the end Paré lost his crusade and the essentially Vesalian vision of the hymen promoted by Pineau won out. Seventeenth-century midwife Jane Sharp accepts the existence of the vaginal hymen without a quibble, and by 1668 we find the anatomical diagrams in the *Anatomy* of Thomas Bartholin prominently featuring a relatively accurate and correctly labeled hymen and hymenal orifice. From this point forward, the hymen is anatomical *terra cognita*, acknowledged universally to exist.

Thus the hymen spent a few relatively uneventful centuries in the medical books, a minor anatomical feature of the female genitalia that could typically be found described as existing in two states, "intact" and "ruptured." Canon and secular law both valued the hymen highly as proof of virginity. On the personal level, the hymen mattered to brides and grooms and mothers and fathers. At the same time, in the heady heyday of Enlightenment skepticism, the Chevalier de Jaucourt, in an article composed for the first Western encyclopedia, could archly question the nature of virginity itself:

> Men, says M. de Buffon, jealous of privacies in every sphere, have always made much of whatever they believed they possessed exclusively and before anyone else. It is this kind of madness that has made a real entity of the virginity of maidens.

Jaucourt's refreshing cynicism was, however, nowhere near as influential as Pineau or Vesalius. By the nineteenth century, the hymen was more firmly entrenched than ever as material proof of a sexual status that was, more and more frequently, being cast as a matter of inherent virtue. Time marched on, but even as the decades of the twentieth century began to slip past, the fundamentals of the medical understanding of the hymen remained essentially the same. It existed, and while it did and was "intact," a woman was a virgin. Once it wasn't, neither was she, and that was all anybody apparently felt the need to know.

It was not until the child sex abuse furor of the 1980s that hymens once again became the object of serious medical study. There was a sudden hunt, as researchers Karin Edgardh and Kari Ormstad put it in their overview of contemporary hymen research, "for a 'gold standard' that could substantiate stories and suspicions of sexual assault." Unsurprisingly given its history and the claims made for it, this hunt centered on the hymen.

Most of the efforts to develop a hymenal standard for abuse diagnosis have centered around two types of anatomical evidence. Clefts or transections of the hymen are the evidence of past tissue tears. Clefts can, however, appear independently of penetration or other sexual trauma. A complete posterior transection of the hymen is considered a red flag in a diagnostic examination looking for signs of abuse, something that indicates a probability of penetration, but it is not by any means definitive.

The other aspect of the hymen that doctors have repeatedly examined in their search for reliable physical proof of abuse is the diameter of the hymen's orifice or opening. Although there are a number of small studies that appear, at first blush, to indicate a positive correlation between an increased orifice size and sexual abuse, larger studies allowing for greater comparison have concluded otherwise. A team led by Dr. Daniel Ingram of the University of North Carolina School of Medicine in Chapel Hill, North Carolina, looked at 1,975 girls referred to a Raleigh, North Carolina, sexual abuse care team over a ten-year period from May of 1988 to May of 1998 and ultimately came to the conclusion that the size of the hymenal orifice could not provide sufficient evidence from which to conclude that a girl was sexually abused.

Other researchers agree. Ann Botash and Abby Berenson, two leading hymen researchers, have both cautioned against interpreting any hymenal findings in isolation. "Medical records of all female children at all well-child examinations should describe the hymen configuration as well as changes in configuration with time. Physical findings do not usually provide clear evidence of sexual abuse and the history continues to be the most important factor when attempting to conclude whether or not a child has been sexually abused." Perhaps with time and study there will be another Vesalius, another skilled and lucky anatomist who is able to detect something we currently cannot, and reveal to us some of the mysteries of this notoriously inscrutable piece of tissue. Until then, all we can say with certainty about the hymen is that it remains an open book, its diagnostic usefulness as much a puzzle to us now as its very existence was for our ancestors.

CHAPTER 5

The Virgin and the Doctor

"I tried to tell her once more," said the grandmother, "that marriage and children would cure her of everything. 'All women of our family are delicate when they are young,' I said. 'Why when I was your age no one expected me to live a year. It was called greensickness, and everybody knew there was only one cure.' 'If I live for a hundred years and turn green as grass,' said Amy, 'I still shan't want to marry Gabriel.' "
—Katherine Anne Porter, "Old Mortality"

IHAVE, MORE THAN ONCE, seen young unmarried women, of the middle classes of society, reduced, by the constant use of the speculum, to the mental and moral condition of prostitutes; seeking to give themselves the same indulgence by the practice of solitary vice; and asking every medical practitioner, under whose care they fell, to institute an examination of the sexual organs," wrote physician Robert Brudenell Carter in 1853. The vaginal speculum, the infamous duck-billed contraption that features as best supporting actor in most gynecological exams, has been with us in one form or another since Roman times, holding open the vaginal walls so that physicians can see inside. It took the nineteenth century's sexual paranoia to turn the vaginal speculum into a weapon of mass feminine destruction.

The nineteenth-century controversy over the use of the speculum contains all the classic elements of interactions between virgins and doctors. Medical and moral claims regarding access to the body coexisted uneasily. The act of examining the genitals by touch was only barely acceptable by the mainstream medical standards of the day, and then only when absolutely necessary. It was by no means clear what sorts of medical need could excuse the more invasive speculum examination. Using the speculum was seen as intrusion into the vagina, not only by an object but by the male gaze, making every woman a potential victim not only of the speculum but of the presumably voyeuristic "speculumizer."

The use of the speculum did not, in other words, merely represent the possibility of a physically disrupted hymen, although that fear certainly accounted for some of the controversy. It represented a wholesale breach of the *hortus clausus*, the "enclosed garden" of the feminine body, the supposedly inherent purity and modesty that tradition generally, and nineteenth-century mores particularly, attributed to women.

As such, the speculum was seen as a first step on a perilously steep slope that could lead straight from purity to perdition. It physically opened a body that was supposed to be closed to all men save a woman's husband. Worse, the insertion of an object into the vagina was thought to give women ideas they shouldn't have. For want of further vaginal stimulation, women who underwent speculum exams—or so argued Carter and some of his colleagues—would begin engaging in the ruinous "solitary vice" of masturbation and perhaps even turn to prostitution. Such fears of uncontrollable transformations set in motion by the use of medical technology, very like the upright Dr. Jekyll's transformation via drug into the murderous Mr. Hyde, were both a fear and a fantasy in a nineteenth century in which genuinely scientific medical practice was just beginning to gain ground.

Both the bodies and chastity of women and the nature and intentions of medical men were at stake in the speculum controversy. Medical examination of women's bodies by men has always been at least somewhat controversial, and particularly so in cases involving virgins. As far back as St. Augustine we can find cautionary tales of virgins whose virginities are accidentally "ruined" by clumsy midwives or physicians. The male gynecological specialist's motivations were suspect because they constituted male intrusion not just into women's bodies, but into a historically all-female realm. For most of recorded history, the treatment of women's sexual and reproductive health was the almost exclusive bailiwick of women, including the "juries of matrons" who performed the genital examinations required in the evaluation of rape and annulment cases and who were among the rare women considered qualified to give testimony in medieval courts of law. Women served as respected and acknowledged medical professionals for other women in evaluating fertility and treating infertility, coping with pregnancy and its complications, delivering babies, and of course in evaluating virginity.

It was not until around 1625 that a term even existed to identify men professionally interested in the health of women and babies. Until the twentieth century, "men-midwives" were often held in disrespect by both women and by other physicians. By crossing over into what had for so long been women's turf, men-midwives crossed not only traditional lines of propriety but also boundaries of class, because midwifery and all it entailed was women's work, a dirty, low trade that could be performed even by those who had not the benefit of a proper, manly Latin education. It was not infrequently presumed that the only interest a man could possibly have in matters gynecological was of the prurient sort. Gynecologists went out of their way to avoid such allegations, frequently conducting examinations by touch alone, perhaps with the patient curtained off by bedsheets, in order to avoid giving the impression of impropriety. It was also not uncommon for doctors conducting gynecological exams to perform palpations of the uterus and ovaries by inserting a finger or fingers into the rectum rather than the vagina, as that was considered less potentially erotic and did not present the problem of possibly damaging the hymen in unmarried women. Men-midwives literally could not afford to be suspected of what was archly termed " 'scientific' rascaldom."

As if this did not already form a sufficiently polarized background for trying to introduce the speculum into gynecological practice, the speculum itself had acquired an aura of guilt by association. In her book *The Science of Woman*, historian Ornella Moscucci describes how the age-old medical instrument became tainted, in the early nineteenth century, by a relationship with prostitution, the police, and venereal disease. Speculum exam became routine in France in the wake of the 1810 legalization and regulation of prostitution. New laws required each prostitute who registered to practice her trade to submit to a speculum exam to be checked for evidence of venereal disease. Because these exams were performed in a public health context, by physicians in the public employ, upon "public women," trainee physicians from all over Europe and the British Isles, as well as the United States, were able to observe these exams during studies in Paris.

Prostitutes, considered to be already ruined and only marginally human, could not only be forced to undergo a type of exam that would scarcely have been considered a reasonable thing to request of a "normal" woman, but they could be forced to serve as living visual aids as well.

By midcentury, an unprecedented number of physicians had seen the speculum in action, realized that it had a great deal to offer them as diagnosticians, and began to use the instrument in their own practice. Outrage followed, and articles, reports, and vitriolic letters to the editor began to litter the medical journals. Robert Lee, the professor of midwifery at St. George's Hospital, London, was one of the speculum's most vocal opponents, delivering a May 1850 paper before the Royal Medical and Chirurgical Society that gruesomely detailed his opposition. Lee's examples "gave a medical veneer to arguments that had little to do with science, and everything with morals," Ornella Moscucci writes. Physiologist Marshall Hall similarly spoke of a degrading "dulling of the edge of virgin modesty," and thundered "what father amongst us . . . would allow his virgin daughter to be subjected to this pollution?" One pseudonymous writer to the 1850 *Medical Times* suggested facetiously that "speculumizers" might consider renting out an opera house for a season of public exhibition.

Indeed, even today, it is not uncommon for gynecologists to either forgo performing internal exams on virgin patients, or to habitually use smaller and narrower speculums with them. This is often explained as being necessitated by the small size of the virginal vagina, but this is not necessarily physiologically true. Prepubescent girls do typically have smaller and narrower vaginas, just as their bodies are smaller overall, and preadolescent vaginas tend not to be as elastic as postpubertal ones due to lower estrogen levels. It was for these reasons that tools like the Huffman adolescent speculum, a smaller, narrower-bladed version of the standard Graves speculum, were developed.

In women who have gone through puberty, however, the vagina is likely to be estrogenized, elastic, and at its adult size. The dimensions of the vagina itself—like the size of the penis—do not change because someone has become sexually active. It is not, therefore, terribly likely that the issue genuinely is the vagina's ability to accommodate a speculum. It is more likely to be a fear of damaging the hymen, or a lingering if unsubstantiated notion that the first object to penetrate a particular vagina, whether it is a penis or a speculum or something else entirely, has a unique propensity to cause damage and pain. It seems that even the most clinical and mechanical penetration of a virginal vagina still seems to carry the distinct whiff of destruction, a potential that at least some gynecologists still prefer, even in the twenty-first century, to avoid.

The Virgin Cure

A common contention during the heyday of the speculum debate, generally brought up in the attempt to dismiss the usefulness of the speculum, was that virgins did not contract venereal disease. Speculum exams were useful primarily for diagnosing VD, the argument ran, and logically virgins (and all respectable women generally) would not be exposed to VD. Without the possibility of VD, there was little or no natural need for any doctor to inspect the interior of the vagina, and thus no need for the speculum.

It was a fine argument as far as it went, but alas, it didn't go very far. In point of fact, virgins have often been the particular victims of sexually transmitted infections (STIs) due to a pernicious, long-running myth that a person suffering from an STI can be cured by having sexual relations with a virgin. We do not know when or where this myth began. Desperate people do desperate things, though, and as such, the practice has probably been around almost as long as people have recognized the signs of sexually transmitted diseases in their bodies and struggled, horrified, to be rid of them. We have evidence that the use of virgins as a VD remedy has been especially rampant in various places at various times, among them in Scotland in the late nineteenth and early twentieth centuries, in various parts of Eastern Europe in the late eighteenth century, and currently in AIDS-ravaged Africa.

Part of what is behind this practice is a naive and hopeful belief in sympathetic magic. Across cultures and eras, virgins have been perceived as having a particular potent purity that acts as a shield and keeps the virgin from harm. In Christian virgin martyr legends, for instance, virgins often do battle with demons or with Satan himself while protected by virginity. Surely, the thinking goes, something powerful enough to vanquish demons can also cure syphilis. All one has to do is to take that something from the body of someone who still possesses it.

Other explanations have also been advanced. It is, for example, possible that the myth either began with or was corroborated by a coincidence. Many STIs have distinctly different symptom stages. Initial symptoms, like sores, blisters, or discharges, may eventually cease, to be replaced by more systemic, but less immediately noticeable, symptoms. If an infected person had sex with a virgin during a shift between symptom stages, or if a shift in symptom stages took place shortly after the sexual interaction, the infected person could easily (if incorrectly) deduce that having sex with a virgin was what had caused the illness to "disappear." If the former virgin subsequently came down with primary symptoms of the STI, it would appear to provide proof that the illness had been transferred to another person. Prior to the time when scientific medicine was finally able to explain how such illnesses were actually transmitted, the idea that STIs could be given wholesale to another person was as good an explanation as any for the sudden disappearance of symptoms in one person and their equally sudden appearance in another.

Lest this sound so ignorant as to be unbelievable, it should be noted that many pre-twentieth-century doctors believed that it was not only possible but common for venereal infections to be transmitted in ways that did not require sexual or even physical contact with others. (Many infections classed as "venereal" or "sexually transmitted" can in fact be transmitted nonsexually, but generally not in the ways most of these doctors imagined.) In the later eighteenth and nineteenth centuries, for example, venereal diseases were sometimes blamed on masturbation, or on any of a number of conditions strongly associated with poverty, such as dirty rooms, bad air, infrequently changed linens, or shared eating utensils. The morality of parents was also at issue; parents' sexual overindulgence with one another was thought to be a potential cause of venereal disease in their children.

This sort of thinking combined in a most insidious way with the nineteenth-century notion that children and "respectable" females of all ages were essentially nonsexual. In a social climate where it was unthinkable for a "good" female to be sexual outside of marriage, it was equally unthinkable to voice suspicions that the woman or girl had been raped or molested. Any "good" virgin or child who showed symptoms of an STI was likely to find the blame landing squarely on her and on her family's socioeconomic status. If STI cases could be blamed on things like dirty underpants or poor housing conditions, perhaps they could also be avoided by providing cleaner or better ones. This was a tidy, charitable, and easily effected change, and one in keeping with the popular, middle-class philanthropic goals of the day. Furthermore, it allowed both doctors and families to maintain reassuring lies: children had not been violated, virgins had not been despoiled, and men did not stoop to such reprehensible things.

This willful dissociation of venereal disease from sexual activity was so strong, in some cases, that in order to prosecute cases in which children and virgins had been raped, lawyers and judges were tasked with proving that the practice of attempting to use virgins as a venereal disease cure did in fact exist. One such case, the 1913 Glasgow arraignment of a thirty-seven-year-old coal miner for the alleged rape of his nine-year-old niece—and the additional of-fense of transmitting to her the "gonorrhoea and other venereal disease with which his private parts were at the time affected"—provided the occasion for a substantial and impressive inquiry into the issue.

Indeed, as numerous eminent physicians testified, the notion of the "virgin cure" was quite widespread. His Majesty's Prison Surgeon Dr. James Devon's testimony in this case was both sweeping and damning: "There is a curiously persistent and widespread belief that a man who suffers from venereal disease can get rid of it by having connection with a virgin. I have been surprised at discovering the existence of this belief in people generally well informed as well as among the comparatively illiterate. I have tried to find evidence for the theory that it is a belief traceable to certain districts but I have discovered it among people of different places and of different occupations—so different that now I should scarcely be surprised to come across it anywhere."

And indeed there was no reason that Dr. Devon should have been surprised to find evidence of this particular myth in turn-of-the-century Scottish society. Since at least the eighteenth century, rape cases involving children had been com-monplace in other British Isles courts: in eighteenth-century London, approxi-mately one in every five capital rape cases on the books involved a victim under the age of ten. The virgin cure myth, as Antony Simpson notes in his analysis of such rapes, was a commonplace excuse offered by accused child rapists, and lawyers and judges throughout the eighteenth century and into the nineteenth knew of the belief and were familiar with its use as a justification for rape.

The belief was never limited to the British Isles, although it remained a no-ticeable presence in British venereal disease surveys until the mid–twentieth century. It was noted as a problem among some subcultures in the nineteenth- and early-twentieth-century United States as well, particularly populations for whom neither higher education nor medical treatment was commonly available. And while the myth is no longer prevalent in the First World, it continues to flourish elsewhere. Since the advent of the HIV/AIDS epidemic in the 1980s, the millions of infections around the world and the desperate straits faced by the

HIV-positive in the Third World have created a tragically fertile field in which the myth of the virgin cure has flourished. In South Africa specifically, where a number of highly visible infant rape cases have brought the issue to the international news pages, the rates of child rape have risen by as much as 400 percent. University of South Africa surveys of South Africans reveal that substantial percentages of those interviewed—as high as 32 percent in Gauteng province, the region that contains the country's capital, Pretoria, and one of its largest cities, Johannesburg—believed that sex with a virgin could cure AIDS.

The virgin cure myth is thus no mere artifact of an ignorant past, but a very real and present problem. A taboo within a taboo, it is difficult to discuss and more difficult to prevent. Merely entertaining the possibility that some people might believe the virgin cure possible, much less attempt it, is so unpleasant that many people take refuge in denial, or blame it on the ignorant, on the poor, and on parents too incompetent or wicked to protect their children from such a fate. Such claims hold up no better now than they did in the nineteenth century. The virgin cure may, these days, be a more pressing concern in black townships in South Africa than in predominantly white communities in the United States or northern Europe, but this is no excuse for smugness . . . or false security. As the historical record shows, when desperate situations make it seem reasonable to think about doing desperate things, interest in the virgin cure knows no ethnic or cultural bounds.

The Disease of Virgins

Sex with a virgin has been believed to be a cure for more than just venereal disease. For over five hundred years it was believed to cure virgins themselves of a very specific medical disorder that only they could suffer. This disease, known as *morbus virginaeus* in Latin, or simply "the sickness of virgins" in English, is no longer considered to exist as a condition in Western medicine. Prior to the twentieth century, however, it was not only a common diagnosis but had a substantial medical literature as well. With its long history, its inconclusive nature, and its sudden disappearance from the medical landscape, the disease of virgins is not only a curiosity, it is also a first-rate medical mystery.

The disease of virgins went by many names. Known in different places and times as chlorosis, "the white fever," *Bleichzucht*, *les pâles couleurs*, greensickness, and *geelzucht*, it was one of the few diseases whose ultimate cure was hinted at in its very name. Marry the girl off and relieve her of her virginity, and a cure was sure to be had, the lyrics to the British Renaissance ballad "A Cure for the Green-Sickness" implied. Deprive her of a lover, on the other hand, and she might well die:

> *A Handsom buxom Lass*
> *Lay panting in her bed,*
> *She lookt as green as grass*
> *And mournfully she said:*
> *"Except I have some lusty lad*
> *To ease me of my pain*
> *I cannot live,*
> *I sigh and grieve,*
> *My life I now disdain."*

Indeed, women sometimes died of greensickness, either due to the course of the disease itself or from suicide triggered by mental derangement, such as "desiring death as a lover," which was sometimes a symptom. And indeed, marriage and particularly childbearing were believed to be a sovereign cure. What this disease of virgins really was, on the other hand, is harder to say.

As implied by the multitude of names used to identify this illness, the disease of virgins was not so much a discrete condition with distinct characteristics all its own, like dysentery or a broken leg, but a syndrome, a collection of symptoms that all seemed related in some way. Some of the symptoms, such as lack of menstruation, paleness, lack of normal appetite, and pica (the desire to eat dirt and other substances normally considered inedible) remained relatively constant over the centuries that the condition was described in medical books. Other symptoms, like a feverish pulse, swelling of the eyelids and ankles, difficult breathing, heart palpitations, delusional thinking, chest pains, suicidal tendencies, swelling of the liver, a supposed "backwards flow" of the blood toward the heart, and the green complexion implied in the name "greensickness," turn up in accounts from some time periods and not others. Perhaps unsurprisingly, given the array of symptoms associated with the disease of virgins, it often overlapped with other diagnoses. A young woman showing symptoms of this disease might also be diagnosed with anything from lovesickness to obstruction of the spleen, and in some cases such a diagnosis might even have been the correct one.

From a historical perspective, however, the most interesting thing about the disease of virgins is that it was a disease *of virgins*, an iconic disease suffered by women at a stage of life when they theoretically were in their prime and full of potential. As a disease of virgins, it also insistently points to virginity as a source of trouble rather than a source of reassurance and safety.

The primary symptom of the disease of virgins was lack of menstruation. In the understanding of the humoral medical system, it was believed that when a woman did not menstruate properly, the blood that should have been purged from her body by menstruation became backed up inside. This excess blood might putrefy and become poisonous (menstrual blood was often considered to be poisonous to begin with), weigh down the woman's womb and limbs, or even cause her circulatory system to become so backed up that blood would be forced to flow backward. According to Hippocratean theory, the backed-up blood might put pressure on the heart and cause mental disturbances and the sensation of being strangled, cause women to see ghosts, or make them try to drown or hang themselves. Virginity might have saved women from the enormous risks of childbirth, but what good was that if it meant that they developed a disorder that might kill them anyway? Virginity, held up for so many centuries as the Christian ideal for women, might save women from the ravages of sexual sin, but it could not save them from the treachery of having a womb.

While the disease of virgins did nothing to make the female body seem less toxic and dangerous, it did provide quite a good argument for the expediency of marriage. It can scarcely be complete coincidence that the emergence of this disease as a distinct and distinctly *virginal* phenomenon in the medical literature, curable by nothing more or less than the topical application of marital sex, coincided very closely with the emergence of Protestantism in Europe. Protestantism, unlike Catholicism, had no real use for adult virginity. It is no coincidence that greensickness appears on the heels of Protestantism. Martin Luther nailed his ninety-five theses to the doors of the Castle Church at Wittenberg in 1517; by 1526 his German mass (the first Protestant service) had been formulated. The first major medical writing on the disease of virgins, in the German physician Johannes Lang's *Medicinalium epistolarum miscellanea*, appeared right on schedule in 1554.

This is by no means to say that the disease of virgins was invented as a Protestant plot to get women married off, or even that it only suddenly began to exist in the sixteenth century. In point of fact, a set of symptoms very similar to those of the disease can be found in the Hippocratean corpus, and certainly the medical literature bears out the fact that young women with menstrual irregularities and mood disorders have always existed. But there was clearly something specific to the mid–sixteenth century that allowed doctors to suddenly begin speaking of a disease of virgins when, previously, they would have spoken about individual symptoms. That something, in a nutshell, was the emergence of a social climate in which virginity could be discussed in a negative light without running the risk of committing heresy.

Not, mind you, that this made the symptoms of the disease of virgins any more genuinely a result of virginity than they had ever been. Such symptoms can strike women of any age and sexual status, and many things may cause them. In fact, one of the curious side notes in the history of the sickness of virgins is that sometimes the absence of menstruation, upset stomachs, and other symptoms associated with it were actually symptoms of something else entirely, namely the rather nonvirginal condition of pregnancy. The fact that absent menses are an ambiguous symptom was not lost on doctors and midwives. In calling for purgatives, medications to induce menstruation, bloodletting, and other treatments, writers cautioned against using them on women who were pregnant. Since early pregnancy can be indistinguishable from the symptoms of greensickness, there was a possibility that treating greensickness could cause miscarriage, and it seems clear that doctors understood that this might, in fact, be precisely what was desired. For legal reasons, however, they dared not give the impression that they endorsed it. The medical disclaimer, in other words, is nothing new.

There were of course other causes than pregnancy for the symptoms associated with the disease of virgins. Various explanations have been advanced over the years, running a broad gamut from Bright's disease to biliverdin jaundice to the rare variant of acute myelocytic leukemia known as chloroma. These and other highly specific diagnoses, however, likely accounted for only a very small number of cases of *morbus virginaeus*. If nothing else, the fact that so many of the girls who suffered from the disease of virgins survived it argues against many of the more terminal explanations. To this end, most of what are considered the likeliest modern-day diagnoses for greensickness or the disease of virgins are forms of anemia, particularly a variant known as hypochromic anemia.

It is conjectured that much of this anemia was caused by insufficient nutrition. Whether because limited food availability and sexism have offered them no better or because the pressures of social conformity have led them to permit themselves no more, women and girls have often gone without sufficient nourishment. It is hardly coincidental that many treatments for the disease of virgins included the recommendation to improve the girls' diets, specifically adding meat and wine, both of which were believed to strengthen the blood (and which red meat, a good source of dietary iron, in fact can), and other nourishing foods. In the eighteenth and nineteenth centuries, when patent medicines for the treatment of what was by then called chlorosis became available, some of the most successful were mineral supplements.

In this light we can understand some of the ways that marriage and motherhood might have helped to cure the disease of virgins. It was not, as was often written, the opening up of the passages of the womb and vagina by intercourse and childbearing that cured the disease by making a straight and ready path for the exit of all that pent-up menstrual blood. Rather, as wife and head of the domestic sphere, a woman was likely to have better access to food. Marriage and motherhood might also have helped to resolve psychological causes of greensickness as well, possibly simply because unnecessary invalidism was no longer an option—her household needed her.

None of this, of course, discouraged the myriad people who pruriently joked about the cure for chlorosis being a simple matter of applying an appropriately virile penis. As this tidbit of anonymous Elizabethan doggerel shows, greensickness and curing it were—a bit like menstruation still is today—the butt of many a bawdy barroom joke:

A mayden faire of ye greene sicknesse late
Pitty to see, perplexed was full sore
Resolvinge how t'amend her bad estate,
In this distresse Apollo doth implore
Cure for her ill; ye oracle assignes,
Keepe ye first letter of these severall lines.

Despite the many cures attempted, jokes cracked, and explanations advanced, the disappearance of symptoms in women who suffered from the disease of virgins remains as mysterious, and has nearly as many possible explanations, as the disappearance of the disease itself. For four centuries the disease of virgins, under all its many names, was the paradigmatic clinical disorder suffered by young women, in much the same sense that depression and eating disorders are the paradigmatic disorders suffered by young women today. As late as 1901, Sir Clifford Allbutt could still write that "the chlorotic girl is well-known in every consulting room, public or private." But somehow, as the first quarter of the twentieth century wore on, the disease of virgins gradually vanished. No longer considered a viable diagnosis, no longer included in current medical texts, young women who presented with the same symptoms that would have gotten them diagnosed with chlorosis a decade earlier were now being told they had other things wrong with them. After five hundred years, the disease of virgins went from ubiquity to nonexistence in the space of a generation.

Where it went, and what to make of the very real disorders and discomforts of the women who had suffered it, are matters of considerable debate among historians of medicine. Dr. Helen King of the University of Reading, United Kingdom, and the author of a monograph dealing with the history of the disease of virgins, offers a number of possible explanations, including improvements in medicine, such as the ability to diagnose and treat anemia, a general improvement in diet, and an increased understanding of the importance of adequate vitamins and minerals in nutrition. Did eating disorders like anorexia nervosa and bulimia gradually take over the cultural position once occupied by chlorosis? King acknowledges the theory, but believes the comparison is inadequate. It seems that the only honest answer to the question of the sickness of virgins is the unglamorous truth: just as virginity itself is wont to do, it disappeared from the scene, its afterlife unknowable and unknown.

Cut to the Chaste

When the vagina doesn't finish canalizing and thus never forms a vaginal opening, what remains is an unbroken expanse of skin that completely covers the vaginal entrance. We call this an imperforate hymen. No one knows why imperforate hymens develop, only that they do so on a fairly regular basis. Imperforate hymen is the single most common anomaly of the female genitals and is, in fact, a birth defect.

Imperforate hymens can cause several medical problems, ranging from the merely inconvenient to the quite severe. Most commonly, imperforation causes *hematocolpos*, a buildup of menstrual blood, endometrial tissue, and vaginal fluids within the vagina that occurs simply because there's no way for any of it to get out. Because the vagina is rather elastic and expandable, quite a quantity of menstrual fluid can build up behind the imperforate hymen, causing abdominal pressure and pain. The fluid puts pressure on the bladder and on the rectum, which can cause constipation and symptoms that may mimic urinary tract infection. Sometimes it also causes *hematometra*, a buildup of blood inside the uterus or fallopian tubes that can be mistaken for tumors.

Fortunately for the numerous young women who find themselves having to deal with the surprise of an imperforate hymen, treatment is simple. Hymenotomy, also called hymenectomy, is precisely what the name implies, the surgical cutting of the hymen. Typically done on an outpatient basis, the standard Western hymenotomy surgery can be done according to any of several different incision styles, including a cross-shaped incision or one shaped roughly like the fictional masked swordsman Zorro's celebrated Z. The incision creates a central opening in the hymen so that menstrual fluids can drain from the vagina. The cut edges of the hymen are either pinned back with sutures or the surgery may be done with a laser scalpel, which cuts and cauterizes at the same time; both methods prevent the cut edges from healing back together. Since neither the opening of the vagina nor the hymen itself is particularly vast, this is only a small incision, usually less than an inch. Once the cut is made, the backed-up menstrual fluid may be removed by suction or allowed to drain on its own. As is common with superficial wounds in the genitals, the healing time is typically short.

The secondary purpose of hymenotomy is to allow vaginal penetration. Hymenotomy is also sometimes used to increase the size of the hymenal opening in women whose hymens are not imperforate, but merely particularly thick or inelastic in a way that makes penetration difficult or uncommonly painful. During the middle of the twentieth century, in fact, there was something of a vogue for gynecologists to perform preemptive hymenotomies on the theory that it would prevent wedding-night trauma from painful first penetration. From the 1930s to the 1960s or so, many gynecologists offered the procedure to patients announcing an impending wedding. Such "just in case" hymenotomies have passed out of fashion as doctors have recognized that they are typically unnecessary, both because most women do not suffer significant pain when they are first penetrated, and because the psychoanalytic theory of wedding-night trauma has fallen out of favor. Contemporary doctors will generally wait until an actual problem arises before deciding to take a scalpel to a woman's hymen.

A Recycled Box?

Contemporary Westerners have an odd, paradoxical relationship to virginity, simultaneously protesting that too much emphasis on virginity is "medieval" and sexist even as we demonstrate that we still believe that virginity goes hand in hand with desirable attributes like purity, self-control, and respectability. In many ways we have a similarly paradoxical relationship to our bodies. We seem to believe that "the body is a temple" and, simultaneously, that these "temples" are private property that can be decorated—tattooed, pierced, transformed through bodybuilding or plastic surgery or corsets or what have you—as the owner sees fit. Little wonder, then, that we have a complicated time coming to grips with surgically rebuilt hymens.

Over the course of the last twenty years or so, the hymen "reconstruction" procedures known as hymenorraphy and hymenoplasty have become increasingly popular. They are performed all over the world, including in countries where they are technically illegal. Unlike hymenotomies, there is no such thing as a medically necessary hymen reconstruction surgery: the hymen does not perform any physiological function, therefore there can be no physiological reason to install one. Hymen reconstruction is a purely elective surgery, performed for no reason other than to give a material presence to a virginal status that may or may not actually exist.

The majority of women seeking hymen reconstructions do so to cover up a history of consensual sex, although others seek it out in the wake of sexual assault, injury to the genitals, or because they are concerned that their own hymens may be too insubstantial to perform "correctly" on a wedding night. For about $2,000, such women acquire a deftly constructed flange of mucous membrane that is basically indistinguishable from something that might easily have been part of the original equipment.

This may be accomplished in one of two ways. Hymenorraphy is a procedure in which the original hymen, or whatever bits of it are still in evidence, are sewn together to approximate an "intact" hymen. Hymenoplasty is somewhat more involved, and is done either when there are not sufficient hymen remnants to work with, or when the hymen is so fragile that it won't hold up to being pieced together like a genital jigsaw puzzle. In a hymenoplasty, a small slice of mucous membrane is lifted from the vaginal wall and sutured into place as an ersatz hymen. Typically, in cases where the reconstructed hymen is being created for an upcoming wedding, these surgeries are scheduled a few weeks prior to the big day.

Some doctors provide their hymen reconstruction patients with advice to help them ensure there will be adequate "proof" of virginity on the wedding night. Patients may be told, for example, to try to time their wedding nights with the onset of their periods. The doctors who perform these surgeries don't always provide this kind of advice, but the fact that some do is revealing: even physicians who've made a business of repairing hymens are well aware that merely having the correct flap of skin in the correct place doesn't mean that it will behave "correctly" when the time comes.

Such awareness of the body's variable responses is the basis for some of the ethical controversy surrounding these procedures. Increasingly we understand that bodies are not identical, nor do they behave identically when women lose their virginity. Many doctors are thus understandably troubled by the implications of the physical and cosmetic uniformity that these surgeries are intended to create. Is a hymen reconstruction surgery just another form of catering to a patently inaccurate and misogynist ideology about women's bodies and sexuality that tries to force all women into the same procrustean bed? Or is plastic surgery just plastic surgery, and a "recycled box" no different from breast implants or a nose job? Some clinics offering the surgery package it as part of a genital "rejuvenation" aimed at increasing erotic sensation (although on whose behalf can be unclear), surgeries that may include narrowing the vaginal entrance or other modifications.

Around the world boyfriends, fathers, and husbands register frequent objections to hymen restoration surgeries, to the point that some doctors and clinics have received death threats for their role in abetting what some men see as an unjustifiable and even criminal deception. Some doctors say that this just underscores the need for the procedures, and believe that by performing them, they are helping women avoid the possibility of the unjust consequences (including beatings, mutilations, or "honor killings") they might suffer as a result of not measuring up to a family's or community's unrealistic virginity standards. One would, of course, prefer a world in which virginity or lack thereof did not represent a burden of proof for women at all. In lieu of this, compassion seems to dictate that other, medical, options be made available.

CHAPTER 6

The Blank Page

And where does one read a deeper tale than upon the most perfectly
printed page of the most precious book? Upon the blank page.
—Isak Dinesen, "The Blank Page," from *Last Tales*

WITHIN THE VAGINA OF EVERY VIRGIN, or so the Spanish Roma
(Gypsy) people called Gitanos believe, there is a grape, an *uva*, that
contains a yellowish liquid. Neither this grape nor its contents exist in any
Western book of anatomy, nor do gynecologists recognize their description.
But the Gitano insist that both the grape and its juice do exist, and that furthermore they are the only reliable signifier of a woman's virginity. What's more,
they've got proof.

The liquid inside the *uva*, called the *honra*, can be spilled only once. When
it goes, the woman's virginity goes with it. It is burst—virginity and *honra*
spilled at the very same time—in a ceremonial defloration that happens as part
of the wedding celebration, for a woman's *honra* should not be permitted to
just trickle away unnoticed. It would hardly be proper. This is an occasion for
witness, celebration, and pride.

In a large room, surrounded by married women from her community, the
bride lies down. Her skirts are tossed up and her bottom bolstered by a pillow to
make viewing easier, and her legs are spread wide. An elder woman expert in

such matters, the *ajuntadora*, examines her vulva, labia, and the entrance of her vagina. They must look small, dainty, healthy, and pink. Any other color, and any other appearance, indicates that she has been fooling around inappropriately with her sexual purity, although that "fooling around" might have been something as relatively innocuous as wearing trousers instead of skirts (trousers are thought to rub against the vulva) or riding a bicycle, which is believed to place a problematic amount of pressure on delicate parts. Sexual misconduct would turn the tissues dark, even black, the Gitano say, and so this is easy to detect.

As long as everything looks all right, the ceremony proceeds on to the pressing of the grape, the manual bursting of the *uva*. To the sound of songs from the other women in attendance, each of whom has once been in her place, the bride watches as the *ajuntadora* takes a handkerchief trimmed with lace and ribbons and wraps it snugly around one finger. This cloth will absorb the bride's *honra*, and as the older woman inserts her well-wrapped finger gently into the bride's vagina—she is honor bound to stop if the bride should bleed, for the blood would spoil the "flowers" made by the *honra*—she deftly bursts the *uva* and presses it to extract the yellowish liquid that will leave a permanent stain on the handkerchief. The examiner presses several times, turning the handkerchief between pressings to expose clean cloth. The more flowers, the more honor: three is considered quite respectable, although even one will do. The handkerchief, yellowish *honra* marking its whiteness, is displayed, and all the women celebrate, singing and clapping and tossing pink and white candied almonds over the bare belly and thighs of the relieved bride.

The rest of the wedding is almost a formality, after this. The most important ritual is over. The bride will go through the church ceremony with her husband, but it is the bride's mother who will keep the handkerchief, and the flowers of her daughter's virginity, forever, safely knotted to preserve the stains that are her proof of having raised a good, traditional daughter fit to carry on the family and clan.

The Gitano may live in the modern cities of Spain—the young bride of contemporary Gitano flamenco star Farruquito was publicly revealed on Spanish television to have been tested in much this way at their 2005 Madrid wedding—but their rituals of virginity seem, to the rest of us, to come from a different place, a different time. They even seem to involve a different body. As a proof of virginity, the Gitano believe that the *honra* is infallible. Blood can be faked, as any fool knows, but the *honra* cannot.

A Western physician might counter that the fluid produced by the Bartholin's glands found near the entrance of the vagina is often yellow or yellowy-gray in color, and can build up within the glands at any time during a woman's life whether she is a virgin or not. Any woman, they might argue, possesses the means of producing these yellowish stains. The Western physician might further add that there is no such thing as the *uva* the Gitano speak of, and therefore the Gitano are mistaking perfectly ordinary and utterly insignificant secretions for something meaningful, making a mountain of social significance out of a mundane anatomical molehill. They would do better to look for bloodstains on bedsheets, or to examine the hymen for evidence of tearing or stretching.

This in turn would make the Gitano sneer. Any Gitano knows that the condition of the hymen is, like the condition of the rest of the tissues of the genitals, capable of providing only secondary, and possibly merely circumstantial, evidence of virginity. After all, is not the *uva* normally burst, and the *honra* spilled, without the loss of a single drop of blood?

Putting It to the Test

Who is right? Perhaps neither the Gitano nor the doctors are. Perhaps both of them are. Proving virginity has never been an exact science. It has not even been an exact controversy. The sort of conflict we see between the Gitano and the Western medical tradition over the nature and proof of virginity seems exceptional, but historically speaking it is reasonably typical. Over the course of Western history, so many different methods have been used to try to prove virginity, and so many different standards of proof invented, that it would take another book of this size to catalog them.

The simple fact is that short of catching someone in the act of sex, virginity can be neither proven nor disproven. We cannot prove it today, nor have we ever been able to. Barring some unprecedented quantum leap in diagnostic techniques, we are equally unlikely to be able to do so in the future.

Not that the notorious ineffectuality of virginity tests has ever stopped anyone from insisting that they be done. Myriad tests, testing myriad things, have been put into use over the centuries, none of them any more definitive than the others. All virginity tests, however, share three very consistent and telling characteristics. They all look for the same thing, they all share a single basic rule of evidence, and they all have a particular, and peculiar, relationship to objective truth.

First, the thing that virginity tests look for is not, in fact, virginity. Virginity cannot be seen or measured, in and of itself. *Virginity tests do not look for virginity, but for signs of virginity*. The difference is subtle but crucial. The quality we call virginity is an abstract, intangible thing. When we look for proof of the existence of an intangible thing, when we look for proof of justice or injustice for example, what we look for is not the thing itself but evidence of the thing. Furthermore, this evidence is gathered and interpreted according to culturally specific systems of thought that attribute particular meaning to particular types of evidence.

This cultural element means that a sign that may seem to prove the existence of virginity according to the ideology of the people of one era or subculture—for example, the evidence of the *uva* and its *honra*—may not be considered to do so by those whose system of thought does not attach the same meaning to the same evidence. The *honra* and *uva* don't work within the standard Western medical system of thought on virginity; bleeding and hymen tearing don't work within the Gitano one. Thus in the virginity tests discussed throughout the remainder of this chapter, the question is never, is this woman a virgin or not? or even, is this test the right kind of test or not? but rather, according to the system of thought of the place and time in which this test was used, was it capable of providing evidence that would have been meaningful for people thinking according to that particular set of guidelines? The criteria by which virginity is tested, in short, are by no means universal or empirical, and they must be considered in their own historical and cultural moment.

This may seem confusing, since virginity tests are performed on individual women. But what they actually involve is not so much the body of the individual being tested, but an idealized standard version of the female body. The results of virginity tests are determined by the degree to which individual bodies (or body parts) conform to the generic virginal ideal. This in turn leads us to the second thing that all virginity tests have in common: *virginity tests cannot tell us whether an individual woman is a virgin; they can only tell us whether or not she conforms to what people of her time and place believe to be true of virgins*.

For all that, there is one constant in virginity testing, and this is the third characteristic that all virginity tests share: *women may not speak for themselves*.

The one form of evidence that is always considered inadmissible in virginity testing is a woman's own verbal testimony. Only her body—or in some cases a magical object that reacts to her physical presence—is allowed to give testimony. Undoubtedly, this is due to the fact that sexually active women have always been presumed to have ample reason to lie about their sexual status. By focusing virginity testing on the body and its physical attributes, tests attempt to bypass hearsay and avoid fakery. In the process, the woman whose virginity is being tested disappears as a person. We cannot forget that the most common virginity test of all time—watching for signs and telltales of virginity during and after the first time a woman is vaginally penetrated by a penis—only looks for evidence of virginity as experienced and reported by the man who penetrates the virgin's body. The standards by which virginity is assessed have nothing to do with what is actually true of a virgin or her virginity in any individual case. They have everything to do with what other people believe is true about virgins as a generic and idealized category.

Signs and Portents

In Washington Square Park, in Greenwich Village, stands a statue of Giuseppe Garibaldi, the Italian (and sometime New Yorker) hero of the nineteenth-century *Risorgimento*. There is an old joke about this statue, which claims that Garibaldi, ever the gallant Italian, will raise his sword and salute any virgin that passes. The punch line? It's been a hundred years since any woman in the Village has received his salute.

Garibaldi's statue isn't the only inanimate object to have garnered a reputation as a magical virgin detector; legions of college campuses boast statuary of similar reputation. Magical virgin detectors have always been popular. Legends and medieval romances are peppered with things like magic drinking horns that act like a prankster's dribble glass whenever an unchaste woman tries to drink from them, making the invisible stain of sexual sin public as wine spills all over the woman's clothes. A friend of mine once told me that at a college party in the 1980s, another student explained quite earnestly to her that only a virgin could remove the label from a beer bottle in one piece. Similarly direct is the medieval story of Floris and Blaunchefleur, which tells of an enchanted fountain owned by the Sultan of Babylon, the waters of which run red as blood if an unchaste maiden washes her hands in them.

These tests, and others like them, rest on the principle of symbolic magic. An inanimate object serves as a symbol of virginity or lost virginity, and behaves in some telltale way when a female body is within range. When Garibaldi raises his phallic sword or a beer bottle label is removed as intact as a virgin's hymen is supposed to be, we understand the symbolism intuitively. When an unchaste maiden is revealed through the fountain water running red or by the drinking horn spilling wine across her front, we know instantly the nature of the vivid red stain the wine imitates. No one need wonder what it means when the unicorn lays his sharp-horned head in the tender lap of a virgin, or why she is the only one who can tame him. Virginity, in these tests, is a form of elemental magic.

Virgin magic substantially predates Christianity. In ancient Greek literature, we find instances where sacred snakes only accept offerings from virgins, spurning those from any other hands. Mythological virgins like Persephone are capable of visiting the world of the dead. Virgin women like Evadne and Leda and a certain Mary (or Miriam) were singled out to bear the children of gods. In Christian martyr legends, virgins could withstand any torture, stop would-be rapists in their tracks, defeat demons, defy parents and kings and even Satan himself. In the Christian apocrypha, we read that a certain midwife named Salome doubts the virginity of the Virgin Mary and goes to perform a virginity test on her only to have her hand burnt to a crisp by the magical force of Mary's holy and virginal genitals. Over and over again, virgins are magical beings.

It only makes sense that we might attempt to use magic to test magic. The magical tattling drinking horns, fountains, and unicorns of our medieval past are kissing cousins to the beer labels and park statuary of the present. In rural black communities of the American South, a folkloric tradition holds that a man can test the virginity of a woman by collecting some earwax on his fingertip, then pressing the fingertip to the woman's vulva. If this exposure to a man's earwax hurts her and she cries out, she is a virgin, her virginity capable of being "burned" by any secretion from the body of a man. It is a classic demonstration of symbolic and sympathetic magic. The incidental fact that it is no more accurate an indicator of virginity than a coin toss is, magically enough, considered irrelevant.

Cucullus non Facit Monachum

Ever alert to the possibility that women might try to lie about their virginity, many tests are chosen because their criteria are difficult, if not impossible, to fake. But neither can many of these tests be passed except by sheer luck. This is particularly true of tests that take a woman's external appearance as evidence of her virginity or nonvirginity.

The most infamous example of this is the breast test. Since the time of Galen and Soranus at least, and probably for many centuries prior, breasts have been bared and pressed into service as a prima facie proof of virginity, with "small, plump, and elastic breasts" being listed as a sign of virginity in the forensic legal literature as late as the early twentieth century. As we know, short of cosmetic surgery that has only become available in the last fifty years, there has been precious little any woman could do to intentionally alter the size, shape, or nature of her breasts. Yet source after source takes the female breast as a source of evidence for or against virginity. Upward-pointing nipples, nipples that were pink, pale, or small in size, and breasts that had not begun to sag were all characteristics that were supposed to prove virginity. If the nipples pointed downward, were dark or overly large, or the breasts appeared to be thin or saggy, they were said to betray a guilty sexual past.

Today the idea of diagnosing virginity on the basis of whether or not a woman can pass the pencil test* seems laughable at best and blindly misogynist at worst. But many currently used popular "proofs" of virginity rest on criteria that are hardly any better.

Humans have often evinced a strong desire to believe that sexual activity must, somehow or another, literally alter the body. The idea that masturbation causes blindness, pimples, or hair on the palms is one manifestation of this theory. When we hear through the grapevine, or read in books, about the loss of virginity being somehow visible in the look in a woman's eyes, the way she

---

*Women's magazines of the mid–twentieth century advised readers to assess the pertness of their breasts by seeing whether the breast sagged sufficiently to hold a pencil in place against the rib cage. Only those whose breasts could not keep the pencil from falling "passed" this test.

walks or sits, in the shape or size of her breasts, or in the curve of her hips or buttocks, we are hearing the same thing. "By me having, you know, a big butt and hips, they think I'm having sex, too, but I'm not, it just runs in my family," one young woman told researcher Kristin Haglund in a 2003 research report. When Haglund asked this young woman why people would believe that she was being sexually active based on how her body looked, the subject responded, "They said because when you have sex your hips spread or something like that."

Although untrue, the idea that a narrow butt or a sexless walk devoid of swaying hips is an indicator of virginity does, like the breast test, have a certain internal logic. The younger and more childlike one's body appears—the high, small, firm breasts, the slim hips, and the less pronounced buttocks are all characteristic of girls who are just past the cusp of puberty—the more likely one is to be judged to be, or believed to be, a virgin. Bodies that appear more sexually mature are more likely to be presumed to be sexually active.

Attempting to derive knowledge of someone's sexual status from the external appearance of her body or even from the way she dresses is uncannily close to the nineteenth-century attempt to use the pseudoscience of phrenology—the measurement of various regions of the skull and the contours of the head—to determine a person's character and personality. It is strange indeed that belief in phrenology has gone the way of the dodo, but we still commonly find examples of people believing that they can tell a virgin by the size of her butt and the way that she walks, or because she's got perky breasts, slim hips, or favors modest necklines.

There is no such thing as "looking like a virgin." One can only look like what one's culture presumes a virgin should look like, and even then, one's success often depends on whether one's genetics have been cooperative. *Cucullus non facit monachum,* our medieval ancestors said, "the cowl does not make the monk." Just so: neither the breasts nor the hips, the clothes nor the comportment make the virgin.

Chemistry and the Piss-Prophets

Even when a woman does "look like a virgin," there are always those who remain unconvinced. The author of the late-medieval text *De secretis mulierum*

(On the Secrets of Women) was one of these skeptics, listing first various traits—"shame, modesty, fear, a faultless gait and speech," "casting eyes down before men and the acts of men"—by which virgins could be known, then turning around and saying that "some women are so clever . . . that they know how to resist detection by these signs." Those who wished more certain proof of a woman's virginity were advised to look for proof somewhere that the woman could not hope to disguise: in her urine.

The premodern "piss-prophets," as uroscopists were sometimes known during the Renaissance, didn't use the kinds of urinalysis techniques used today. Rather, they listened to and watched patients while they urinated, administered potions and decoctions, and observed urine under a variety of supposedly informative conditions. A virgin "urinates with a subtle hiss," wrote thirteenth-century William of Saliceto, "and indeed takes longer than a small boy" to complete her urination, implying that because her genitals had not yet been opened by intercourse the flow of urine would be constricted. A commentator on the *De secretis mulierum* claims that the virgin's urine comes from a place higher up in the vulva than it does for nonvirgin women, one of the innumerable examples in the medical literature in which it is implied that intercourse somehow fundamentally alters a woman's anatomy.

The way the urine looked was important. A virgin's urine was clear, sparkling, and thin in consistency, according to many sources, and never muddy or cloudy. Optimally, their urine would be colorless. Golden urine was believed to indicate an appetite for pleasure, which was not necessarily desirable. It was believed by some that if a woman was not a virgin, sperm in her urine would precipitate out if the urine were left to stand, forming a cloudy layer in the bottom of the jar.

Another way that urine was used to test virginity was by seeing whether a woman could be forced to urinate by special means. In his treatise on minerals, thirteenth-century scientist Albertus Magnus wrote that if a woman drinks water in which jet stones have been washed and to which small scrapings of jet have been added, and she immediately urinates, she is no virgin. Other authorities claimed that various other substances, including lily petals and stamens, coal, and lettuce would have the same effect. Lettuce, in fact, was considered so potent that one had only to smell it. "Take the fruit of a lettuce and place it in front of her nose," one early Renaissance writer directed, and if the woman is no virgin, "she will urinate immediately."

Road Trip

A different sort of urine-related test could be performed by fumigating the body with smoke or fumes. A fumigation was performed by introducing vapors, for instance the smoke of particular herbs, into the interior of the body. Fumigations of various body parts were used as treatments for a variety of illnesses, but fumigations of the vagina could be specifically used as a means of diagnosing virginity. In these fumigations, a pan containing the fumigating material would be placed on the coals of a small fire, then the woman being tested would be seated on a special frame with her legs spread over the pan. Her body might be draped with a blanket or heavy cloth to trap the smoke, or perhaps the procedure would be simplified and a pan containing burning resins and such might simply be thrust beneath her long skirts as she stood and straddled it. If her examiner were especially well equipped and sophisticated of technique, the smoke and fumes might be channeled directly into her vulva or vagina through a reed stuck through the stopper of a jug containing the volatile substances. On the other hand, she might simply be instructed to hike up her dress and straddle an open wine barrel or a jug of onions and let the fumes rise up into her body. Fumigations with "the best coal," according to Gilbertus Anglicus (late twelfth to early thirteenth century), or with dock leaves, according to the fifteenth-century writer Niccolo Falcucci, would produce the same result as waving a lettuce below a woman's nose: if she were a virgin, she would feel nothing, but if she were "corrupt," she would urinate involuntarily.

Other fumigation tests worked on a different principle. For centuries, the internal plumbing of the body was understood to function on the basis of the Greek concept of the *hodos*, or road. The Greeks understood that food, water, and air went into the body, and urine, feces, and menstrual blood came out of it. To them, the logical conclusion was that the openings for the outbound traffic, the genitals and anus, were directly connected to the openings for the inbound traffic, namely the mouth and nose. What connected them was the inner bodily path of the *hodos*. The only reason that the *hodos* should fail to be a reliable thoroughfare between the upper orifices and the nether ones would be if some part of it were closed off.

On the assumption that the vaginas of virginal women were held closed by webs, knots, folds, or gathers of blood vessels and other delicate tissue, women whose virginity was to be tested were fumigated from below to see whether or not the smell of the fumes could be detected up above. If one could smell the fumes on her breath, it would mean that the vaginal entrance to her *hodos* had been opened and the fumes had traveled all the way up the internal "road." If nothing could be smelled, on the other hand, she was closed, and thus a virgin. Given some of the substances used in fumigations and the ways the fumes were released—open wine barrels or kegs of chopped onions and garlic figure in some descriptions—it seems that everything in the immediate vicinity would have been likely to smell of them. One wonders just how many women were deemed nonvirginal on the basis of something that was quite literally in the air.

Other tests likewise traded on the notion of the *hodos*. These tests had to do with the size or character of the neck and throat. The vaginal canal, often known as "the neck of the womb," was and often still is, in the popular imagination, considered to be vulnerable to the broadening influence of the invading penis. In an era when the theory of one-to-one correspondence between the neck of the womb and the neck between the chin and collarbone was current, many believed in the principle "as below, so above." If the lower neck broadened, the upper one would, too.

From this came the theory that measuring the throat, and in some cases merely listening to the voice, could tell an examiner whether the individual had been sexually active. A broader, wider, or thicker neck, a lower or coarser voice, or a throat that was out of proportion in its thickness might all be considered telltale signs of lost virginity. Various tests recommended measuring the neck in different ways, but a classic example is found in the December 16, 1660, entry in the diary of British man of letters Samuel Pepys: "From thence with Tom Doling and Boston and D. Vines (whom we met by the way) to Price's, and there we drank, and in discourse I learnt a pretty trick to try whether a woman be a maid or no, by a string going round her head to meet at the end of her nose, which if she be not will come a great way beyond."

This test, which Pepys seems to have regarded as nothing more than a good game to play if the barmaid would hold still for it, is described in other writings from the early 1500s to the early 1800s. Each version of the test gives its specific version of the instructions, but a common variant—perhaps the very one Pepys learned—is performed as follows. One end of a string is held against the bony ridge at the base of the skull and the string brought up over the head along the midline. Held down against the skin so that it follows the bridge of the nose, the point at which the string meets the tip of the nose is marked. The string is cut at that point, and it is then wrapped around the woman's throat like a necklace. If she is a virgin, the ends of the string will just meet, its length neatly measuring her neck. If she is not a virgin, on the other hand, the ends will not meet because the woman's neck has expanded, implicating a similar widening of the "neck" below.

Interestingly and unusually, the widened or broadened neck as a sign of lost virginity was not believed to be true of women only but also of men. Though they of course lacked vaginas, boys' voice change was nonetheless sometimes linked by scholars and singing masters to the onset of sexual activity. This might take the form of masturbation or, as one eighteenth-century German writer darkly hinted, the possibility of homoerotic acts with other choirboys: "In cities, where choirs exist, one should especially watch out for boys who sing soprano parts. If their treble voice darkens before they are seventeen, even though they observe the dietetic rules of a soprano singer, it is obvious what is the matter with them."

Pucker Up

Across history, the two most common tests of virginity are not really tests so much as they are things observed during and after the process of penetrating the vagina during first heterosexual intercourse: the degree of tightness of the vagina and the bleeding associated with virginity loss. Both are described as being found only once and as vanishing as virginity does, and so their appearance has a definitive air about it. Sources ranging from the Talmud to the eighteenth-century standby *Aristotle's Master-Piece* debate the meaning and importance of these two characteristics. Debates on the matter continue apace in the world's locker rooms and on Internet bulletin boards. It remains an ironic fact that the two "proofs" are only capable of being assessed when virginity is destroyed.

This is all of a piece with the ideology that holds that virginity is a sort of placeholder, something that exists until such time as it is removed or destroyed by a man. Presumably the "right man," to be sure, but nonetheless, virginity exists for him and for his use: many people over the centuries have described virginity as a gift that a woman is given by God for the purpose of giving it to her husband. The fact that the man is then entitled and even expected to assess the quality and existence of the virginity he has been given—particularly in regard to whether he happens to perceive the woman's vagina as being adequately "tight"—merely emphasizes that virginity has fundamentally little to do with actual women and a great deal to do with men's fantasies.

Ironically, such standards of "proof" make virginity relatively simple to counterfeit. Unlike with penises, where what you see is pretty much what you get, female genitals are conveniently amenable to being rigged, treated, toned, and primped. The subject of artificially narrowing or tightening the vagina is, in fact, taken up in many premodern medical treatises. The practice no doubt handily predates the second- and third-century writings of Galen and Soranus, who recommend, in a tone that suggests the practice was well known, the insertion of perfumed pessaries made with oils and fats to "rejuvenate" the vagina and its appearance. These and other ancient recipes that would assist in the manufacture of the signs of virginity—a practice known as "sophistication" to later European writers—make it clear that women have for millennia been doing vaginal renovations for the purpose of placating men.

Some of the best-known early recipes "for the violated woman, that this be kept secret," as Theodoris Priscianus put it, come from the lineage of what are known as the Trotula texts. These tenth- and eleventh-century writings were by a woman or women whose real name(s) we do not know, and they exist in many different forms and formats. At the time they were written, however, the recipes might not have been used only as sophistications but as a genuine medical therapy. It was believed for many centuries that a narrow, tight vagina was necessary for successful conception, because a too-wide or too-loose vagina would allow the male seed to pour right back out of the woman's body so that pregnancy could not occur. Helping a woman to tighten her vagina to improve her chances of conceiving was quite legitimate. If such a recipe had an alternate use, so be it: *honi soit qui mal y pense.*

Most of the recipes for tightening and narrowing the opening of the vagina and the tissues of the vulva are astringents, applied topically as baths or poultices and more rarely internally as douches or pessaries. A thirteenth-century recipe tells the "girl who has been induced to open her legs and lose her virginity by the follies of passion, secret love, and promises" that when it is time for her to get married, she should keep her husband from knowing the truth by taking ground sugar and egg white and mixing them in a decoction made from alum, fleabane, the dry wood of a grapevine, and other astringent and drying plants, then bathing her private parts with the resulting mixture.

The highly caustic compound alum, otherwise known as aluminum sulfate or potassium aluminum sulfate, was a frequent star in these recipes. A common household and culinary chemical until reasonably recently, it is still used in pickling and as an ingredient in baking powders. It generally represents the strongest active ingredient in vagina-tightening mixtures.* The herbs in these mixtures, however, were also active components. The seeds of fleabane (*Inula dysenterica*) were a well-known and popular astringent, shrinking and tightening the tissues to which they were applied. Numerous recipes call for members of the mint family. Mint oil is an irritant that would cause a certain amount of puffiness and swelling and thus help give the appearance of a plump and youthful vulva and vagina. Many recipes require pennyroyal (*Mentha pulegium*), a mint long known to women around the world as an emmenagogue, abortifacient, and contraceptive, and thus one with a long-standing association with women's reproductive concerns. Another popular ingredient in these recipes was bearfoot or lady's mantle (*Alchemilla vulgaris*), likewise a popular astringent and styptic plant of well-established medical utility.

Doctors and midwives, in essence "double agents" when it came to virginity, have always been aware that sophistications were available and have, in many cases, helped women to employ them. But they were also well aware that the men who paid their fees as virginity testers would expect the doctors to be able to uncover a fake. Sensibly enough, they developed sophistications with which to counter sophistications, or put another way, tests to foil women's attempts to foil virginity tests. Nicholas Venette, the French author of the eighteenth-century sexual self-help blockbuster *L'amour conjugal* (The

---

*Indeed, it still is. On the shelves of many an adult bookshop one can find vaginal creams called things like China Shrink Cream and Tighten Up. Though touted as containing "secret herbs" and various oriental essences, the active ingredient in such concoctions is often alum in the form of food-grade potassium aluminum sulfate. Mixed with polyethylene glycol, a water-soluble waxy substance often used as a base for medicated ointments and cosmetics, it becomes a lotion or cream that is touted as being able to increase sexual pleasure by tightening the vagina so that it is "as tight as a virgin's."

Mysteries of Married Love), describes one of these in considerable detail.
Venette's countertest is given just prior to his instructions on how to go about
counterfeiting virginity—he is nothing if not comprehensive.

> We ought to examine the means, by which a counterfeited Maiden-head
> may be discover'd . . . make a Bath of a Decoction of Leaves of mallows,
> Groundsel, with some handfuls of Line Seed and Fleabane Seed, Orach,
> Brank Ursin or bearfoot. Let them sit in this Bath an hour, after which,
> let them be wiped, and examin'd 2 or 3 hours after Bathing, observing
> them narrowly in the mean while. If a Woman is a Maid, all her amorous
> parts are compress'd and joyn'd close to one another; but if not, they are
> flaggy, loose, and flouting, instead of being wrinkled and close as they
> were before when she had a mind to choose us.

Fleabane and bearfoot, astringents both, were common ingredients in recipes
for tightening the vagina. Orach (*Atriplax hortensis*), on the other hand, is another name for a variety of purslane, a plant that was used for various purposes, often as a means of bringing down swelling and reducing lesions.
Mallow (*Althaea officinalis*) and groundsel (*Senecio viscosus*) are similar in effect. They are demulcents, emollients, and topical anti-inflammatories, and
would have helped to bring down any inflammation that had been artificially
induced in the name of plumping up the genital tissues.

One wonders just how consciously Venette was pandering to his public by
offering such a countertest to begin with. Venette, after all, was neither an un-
sophisticated observer nor unsympathetic regarding the various reasons that
women might choose to feign virginity. He understood quite plainly that the
appearance and dimensions of a woman's genital anatomy didn't necessarily
prove anything at all about her virginity, and in fact says flatly that he realizes
that some women's genitals simply don't give the impression of being small,
narrow, or tight: he offers advice on how to pass oneself off as a virgin on the
behalf of women who are "naturally too wide."

Furthermore, he believed that a woman might have legitimate, defensible,
and ethical reasons for wanting to falsify her virginity in order to "secure her
Husband's good Opinion the Wedding night." "May it not be allowable,"
Venette asks, "for the Preservation of Peace in her Family, to take all the pains
imaginable to be thought a discreet Woman by her Husband." Indeed, as

Venette pointed out, it might be what made it possible for even a prostitute to become an honest married woman, and thus but a small evil that could help to erase a far larger sin. Venette's generosity is all the more striking, and his candor all the more remarkable, given his status as a medical authority: writ large, it is nothing less than an admission that if one is sincere and well meaning, virginity need not matter at all.

Blood Simple?

Probably the oldest and foremost belief about female virginity is the notion that when a woman loses her virginity, she bleeds. Many women do bleed, in quantities ranging from the common light spotting to extremely unusual and medically dangerous hemorrhaging requiring emergency treatment. But not every woman bleeds.

While it is by now fairly well established that not all women bleed on the occasion of their first sexual penetration (indeed, many older sources, too, mention that there may not be any bleeding, although bleeding is assumed as the norm), little research has been done on just how many people bleed, how many don't, and *why* some do and some don't. One of the only articles in the medical literature on the subject is an anecdotal study of fewer than a hundred women. The women in this study were the colleagues of English doctor Sara Paterson-Brown, who, when she was unable to find any good statistics on the subject of bleeding at virginity loss, began sensibly enough to ask her colleagues about their experiences. While it is perhaps unreasonable to assume that Paterson-Brown's sample is truly representative of the population of women as a whole, it is noteworthy that fully 63 percent of her respondents—and possibly more, since some of the women she asked could not remember—had not experienced any bleeding when they lost their virginity.

The responses in Paterson-Brown's study shed an interesting light on part of the Gitano ritual defloration described at the beginning of this chapter. When readers reared in the mainstream of Western sexual ideology hear about Gitano defloration rituals and discover that the appearance of blood during the defloration ritual stops the proceedings cold, they are often surprised, even shocked, to discover that the bleeding they had presumed was universally recognized as a sign of virginity simply isn't always recognized that way. As both

Paterson-Brown's study and Gitano deflorations prove, not only is coitarche (first intercourse) bleeding not universally recognized as meaningful in terms of virginity, it isn't universal, either.

This is a valuable corrective. For literally thousands of years, Western culture has presumed that first sexual intercourse creates a wound in a woman's body. Blood is evidence that this is an injury, a thing that is inflicted upon women by men, with all that implies. From Avicenna to Freud, the "primal wound" inflicted by the simple insertion of a penis into a vagina has been painted as one of the major events in the life of any woman, a milestone marked in pain and blood. Historically, many physicians, expecting that intercourse was going to prove both violent and forceful (if not forcible), have provided advice for treating the injuries of defloration. These include soothing baths and styptic waters to stop bleeding and reduce inflammation: Avicenna recommends rose and myrtle infusions. Seventeenth-century French doctor François Ranchin, writing in 1627, described a class of disorders associated with defloration that included not only soreness and bleeding but hemorrhage.

We have no reason to believe that bleeding was any more inevitable a part of virginity loss for our foremothers than it is for us now. But it was, probably due in part to the cumulative weight of received wisdom and written authority, more inevitably expected and even required. Bloody bedclothes or personal linens have, for centuries, been the standard of proof by which a bride's honor was judged in many communities, and some still expect to examine and display them today. The "tokens of virginity" described in Deuteronomy almost undoubtedly consisted of blood on a cloth or garment. Certainly blood was given primary consideration by Soranus and Galen, Gilbertus Anglicus, Albertus Magnus, Nicholas Venette, Jane Sharp, and legions of juries assigned by canon and secular judges to assess evidence in courts of law. In some parts of the world, including certain communities in the West, the absence of blood on a woman's wedding night might still mean repudiation or even murder.

We still share a fantasy of blood when it comes to women's bodies and women's virginity, and the stakes that ride on the realization of that fantasy can be enormous. When the stakes are high, so is the incentive to counterfeit. As with vaginal narrowness and the appearance of the inner labia and vaginal opening, blood is a fairly simple thing to fake.

The mechanisms are simple. A modern-day woman might resort to methods not too dissimilar from the recommendations of the ninth-century Persian physician Rhazes, who said that women who wished to feign virginity should combine the application of substances to constrict and tighten the vagina and vulva with the insertion into the vagina of a section of dove's intestine filled with blood. The bladders of fish and the innards of songbirds, the blood of chickens and ducks and doves, and sponges soaked in pigs' blood have been pressed into service, as have modern-day expedients such as gelatin capsules and surgical sponges. True, we are no longer likely to heed the advice of an eleventh-century Trotula manuscript that tells us that "best of all is this deception: the day before her wedding, let her put a leech very cautiously on the labia, taking care lest it slip inside by mistake, then the blood will flow out here, and a little crust will form in that place. Because of the flux of blood and the constricted channel of the vagina, thus in having intercourse the false virgin will deceive the man." But that is merely modern squeamishness.

Even today, women sometimes try to time the wedding night with the onset of their menstrual periods on the theory that blood is blood, and no one will look too closely. Every once in a while stories surface of a woman employing some form of self-mutilation—inserting ground glass into the vagina, for instance, or nicking the entrance with a razor blade so that the cuts will later be rubbed open and bleed during sex, for example. As these sorts of things are typically done very much in secret, however, they are difficult to verify. Some people even find such stories difficult to believe, but it seems fairly clear, given the popularity of things like hymen reconstruction, that even in the supposedly "postfeminist" West some women do indeed continue to undertake these kinds of efforts to ensure that their blood flows at the right time. Around the world and right here at home, women silently cut into their own genitals in the name of an expectation that may be far from fair and is definitely far from biologically realistic, but is nonetheless still widely viewed as utter and absolute proof.

Doctor, Doctor, Gimme the News

Many people are willing to believe that our forefathers couldn't diagnose virginity, but are unwilling to believe that modern doctors cannot do the same. After all, as the American College of Obstetricians and Gynecologists put it in a 1995 technical bulletin, "The physician should be able to differentiate a normal and an altered hymen." But can they? And if they can, does this mean that they can tell us for certain whether or not any woman or girl is a virgin?

The answer, in both cases, is no. This is due partly to the fact that despite what we fantasize, sexual activity simply does not necessarily leave distinctive marks on or in the body. This is true not only for adult women but also for girls. "Only a few vulvar or hymenal findings are reliable indicators of abuse among prepubertal girls," Dr. Abby Berenson writes in the *American Journal of Obstetric Gynecology*. "Furthermore, these findings are infrequently observed among children who are examined at a sexual assault center. In fact, findings strongly suggestive of sexual abuse were observed in < 5% [less than five per cent] of abused children." As the title of another medical journal article on hymenal evidence of sexual assault put it, "it's normal to be normal."

Expecting the genitals to provide definitive evidence, however, is really putting the cart before the horse for the simple reason that the results of any genital examination are dependent upon the practitioner who conducts it. Many, probably most, doctors are honestly and simply ignorant when it comes to hymens, and unfamiliar with the literature that has shown them to be all but useless as a basis for virginity diagnosis.

In the doctors' defense, it must be said that since hymens so rarely present medical problems, there is no particularly good reason for most doctors to know anything about them, or for hymens to be taught in depth in medical schools. Additionally, since only a subset of practitioners will ever practice in branches of medicine in which they would likely be encountering hymens at all, most doctors really have no need to know.

The trouble is that there is some research to suggest that even those who really ought to know what they're talking about when it comes to the human hymen, namely gynecological specialists, do not always pay attention to the hymen, and when they do, they may not know enough to usefully interpret what they see. In 1999 Emma Curtis and Camille San Lazaro of the Royal Victoria Infirmary in Newcastle-upon-Tyne, United Kingdom, published, in the *British Medical Journal*, the results of a survey they took of 126 of their pediatric, obstetric/gynecological, and genitourinary medical colleagues. Only 28 out of a subgroup of 75 of those surveyed regularly examined the hymen as part of a genital examination on an adolescent at all, and of that 75, fewer than half were certain of how to interpret what they saw when they looked at hymens. Asked whether they believed that frequent sexual activity resulted in ongoing loss or damage to the hymen, 44 of the 75 said they simply didn't know.

An astonishing lack of informed agreement among specialists in regard to the diagnosis of sexual history has been borne out by other studies as well. In 1997 and again in 1999 the *Archives of Pediatric and Adolescent Medicine* and the journal *Pediatrics* featured the results of a pair of studies that revealed just how difficult and unlikely it can be to obtain an accurate and objective diagnosis of sexual history. In the first study, a team of researchers headed by Boston University School of Medicine's Dr. Jan E. Paradise mailed out questionnaires that included seven simulated case histories to members of four physician organizations concerned with issues of child abuse or pediatric gynecology. Each case history contained a relevant clinical photograph to be used in making diagnostic assessments, along with questions about what the doctors believed they saw in the images or read in the written histories, as well as what they interpreted as being medically true of the individuals depicted in those images and case histories.

When the responses came back, Paradise's team correlated them with standard "textbook" interpretations for the types of evidence with which the doctors had been presented. Startlingly, only about half of these physicians' descriptions of what evidence was mentioned in the written histories or visible in the photographs conformed to those interpretations. Fewer than three-quarters of the doctors' interpretations of what that evidence meant conformed with standard versions. Last but not least, as many as 21 percent of the doctors reported phenomena that were not in fact shown or indicated in either the case histories or the photographs they were given.

In the second of these two studies, 604 physicians evaluated a set of clinical photographs of the external genitalia of seven girls, presented with brief case histories. Four months later, they were asked to evaluate the same photographs, with the difference being that the second time, six of the seven written case histories that were distributed along with the photos were altered in terms of the extent to which they suggested that the subject of the photograph was the victim of sexual abuse. Both times, the physicians were asked to identify whether they interpreted the photographs they were given as indicating "no [sexual] abuse" or "probable [sexual] abuse."

When the returns were in, the two sets of responses were compared. The degree to which physicians were likely to revise their opinions of the physical evidence visible in a photograph based on a written case history varied dramatically. The least experienced doctors' interpretations changed nearly one-third of the time. More experienced physicians were a harder sell, more likely to rely on their own impressions of the physical signs they could see in the photographs than on the information they gleaned from the written case histories, but even they revised their opinions as often as 6 percent of the time. This is a substantial margin of error.

This is in no way intended to denigrate the abilities of intelligent and ethical physicians, but rather to bring to light three vital truths about medical diagnosis. First, diagnosis is a matter of interpretation, and thus always, and inevitably, a matter of opinion. This is one of the reasons why, when a particularly disquieting diagnosis is made, we often seek out a second opinion before starting a course of treatment. Second, the discrepancies Dr. Paradise and his coauthors discovered give us pause to recall that medical diagnosis is not always as simple as we laypeople want to imagine. No single physical sign can tell a physician all the things he or she might wish it would. Making educated guesses is part of any doctor's job. Last, these studies remind us that observer bias is an objective reality: even the best-trained and most high-minded of us will sometimes see precisely what we look for.

What are we to do, then, if we want to know whether a woman is or is not a virgin? Where can we turn for an answer, if the doctors cannot tell us? The only honest answer is that there is in fact nowhere to turn, and nothing that can give us anything more ironclad than a maybe. In truth, if for some reason we care whether someone is or was a virgin, it would seem that the best solution is simply to ask.

The Blank Page

In Isak Dinesen's 1957 short-story collection *Last Tales*, there is a story that beautifully encapsulates the dynamics of virginity testing. A story within a story, the narrator of "The Blank Page" is a toothless old crone, a professional storyteller. Describing an isolated Carmelite convent high in the hills of Portugal where ceremonial white linens that will later be used on the wedding nights of the aristocracy are made, Dinesen deftly outlines the anxiety, pomp, and circumstance of producing a proof of virginity. *"Virginem eam tenemus,"* Dinesen has an aristocratic chamberlain pronounce, publicly displaying a princess's bridal sheet from the palace balcony with the formulaic Latin "we declare her to have been a virgin."

These sheets, the story continues, are never washed or used again. Rather, their stained centers are scissored out and delivered back to the convent in whose fields the flax was grown and there hung in ornate gilt frames on the walls of the convent's gallery, a small golden nameplate beneath each one. "In the midst of the long row," however, "there hangs a canvas which differs from the others. The frame of it is as fine and as heavy as any, and as proudly as any carries the golden plate with the royal crown. But on this one plate no name is inscribed, and the linen within the frame is snow-white from corner to corner, a blank page."

In Dinesen's tale, this blank page is the object of great and grave curiosity, an arresting memento . . . but of what? No speculations are given, no projections made. Dinesen does not tell us what to make of this unsullied cloth, nor does she hint at what the royal ladies who make the pilgrimage to the convent might think as they stand before it, lost in thought.

There is no single virginal body, no single virginal experience, no single virginal vagina, not even a single virginal hymen. There is only the question, how do we know whether this woman is a virgin? The answer has been written innumerable times, with alum and doves' blood and urine and decoctions of mint and lady's mantle, with charts and graphs and clinical photography. But no matter how many times someone attempts to inscribe it, no matter how firmly they press the pen to the paper, we are left forever with the same blank page.

CHAPTER 7

Opening Night

A Virgin's Bath: If a young woman about to have sex for the first time bathes
in mint tea, rubs her body with vetiver oil, and drinks a cup of sage tea warmed
with a dash of whiskey, her first sexual experience will be good.
—Traditional hoodoo recipe, related by catherine yronwode

SHORTLY AFTER I BEGAN WORKING on this book, I discovered that it
was next to impossible to actually have a discussion about virginity. Every
time I tried, the conversation was inexorably yanked to the topic of "losing it."
It was as if there were some strange force that kept pulling conversation away
from virginity and toward the moment of its end. Wanting to discuss other
things—virginity in religion, the myth of the *droit de seigneur*, season two of
Buffy the Vampire Slayer—this vexed me. I wasn't writing a book about virginity loss, after all.

Eventually it dawned upon me that this wasn't just my friends' oversexed
imaginations at work, but rather the nature of the beast. Virginity is invariably
defined in terms of what it is not, and is believed to be proven most incontro-
vertibly by whatever signs (blood, pain, etc.) become obvious only in the moment of its obliteration. We usually describe our own virginities starting from
the point at which we ceased to be virgins at all. In retrospect I realize that the
tendency to speak of virginity *loss* rather than of virginity itself should not

have surprised me. Virginity *is* because it ends. For this reason if for no other (and there are plenty of others), it makes sense for a book about virginity to also be a book that is, at least in some small part, about the loss of virginity.

The Ritual

Throughout history, losing one's virginity has been viewed as a ritual of transformation. Not merely the transformation from being one of the people who hasn't slept with anybody to being one of the ones who has, but a ritual that transforms a boy into a man, a girl into a woman, a child into an adult. But why?

Simply experiencing sexual curiosity or even engaging in genital acts isn't what makes the difference between child and adult. Sexual play is part of childhood in many cultures around the world, but we don't consider a child an adult just because he or she gets caught "playing doctor." Neither do we attribute adulthood to a child who has been sexually abused, even if he or she has experienced what we might think of as adult sexuality. If anything, we are prone to see such a child as even more vulnerable and in need of greater protection.

Losing one's virginity in a socially significant sense, the kind of virginity loss that "makes a woman" or "makes a man" out of someone, is clearly not just a matter of having gone through the motions. Something more than mere mechanical genital activity is at stake. That "something more," it would seem, lies somewhere in the tangled intersection of reproductive capacity, sexual desire, physical maturation, and the massive social importance of parenthood.

Children's sexual curiosity and adult sexuality are different in many ways. Perhaps the most important difference is that adult (hetero)sexuality has the potential of producing pregnancies, which in turn tends to lead to the assumption of that most adult of responsibilities, the rearing of the next generation. When sexual activity can be directly linked to parenthood—as has been the case for most of human history, since reliable contraception is a fairly recent thing—then it makes perfect sense that sexual activity also gets linked to adulthood and the assumption of adult responsibility. For centuries our social structures have institutionalized this principle, making a tidy tautological circle in which the biological activities of sex and reproduction are yoked to the social assumption of fully adult status in the community. Reproductive sexual capacity becomes the linchpin around which we organize the assumption of social adulthood.

Historically, few people have felt a need to try to separate out the elements of this process. As long as puberty, marriage, and virginity loss all generally followed fairly closely on one another's heels, a woman's social and biological adulthood could not only appear to unfold as a single streamlined entity, it could actually do so. The rituals that were created to mark the culmination of this process were often structured in ways that supported this impression of a single unbroken unfolding into adulthood—for example, as the ancient Greeks did, by incorporating virginity loss into the wedding. Their wedding festivities, which often took place when a young woman was somewhere in her early to mid teens, commonly included a noisy processional that conducted the bride and groom into a private room or enclosure near the site of the wedding feast. Then and there, with their friends and family just outside singing hymns to the god of marriage and generally carrying on, the marriage was consummated and the wife—no longer a bride—and her husband would emerge to cheering and revelry.

This custom, seamlessly weaving together the wedding and loss of virginity, survived in various forms in various cultures around the globe, including both Jewish and Christian weddings in the West. Even today it's a common custom for the bride and groom to retire together, at the end of the ceremony, to some area set aside from the rest of the wedding party. It's also commonplace for the guests at the party or reception to cheer when the newlyweds enter the room for the first time as a married couple, just as the guests would have cheered the ancient Greek bride and groom as they left the nuptial chamber and returned to the wedding feast. These days there probably aren't too many couples who seize the opportunities for privacy offered at the end of the wedding or before the reception to consummate their union (one imagines it would rather shock the guests), but that is where the custom arose.

Symbol and Substance

Fortunately for those who prefer less pressure and greater privacy, the seclusion of the bride and groom has, over the years, become just another symbolic gesture. But symbols and symbolic gestures are critical to rites of passage. Weddings are correspondingly full of such symbolic images and moments: the throwing of rice to symbolize fertility, the custom of wearing something blue on one's wedding day as a symbol of fidelity, the idea of passing on one's luck and happiness by tossing the bouquet, and so on. Of all the common wedding customs that we currently observe in the West, though, the seclusion of the bride and groom is the only one with a demonstrable link to the issue of the bride's virginity.

This may come as rather a surprise, given what is often said to be true of other popular wedding customs and symbols. But the historical record bears it out. Take, for instance, our penchant for dressing brides in white. The white wedding gown is popularly supposed to indicate a bride's virginal purity. Many people, including some misinformed scholars, have endorsed this association, perhaps thinking that the gown symbolizes the white sheets upon which some cultures traditionally expect a bride to bleed in order to provide proof of her wedding-night virginity. The two things actually have nothing to do with each other. If they did, we might expect that white would be a pancultural preference in bridal clothing, used wherever virginity is valued. But white has only rather recently become the color associated with brides, and only in the West—China, India, Japan, and other cultures also recognize and value virginity, but do not traditionally favor white for brides.

The white wedding gown is an inheritance from none other than England's Queen Victoria. At her 1840 wedding, she made the unprecedented sartorial choice—the traditional wedding color for royal brides at the time was silver—of wearing a splendid white satin gown trimmed with orange blossoms, along with a veil of Honiton lace and a tasteful array of diamond jewelry, some of which had been given to her by her groom, Prince Albert of Saxe-Coburg and Gotha. Victoria's dress unintentionally kick-started the tradition of the white wedding dress: how better to feel like a queen, particularly one who had been enjoying a highly public storybook romance, on one's wedding day than to dress like one? In an era where most women married in whatever constituted their Sunday best, a white gown was also a form of conspicuous consumption, a lavish display of the fact that a bride's family could afford to spend large sums on a garment that the bride would, by definition, never wear again. White is also difficult to keep clean, and thus a spotless white gown had associations both with purity (although not necessarily specifically sexual purity) and with attaining a pristine remove from the grimy workaday world. Fine symbolic meanings to take to the altar, indeed.

Had Victoria chosen to be married in blue, a popular choice at the time, Billy Idol might have sung about it being a nice day for a *blue* wedding, not a white one. Blue, yellow (the color associated with the Greek god of marriage, although in other places and times, also the color associated with prostitution), joyous reds, and even black, gray, and brown were common choices prior to Victoria's wedding, and blue and yellow remained popular into the early years of the twentieth century. But gradually, no doubt partly because of the spread of the popular belief that white dresses conveyed some elemental truth about the virginity of the women who wore them, the white wedding gown ascended to its current status as icon of the sexually untouched bride.

The veil shares the wedding gown's reputation for having some relationship to bridal virginity. Some sources have asserted that the custom of the veil arose from the desire to visually depict the bride's virginity, a sort of symbolic open-air hymen. Alas for the imaginative souls who came up with this interpretation of the bridal veil, none of the evidence we have on the custom of veiling suggests that this is the case. Rather, the primary function historically ascribed to facial veils is protection: against dirt and insects; against the gaze of potentially predatory men; and, most important in terms of weddings, against evil spirits, demons, or the evil eye. Veiling the face and thus the identity of a bride was long believed to render her immune from attacks by demons and witches, who depended on either seeing the eyes of the intended victim or on knowing her exact identity. A closely related custom, dressing the bridesmaids in identical dresses, was similarly intended to confuse evil spirits or those who wished to harm the bride. What becomes clear when we look at customs like white wedding gowns and bridal veils, at their historical meanings as well as the specifically sexual meanings we have attributed to them more recently, is that we are master creators of symbolic gestures. Socially significant moments tend to acquire symbolic meaning, even if we have to stick those symbolic meanings on with glue.

Equal Rites?

Rites of passage are not, in and of themselves, changes of status or stage in life. Rather, they are the social and cultural acknowledgment of changes that are either in the process of taking place or which have already happened. The most common rites of passage exist around the events of birth, menarche, attainment of adulthood, marriage, and death. Logically enough, as cultures change, rites of passage change, too, in scope and style. We do still observe some of the rites of passage we have observed as a species since time immemorial, most prominently funerals and weddings. We have also evolved new rites of passage that invoke and serve the kinds of social transitions that are meaningful to us today. One of them is the rite of passage of "the first time."

Virginity loss gets enacted, as a rite of passage, in a way that is partly private, partly public, partly symbolic, and partly explicit. It is diffuse, happening on an informal basis through peer-to-peer communication, not concentrated in the form of a group event or ceremony. The confirmation of social status change is slow, relying upon multiple retellings of virginity-loss stories in different contexts, for different and usually very private audiences. In many ways it is the opposite to the announcements, invitations, formal ceremony, eventfulness, and public witness of weddings. But it is very similar in its function as a rite of passage that marks the borderland of adulthood, and very similar, indeed, in being a social performance.

We might well wonder how it became possible for such a seemingly private experience to take on such a central role in the process of becoming socially adult. Part of the answer is that it has always been this way—for men. Men have always commemorated virginity loss and the acquisition of sexual experience on a peer-to-peer basis. In most Western cultures, the bulk of any young man's sexual learning traditionally comes from other men. This takes many forms: locker room braggadocio, the creation of and trade in pornography, young men being taken by male relatives to a brothel for their first experience of intercourse (still common in much of Central and South America; recent studies reveal that around a quarter of contemporary Ecuadoran men lose their virginity in such a setting), bachelor parties, and even ancient Greece's system of *paidika*, where older men took on younger men as protégés and sexual partners. Men are mutually complicit in one another's sexual upbringings. Among other things, this means that for men, sexuality can and does exist in an independent frame of reference that includes neither women as individual people nor heterosexuality as part of a meaningful human relationship. Men *have* sex. It is something they do and something they acquire.

Women, on the other hand, have often been construed as *being* sex. Women's sexuality, unlike men's, has never really been allowed to exist as a frame of reference unto itself. The K-strategist's dilemma, the need for resources with which to rear resource-intensive offspring, has kept female sexuality tied to socioeconomics. Men could experience their own sexual milestones as occasions for private celebration because there is no direct material consequence, for men, to sexual activity. Women, however, often learned the hard way to capitalize on the protections offered them by the public ritualizing of their own sexual milestones. This is not to say that in the past, all women waited until marriage to have sex, or that modern women have become sexual in unprecedented ways. Rather, it is to say that in the past, women who had sex prior to marriage, even if they were victims of sexual violence, typically had to hide it under pain of severe punishment, whereas modern women have acquired the unprecedented ability not to have to do so. The difference is vast. Women's newfound ability to be known as independently sexual is a large part of what has gone into making virginity loss a modern rite of passage all its own.

Telling Stories

Marriage has, in the past hundred years, lost much of its gravitas as the rite of passage through which women assume the mantle of adulthood. This is in large part because marriage today rarely takes place at the onset of adulthood. Most contemporary Westerners have completed their education, spent several years as self-supporting members of the workforce, lived on their own and run their own households, and, in most cases, had at least some experience with romantic and/or sexual relationships before they marry for the first time (if indeed they marry at all). But except for weddings, we have no formal public rite of passage that exists to acknowledge the achievement of female adulthood. We come of age in myriad ways, and more often than not we do so long before we marry. Drifting along as we do on the currents of cultural change, the element of the adulthood rite-of-passage to which we seem to cling tightest is not marriage but the onset of sexual activity. Having sex is a true centerpiece of our traditional values.

As is typical of rites of passage, the actual act or acts—in this case, first-time sex—are only part of the picture. The bulk of a rite of passage is the social acknowledgment of the transition. In the case of virginity loss, the vehicle for this acknowledgment is storytelling. Both before and after the actual event(s) of first-time sex, we both prepare for and commemorate the transition, this entry into the world of the adult, by rehearsing expectations, fears, experiences, and lore "through the grapevine."

Virginity researchers Laura Carpenter and Sharon Thompson are among the few academics to have looked at how this rite of passage works, gathering hundreds of examples of the stories contemporary teenagers tell one another about their experiences of virginity loss. It is through telling, comparing, and validating such stories that adolescents confirm to themselves and one another that they've officially crossed the threshold into the world of adulthood. Tales from the trenches provide models for those who have not yet lost their virginity, giving the uninitiated a selection of blueprints for the ways the experience is supposed to happen. They teach us what is considered desirable and undesirable, right and wrong. The social styles of our cultures and peer groups, reflected in the stories we tell, shape our understanding of what our sexual lives mean and are, including what we're likely to say about our own experiences.

This is why, as collections of virginity-loss narratives like Karen Bouris's *The First Time* and Louis Crozier's *Losing It* demonstrate, despite the infinite variety of our personal experiences with first-time sex, we tell a fairly limited number of stories about it. There are positive versions and negative versions, and variety in the details, but over a broad sample, virginity-loss tales are for the most part quite similar. Objective facts—what happened and how—are less important than communicating symbolic truths. The stories that we tell say less about what was literally experienced than they do about how we felt about the experience, how we wanted to feel about it, and how our culture expects us to feel about it. They are the way in which we contemporary Westerners transmute a physical moment into a social fact, hearing and telling our stories of first-time sex as our adult rite of passage.

Male-Order Brides

Historically speaking, one of the favored ways of resolving the rape of a virgin was to see to it that the victim married her rapist. More than a few legal codes, pre-Christian and post-Christian alike, have indicated this as a preference. The woman's feelings in the matter were of no import in these decisions. From the perspective of property, it was the way to make the best out of a bad situation. If the man who stole a woman's virginity was given the right to it through marriage, at least the woman was (in theory) provided for, and no other man would find his fortunes undermined by having a new wife bear another man's child.

While callous, cruel, and gobsmackingly sexist from our perspective, this solution is perfectly sensible in its own context. Over the centuries, marriage has far more often been about economics than it has been about romance. Marriage as an outgrowth of romantic love only became common in the West within the last three hundred years: romance, after all, is rather peripheral to the functioning of a society, whereas resources are crucial. As a means of maximizing wealth, cementing alliances, solidifying land and other holdings, and organizing the transfer of property across generations, marriage has been an institution of the utmost pragmatic and strategic importance.

As part of the apparatus of this institution, virginity was materially important because of what it meant in terms of verifiable paternity of children. It was also important because it signified a woman's willingness to put the priorities of her family, her future husband, and her community ahead of her own desires. A bride's virginity was considered an indicator of her good upbringing, her fitness to be taken into a new household and family line, and her trustworthiness as a wife. It represented a symbolic guarantee of a woman's behavior and value system, and a material guarantee that at least the first child born within her marriage would verifiably be sired by her new husband, not some potential competitor.

Virginity, in short, was a critical element of the material and symbolic value any bride had to offer to a potential husband. One could even call it a part of her dowry. Dowry, like its inverse practice, bridewealth, is a one-way transfer of wealth that takes place at marriage. Dowry means a transfer from the bride's family to the groom's household, so that property accompanies the bride. In cases where wealth is given to the bride's family by the groom in exchange for the privilege of absorbing their daughter into his household, we call it bridewealth instead. Bridewealth was never widely practiced in the West. Dowry, on the other hand, was nearly ubiquitous, only eventually fading out in the nineteenth century as a combination of socioeconomic forces and the rise of the romantic marriage rendered dowries less important and less popular. Even so, vestiges of dowry, like the hope chest and the bride's trousseau, remain fairly popular as wedding customs.

Like the rest of the items in her dowry, virginity was one of the valuable goods that went with a woman from her own household to her husband's household when she married. Like the linens and clothing, household goods, livestock, and other items that might be part of her dowry, it became her husband's property, of which he would dispose in the process of consummating the marriage. In essence, this means that the Western tradition was not only to enhance the value of daughters on the marriage market by keeping them virgins prior to their weddings, but to actually pay the men to marry them, too. If this seems paradoxical, it is.

Or is it? The common presumption has long been that if virginity is valuable, men will give a good deal in order to acquire virgin brides, and the potential of an increased bridewealth would be one of the major motivators for a family to keep its daughters virginal. But as the studies of researchers including Jack Goody and Alice Schlegel have shown, it doesn't quite work that way. In cross-cultural surveys of marriage practices, in fact, it has been shown that cultures that practice bridewealth transactions place less stress on the premarital virginity of women, not more. It is the dowry-giving cultures (wealth going from the bride's family to the groom), not the bridewealth-givers, that tend to care the most about virginity.

Anthropologist Schlegel posits that this has to do not with religion or morals but with good old-fashioned social climbing. Essentially, if a family wants to ensure that its daughters get married to men of optimal rank and status, it needs to make its daughters as appealing as possible to the kinds of families with which they wish to become allied. Simultaneously, they must keep their daughters away from all inappropriate suitors. In cases where the stability or improvement of family status depended upon the marriages of its daughters, as was certainly true throughout the preindustrial West, virginity was co-opted as a primary asset for increasing a family's leverage in the husband-finding market. If Schlegel's conjectures are true, then men wouldn't have had to pay for virgin brides for the simple reason that families with daughters would already be using virginity as a means of attracting better grooms. In effect this would ultimately mean that most any man could comfortably expect to marry a virgin, because virtually every family would be invested in the possibility of one of its daughters "marrying up," something it would be impossible to do without a virginal daughter to offer in marriage.

We cannot say why the system evolved this way in the West when it didn't in other cultures. For instance, cultures that practice bridewealth or potlatch in conjunction with weddings rather than dowry often have a radically different perspective on bridal virginity. The fact remains that not all cultures handle virginity in the same way, however; indeed some don't recognize or value it at all. The value we place on virginity is precisely that, placed upon it, and not intrinsic either to human beings or to virginity itself.

Despite occasional claims to the contrary, human males do not have an inherent desire for female virgins. It would be a fine trick indeed if they did, since virginity is an intangible quality that one cannot see, touch, smell, or reliably identify. To claim that men innately desire virgins is every bit as baseless as claiming that people have an inborn yearning for sexual partners who are philanthropic or insightful, or have a keen sense of fashion. Which is not to say that we do not ever desire intuitive, well-dressed altruists, but rather to say that our desire for these qualities and these people is neither biological nor inborn. We learn to desire these attributes because we learn that within the context of our culture, they are valued and desired.

So it is with virginity. Men learn to desire virgins over nonvirgins when they live in cultures where virginity is construed as being valuable. In such cultures, there are few sexual acts that can increase a man's image of sexual success like laying claim to it. When it comes to the kinds of things that men have developed the habit of acquiring in order to show off their superior status to other men, the maidenheads of young mistresses are worth at least as much as the canvases of old masters. Like winning an athletic trophy, winning the "prize" of a woman's virginity implies a certain type of physical prowess. Like the stuffed head of a moose or tiger on a club room wall, it evokes the idea of a successful hunter capable of bagging his quarry. Like tales of exotic travel, it carries connotations of having been the first person to lay claim to a new and previously unclaimed territory.

Where virginity is a sought-after commodity, a conquered virgin can reflect a multitude of stereotypically masculine virtues. Little wonder that some men have made a fetish out of the destruction of virginity. It's a surprisingly

egalitarian pastime. A career in popping cherries requires few resources beyond audacity, charisma, and a penis. It rewards traits that aren't dependent
on rank or wealth, such as ingenuity and a gift for gab. It's sexually gratifying, and, at least from certain angles and to certain mentalities, it can definitely make a man's social stock soar. As a venue for conspicuously
participating in sexual competition, the acquisitive defloration of virgins has
few equals.

One of the reasons that the claiming of women's virginity works so efficiently in this sense is that virginity is not merely acquired when it is taken; it
is destroyed, removed permanently from the available pool. The virginity of
any woman, at least the way virginity has classically been construed, can only
belong to one man. This finality makes the defloration of virgins a potent social weapon. Women, however, aren't the only ones who have reason to fear it.
Men fear "virginity poachers," too. Taking the virginity of a man's daughter
without intending to marry her, whether by force or seduction, has long been
thought of as one of the most underhanded and devastating blows one man
could deal another. Seducing another man's fiancée and taking her virginity is
closely related and very nearly as bad. As sexual mores and gendered expectations in regard to sex have changed, these sorts of sexual attacks have become
less common, or at least less likely to be interpreted as attacks. But within some
social groups, this sort of sexual theft is still considered a mortal insult to a
man's virility, authority, honor, and strength.

As a result of the stress put on the redemption of a stolen virginity, men
have not infrequently been known to deflower women precisely because it was
a way to force marriages the women's families might otherwise have opposed.
This Machiavellian use of virginity sometimes involved genuine rape, but in
other cases the "rape" was a consensual event a woman participated in with a
man she wanted to marry over parental objections. Presented with a fait ac-
compli of such major and potentially pregnant proportions, it was fairly likely
that her family would throw in the towel and call for a priest. In other words,
shotgun weddings may have been a matter of wife or death in some cases and
entrapment in others, and yet for some women they may have represented one
of the few times that they could use the significant value of their own virginity
to their own ends.

Unforgettable

Is it true that, in the words of the ad campaign for the 1999 movie *American Pie*, "you never forget your first piece"? For centuries, one of the things that has frequently been believed to be true about losing one's virginity is that the experience is indelibly and automatically etched upon one's brain. Some believe, for instance, that people, especially women, form an instantaneous and unshakable emotional bond with their first sexual partners. Others claim that the quality and nature of your first sexual experience is an indicator of the kind of sex life you will have for the remainder of your days. The virgin is thought of as a blank slate, an empty canvas, and the first sexual experience she has is seen as making an inevitable and permanent mark. It is a somewhat poetic sentiment, but it is also false. A first sexual experience is no more and no less likely to permanently shape one's sensibilities, identity, or responses than any other milestone in life, from a first step to a first parking ticket. Nonetheless, over the years many people have believed that the way you lose your virginity not only can but *will* influence you for the rest of your life.

The idea has a long history, but its current incarnation is largely the result of the work of Sigmund Freud. The third of three essays in his *Contributions to the Psychology of Love*, the 1918 essay "The Taboo of Virginity" was for decades considered one of the definitive scientific discussions of the topic of virginity. In this essay, while admitting that our Western ideology of virginity is simultaneously deeply rooted and essentially inexplicable, Freud nonetheless did not hesitate to profess a number of wholly unsubstantiated "truths" about virginity and its loss.

Chief among them—prominently placed in the second paragraph of the essay, so no one could miss it—is the idea that the experience of losing her virginity "brings about a state of 'thralldom' in the woman that assures the man lasting and undisturbed possession of her and makes her able to withstand new impressions and temptations from without." Without so much as a footnote to back up this amazing assertion, Freud takes the notion of female emotional dependency on sexual partners (an idea he borrowed uncredited from the notebooks of his sexologist colleague Richard von Krafft-Ebing) and claims that it is the nearly inevitable result of women losing their virginity. The idea is completely in line with late-nineteenth-century middle-class notions of the proper relationship between the sexes, but the mechanics of this "thralldom" are a classic example of magical thinking. This is Sleeping Beauty's story: the woman is "awakened" into instant and permanent pair-bonding by the first sexual touch of a man.

Freud acknowledged that this hapless, helpless relationship dynamic was not benign. Those who still believe in the existence of this spontaneous, unasked-for bond between virgins and their deflowerers think likewise, and see it as one of the major pitfalls of having sex with a virgin. The flip side of this myth is no prettier. Many a woman has gone into her first sexual experience convinced that losing her virginity would produce an automatic commitment on the part of the man to whom she lost it.

However, as many women have discovered to their dismay, the magic is a myth. Historian Ginger Frost relates numerous occasions where late-nineteenth-century men, arraigned and charged with breach of promise after having seduced women they'd promised to marry, replied with the predictable response that of course they'd promised commitment to get sex, that "all men do." It seems almost superfluous to mention that this phenomenon is by no means limited to the Victorians. Indeed, if there is anything as timeless as losing one's virginity, it may be the empty promises that often precede it: an old Arab proverb laments it with the poetic formula "He promised me earrings, but he only pierced my ears." Whether faced with desperate clinging when one wanted cool independence or dealing with cool independence when one wanted clinging, the former virgin and her partner may both, in the end, view virginity loss as little more than a basket of terribly sour grapes.

But there were other ways that the supposed "imprinting" of virginity loss might, or so Freud claimed, turn into a fiasco. There was a very real risk that a woman would reflexively and inescapably despise her deflowerer for what he'd done. As "The Taboo of Virginity" explains it, such fury is due not to any conscious personal animosity but by the (supposedly) inevitable pain of defloration. This pain was not just physical, according to Freud, although he presumed that women did suffer bodily pain and bleeding. There was also the deeper pain of an inevitable psychic "wound" caused by the destruction of "an organ" (whether Freud meant the hymen specifically or virginity itself is less than clear). The resulting wounded-animal rage could take the form of verbal and physical assaults. Freud reported cases of women who tongue-lashed, physically threatened, or actually struck their husbands after not only the first act of intercourse, but every sex act thereafter. Turned inward, Freud argued, the same fury caused frigidity.

Freud wasn't alone in believing that the wrong first experience of sex, or even the right experience improperly handled, could result in catastrophe. Nineteenth- and early-twentieth-century sex manuals are rife with descriptions of how a husband could cause his wife permanent damage if he bungled the wedding night. Victorian-era writer John Cowan, for instance, warned that a naive bride's refined sensibilities, to say nothing of her delicate constitution, might well be overcome by violent or crass boudoir tactics: "The husband, in the exercise of what he is pleased to term his 'marital rights,' places his wife, in a very short time indeed, on the nervous, delicate, sickly list." Later, British sex education reformers such as Stella Browne and Marie Stopes downplayed the inevitability and permanence of such damage, proposing instead the much more reasonable notion that anyone's first experience of sex can be made better, and the associations they will have with sex improved, if they are given a chance at both sex education and sexual experiences that are unpressured and noncoercive. But even the resolutely progressive Stopes, in her bestselling *Married Love* (1918), could not entirely get away from the notion of the permanently ruinous first sexual experience, relating that there have been "not a few brides whom the horror of the first night of marriage . . . has driven to suicide or insanity."

It took most of the twentieth century for the notion that virginity loss permanently shaped one's sexual existence to fade from the sex manuals and psychology texts, and even now one still occasionally finds traces of it in the literature. As late as 2003, analysts Deanna Holtzman and Nancy Kulish were still hard at work, in an issue of the *Psychoanalytic Quarterly*, debunking the Freudian "vengeful virgin" theory with a curt "we feel this idea of revenge against the deflowerer is an example of a male fantasy projected onto the female." Few if any reputable professionals still espouse the idea that virginity loss gives rise to these spontaneous, uncontrollable reactions, but the belief lives on despite the change in the psychoanalytic party line. A bad first experience of sex, particularly if a woman loses her virginity as a result of rape or incest, is still often popularly touted as the cause of frigidity, inability to orgasm, or lesbianism. (It is sometimes similarly claimed that a bad first experience with a woman can "turn a man gay.") Conversely, in the long tradition of making a disease of female sexual desire, a woman who enjoys her first sexual experience might become a nymphomaniac or a "sex addict," instantly and permanently dependent not on the specific man in question but on the act itself. With the recent resurgence of emphasis being placed on virginity (or "premarital sexual abstinence" as it's often called in today's rhetoric) for teenagers of both sexes, we sometimes find young men turning this mythology on themselves as well, embracing virginity out of fear that if they taste the forbidden fruit, they might not be able to keep themselves from becoming "man-whores."

What all of these beliefs about virginity loss have in common is the idea that there is a deep, core portion of the self that cannot be altered consciously, yet is completely reshaped in an instant by a single sexual experience. Newly deflowered virgins are imagined as the helpless recipients of some sort of automatic imprint, helplessly following in the wake of their own virginity loss like baby ducks following their mother. In reality it's just another manifestation of the fantasy that losing our virginity should by rights leave traces. For better or worse, however, what we generally take away from losing our virginity are only the same sorts of memories, variegated in type and intensity, prone to distortion and fading, as we have of the other memorable events in our lives.

Blood and Pain

No book on virginity could possibly omit a discussion of blood and pain. Considered proof positive of a woman's virginity since the very earliest documents we have on the subject, pain and bleeding have been so strongly associated with virginity loss that we scarcely speak about first-time sex without talking about them. Generally pain and bleeding associated with first-time sexual penetration—if they happen at all—are both short-lived and minor, but this is a very personal and variable thing. While it is true that some women do report intense pain and/or extensive bleeding, it is extremely rare for a physically adult woman's first experience of sexual penetration to result in injuries severe enough to require medical attention. That the physical consequences of virginity loss occupy a sizable continuum has been a known factor for hundreds, even thousands, of years. Even the rabbis of the Talmud recognized that not all women's bodies react to virginity loss the same way.

We look for blood and pain in virgins because we attach enormous symbolic meaning to these things. Depending on one's viewpoint, blood and pain can be understood as symbolic of virtue, morality, sacrifice, and even of sacramental covenants and the grace of God. Sociologist Sharon Thompson's research has shown that in telling their virginity-loss stories, some women seem to positively revel in gory (and in some cases clearly exaggerated) details of how much it hurt and how much they bled and suffered. While some cast losing their virginity in the light of romantic sacrifice or "proving their love," others frame it as evidence that sex inevitably makes victims of women or as proof that sexually active women deserve to suffer. Still others cite it as the physical embodiment of all the betrayal and disappointment they felt when they realized that sex wasn't necessarily going to be the be-all and end-all they'd been led to expect. "They almost seem to be scaring each other off," Thompson writes, then adds, in a perceptive alternate take, "or playing dare double-dare."

In a very different interpretation, some evangelical Christian youth educators like Dannah Gresh, the author of the popular *And the Bride Wore White: Seven Secrets to Sexual Purity*, draw an explicit connection between the idea of a blood sacrifice, blood covenants, and the blood of defloration to emphasize the ideals of premarital chastity and a sanctified marriage bond. "You see, God created you and me with a protective membrane, the hymen, which in most cases is broken the first time that we have intercourse," Gresh writes. "When it breaks, a woman's blood spills over her husband. Your sexual union is a blood covenant between you, your husband, and God." Gresh wins points for acknowledging that this blood loss doesn't happen every time ("in most cases"), but one can only wonder how a reader might react who'd internalized Gresh's characterization of this spilling of blood, only to discover when the time came that she hadn't bled a drop. Such are the risks of attaching heavy symbolic meaning to a physical phenomenon that may or may not happen.

Whether in the painful bloody first times showcased in romance novels and pornography, the ancestral custom of proving virginity through the evidence of post-wedding-night blood on the sheets, the way young women use their virginity-loss horror stories as an arena for female bonding, or in religiously based interpretations like Gresh's, the message is clear: blood and pain equal virginity loss, virginity loss equals blood and pain. On some level, it seems as if our culture believes that women *should* bleed and suffer when they have sex for the first time. Whether it is framed as a consecration or as a punishment is but a matter of perspective.

From antiquity forward, numerous medical writers likewise noted that it was eminently possible for a virgin not to bleed. It is discussed extensively in Tractate Ketubot of the Talmud, and a range of Greek, Egyptian, Carthaginian, biblical, and other sources on the subject are cited in Robert Burton's 1621 *Anatomy of Melancholy*. But if some women bleed and others don't, it rather raises the question why. One fairly common explanation, advanced by writers including seventeenth-century midwife Jane Sharp, was that women who lost their virginity after they had been menstruating for some while were less likely to bleed because the passages were already accustomed to having substances pass through them on a regular basis. Other writers simply admitted ignorance. The late-seventeenth-century sexual self-help best-seller *Aristotle's Master-Piece*, which remained hugely popular throughout England and America for over a century, was firm in its insistence that an absence of blood was not con-clusive evidence of a misplaced maidenhead, and happy to equivocate as to the reasons the blood might not appear:

> When a man is married and finds the tokens of his wife's virginity, upon
> the first act of copulation, he has all the reason in the world to believe her
> such, but if he finds them not, he has not reason to think her devirginated,
> if he finds her otherwise sober and modest: Seeing the Hymen may be bro-
> ken so many other ways, and yet the woman both chaste, and virtuous.

The answer to the question of why the experience of first intercourse is so variable is no clearer today than it was in the seventeenth century. We still don't know exactly why some women experience pain and bleeding along with their first experience of penetrative sex and others don't. We don't, in fact, even necessarily know what aspect of penetration or what part of the anatomy is being affected when pain and bleeding do occur. There are, after all, quite a few possibilities.

Many people simply assume that first intercourse tears the tissues of the hy-men, and this tearing is what causes both pain and bleeding. This may be true in some cases, but we also know that not all hymens are equally traumatized by penetration and some are not traumatized by it at all. What kind of hymen is most likely to prove a source of pain? We don't know, and the research doesn't provide an answer. It would seem prudent, though, to surmise that the hymen itself must not be the sole factor in the equation that determines what a woman experiences the first time she is sexually penetrated.

After all, intercourse does not take place between a penis and a hymen. Hymens do not exist in isolation. The hymen is a landmark within the larger landscape of the entrance of the vagina, much in the manner that the frame of a door is a landmark in the larger landscape of an entryway to a house or room. You can't go through the doorway without going through the door's frame, but you also can't go through the door's frame without going through the doorway. The same is true of the hymen and the entrance of the vagina. If the hymen is present at all, it's present as part of the vaginal entrance. It is made of the same types of tissues as the rest of the vagina, and is subject to the same conditions and forces as the rest of it.

And the vagina, hymen very much included, is a complex thing. Vaginas vary from one to the next in numerous aspects, including their at-rest size, the degree to which they can potentially be dilated or opened, and the relative elasticity of their muscles and tissues. There are also characteristics that change not only from woman to woman, but also over the lifetime of any individual woman, including general health, arousal, naturally occurring mucous lubrication, and susceptibility to *dyspareunia* (a generic term meaning painful intercourse), a condition which has a number of possible causes. All of these things, plus the subjective wild cards of attitude, emotional and intellectual comfort, feelings toward one's partner, sexual guilt or shame, and many other such intangibles, play a role in what a woman experiences and how her body reacts during any given sexual episode, including a first time.

Research suggests that experience, knowledge, and patience go a long way in helping women have less painful, more pleasurable experiences of first-time penis-in-vagina sex. We know that women who have nonintercourse sexual experience prior to their first intercourse usually report less painful and more pleasurable experiences when they do have penetrative sex. Relaxation counts for a great deal as well: a recent German study of 669 young women and their experiences with first gynecological exams revealed a significant relationship between anxiety and painful penetration of the vagina. In this light, we might read some of the advice often found in old sex manuals and medical texts very differently. When old sex manuals encourage a woman (and/or her husband) to gently stretch the opening of the vagina with the fingers a little bit at a time before attempting intercourse, we can see this not merely as instructions for gradual dilation of the hymen but as a prescription for a gradual introduction to sex in the form of digital stimulation.

It's not glamorous, it's not titillating, and in fact it's downright mundane: studies show that women who have a comprehensive, nonjudgmental sexual education and who develop affirming, self-empowered attitudes about their own sexuality are more likely to report positive experiences when they lose their virginity. A woman is also more likely to have a painless experience, as well as a more positive impression of losing her virginity overall, research tells us, if she is not coerced or pressured, feels safe and secure with her partner, and is not worried about being interrupted or discovered during sex. Women who are somewhat older than the average for their demographic when they have sex for the first time are more likely to have more positive experiences when they lose their virginity, possibly because they have simply had more time to learn and experience things and gained more autonomy over their lives than those who first had sex at earlier ages.

The research repeatedly indicates that a nontraumatic and perhaps even pleasant introduction to sex for women may be as simple as educating them and letting them do it on their own terms and in their own time. Could it be that the early progressive sex educators, like Stella Browne, Marie Stopes, and Margaret Sanger, all of whom strongly advocated sexual education and autonomy as being central to good sex lives for women, are finally finding vindication in quantitative analysis? Indeed, it seems to be so. *Plus ça change, plus c'est la même chose.*

PART II

Virgin Culture

But whatsoever is the object of any man's appetite or desire,
that is it which he for his part calleth good;
and the object of his hate and aversion, evil;
and of his contempt, vile and inconsiderable.

—Thomas Hobbes
Leviathan, 1651

CHAPTER 8

In a Certain Way Unbodily

Virginal integrity, and the freedom from all sexual intimacy that comes with
the devout practice of celibacy, belongs with the angels, and in corruptible
flesh it is a foretaste of eternal incorruptibility . . . those whose bodies are
already in a certain way unbodily have something special
over and above what others have.
—St. Augustine

VIRGINITY OFTEN FEELS MONOLITHIC, so huge, pervasive, and old
that it must have been with us since the dawn of time. In a certain sense
this is even true. We do not know how the idea of virginity first arose, what
sorts of ideas and ideals—if any at all—were associated with virginity in its
earliest days, or anything else about how it might have been relevant to the
lives of those who first established the notion. But as long as people have been
writing about themselves, they've also been writing about virginity. We can't
trace virginity back to the origin of the concept, but we can follow it back as
far as we have written references: to the world of antiquity and its Judaeans,
Romans, Greeks, and Egyptians. The fact that a concept of virginity existed
for the Egyptians, Greeks, and Romans and was discussed in the Torah (or
Old Testament) and Talmud doesn't mean, however, that their ideas about
virgins and virginity were anything like ours. Our understanding of the

physical nature of virginity has not been historically uniform, and neither has our understanding of any of its other aspects.

It is often claimed, and accurately so, that "the past is another country." When it comes to discussing virginity, the distance between the culture into which Jesus of Nazareth was born and the culture that grew up around the religion founded by his followers is huger than we can easily comprehend. When we look back to the ancient world—a necessary first step if we are to gain any perspective on the roots of our own Western Judeo-Christian ideologies of virginity—we are truly looking at a different place that functioned according to different paradigms of religion, philosophy, medicine, and human relationships. Indeed, we are looking at the other side of a paradigm shift in terms of the ways in which the body and sexuality were understood. This shift, which was a direct result of the emergence of Christianity, began along the shores of the Mediterranean about a hundred years before the time of Christ and solidified during the fifth century C.E., around the time of the death of the inimitable St. Augustine. To understand the nature of this shift, its incredible momentum, and the inestimable degree to which it changed Western civilization, we must know what preceded it, what virginity was and meant to the ancient world.

Unearthing Ancient Chastities

We think of chastity as a kissing cousin to virginity, a state of sexual abstinence, celibacy, and purity. We frequently think of it as being an aspect of religious belief, and also tend to consider it an expression or embodiment of a particular sort of morality. When we read the fifth-century-B.C.E. Greek lyric poet Bacchylides' statement "as a skillful painter gives a face beauty, just so chastity gives charm to a life of high aims," it makes immediate sense to us. It fits our notions of what the word "chastity" means, the type of people we assume would seek it out and practice it, and the kind of lifestyle we think such people would lead.

So it comes as something of a surprise when we discover that for Bacchylides, as for the rest of the pre-Christian world, chastity did not mean celibacy at all. Nor did it necessarily mean sexual abstinence except for certain brief periods. Ancient-world chastity was just as likely to be a matter of physical health as it was of spiritual fitness.

For Roman citizens, marriage and procreation were often legally required in the name of the state, neither optional nor truly voluntary. The same pertained in much of Greece. This was a world in which virtually everyone married and virtually everyone begot or bore children. It was also a world in which men of the elite (and the elite are the only ancients who had the means and the material wealth to leave behind historical documents, and are, therefore, the people whose history we know the most about) commonly had not only wives but concubines, and slept not only with them but with *heterae*, or courtesans. They were, as landowners and slaveowners, also entitled to have sexual access to the bodies of the people they owned. For a man, confining sexual activity to the marital bed was scarcely mandatory. Simply keeping it within the household would do admirably. In Greece, though less commonly in Rome, a man's sexual activity might also include liaisons with adolescents of his own sex. As they grew up, boys learned to become part of the "old boys' club" of the elite ancient Greek world through intense, loving, and often sexual relationships with older men who were their mentors, champions, and friends.

What, then, did a person of this era consider "chastity" to be? The Greeks had a word for it, *sophrosyne*, a quality of temperance characterized by self-knowledge, maturity, and control. Discussed at length by Plato and praised in Aristotle's *Nichomachean Ethics* as the primary characteristic of the sought-after middle road of personal conduct, *sophrosyne* was the ethical and spiritual force that would cause a man not to eliminate his various passions—hardly a moderate's move—but to discipline them, consciously limiting himself to those actions and activities that most contributed to the general good.

This general good was both social and physical. Sex was an integral aspect of the life of the body, and everything that affected the body could also affect health. It was common for men to consult physicians to discover what kinds of imbalances might exist in the humors of their bodies. On doctors' advice they would tailor their sexual activities as well as their diets, exercise, massage regimens, and work and bathing habits. Pythagoras, for example, counseled celibacy during the summers, for he believed that the humoral heat of sex combined with summer weather might overwhelm the system and cause illness.

Ancient authorities sometimes counseled periods of temporary celibacy, but this did not mean that more celibacy would be better. Quite the contrary: Hippocrates, Rufus of Ephesus, Galen, and other medical men were adamant that insufficient sexual activity in both men and women could lead to illness due to *plethora*, an overabundance of moist humors that would clog the body and weigh it down. Finding the right balance between sexual heat, loss of semen (women as well as men were believed to produce and ejaculate semen), and the tendencies of one's individual body could be tricky.

Neither sex nor ejaculation was seen as problematic, in and of itself. Indeed, a Roman boy's first ejaculation was something to celebrate, both within the household and at the annual March 17 festival known as the Liberalia. Frequency and timing of sex and ejaculation, on the other hand, were issues with which a man who wished to be healthy and wise had to grapple. Not enough and one might succumb to *plethora*; too often and one might become enervated and withered. Getting the balance right was the key to exceptional health. Such health was even reputed to affect the body in visible ways: Aline Rousselle relates that chaste men were believed to be taller and stronger than men who were too profligate.

Women, too, were expected to be chaste. Their chastity was a bit closer to what we today think of as chastity, namely premarital celibacy followed by married monogamy. An adulteress could be killed, potentially even by her own father, for disgracing herself and the houses to which she belonged. But at the same time, women's sexual desire was a recognized aspect of life in the ancient world. The women of Aristophanes' *Lysistrata* complain just as loudly and long about their heavy loins and unmet desires as do the men from whom they're withholding their sexual favors. Women's sexual needs were such an uncontested reality to Jewish thought that the rabbis of the Talmud protected women's sexual interests by delineating the frequency with which wives had the legal right to demand sexual satisfaction from their husbands.

Medical opinion seconded the perception that sex was important for women. Contemporary medical theory held that women's reproductive systems and overall health benefited from regular intercourse and the salubrious effects of keeping the uterus regularly moistened with semen. Without active sex lives, women could fall prey to potentially fatal illnesses like *plethora* and "suffocation of the womb," better known as hysteria. Sexual pleasure was also acknowledged as beneficial. A couple would draw closer to one another and increase the harmony in their relationship through *charis*, a sense of gracious trust and affection born of mutual intimate delight.

A chaste woman of the ancient world, in other words, did not shun sex. Rather, she indulged in it with her husband in a manner befitting her class and upbringing and demonstrating the quality of *sophrosyne*. For both women and men, the various aspects of unchastity, such as excessiveness, decadence, and lack of self-discipline, were to be shunned. But at the same time, complete celibacy or adult virginity were considered physically harmful, philosophically extreme, and socially bizarre.

Virginity Before Christianity

Whether dictated to do so by law, pressured to do so by tradition, or merely out of personal inclination, virtually everyone in the ancient world who was eligible to marry did so. In the patriarchal cultures of the early Mediterranean and Adriatic, marriage was (as it still is in preindustrial societies) a means of expanding one's household, of bringing in new blood, and of providing for the future. Because provable paternity was important, so was the virginity of brides, and the honor of entire families was often bound up in whether or not the daughters who left them and the brides who entered them went to their bridal beds as virgins.

It is likely that most of them did, but not necessarily because each individual woman had an enormous personal investment in doing so. Rather, it was just what was done, part of their culture. Also, the framework of daily life would have made illicit premarital affairs logistically difficult for many, although not necessarily impossible. Men and women of the ancient world had largely separate physical and social spheres, including, in many socioeconomic brackets, largely separate working lives. Additionally, we have to recall that women of the time were usually married off quite young by our standards. Roman brides might not even have begun to menstruate yet, while Greek brides tended to be a few years past menarche.

Premarital virginity was also encouraged by the extraordinary penalties that one could incur by losing it. Under the Roman Empire, *stuprum*, or sexual impropriety, with an unmarried young woman was considered equivalent to adultery. If the young woman had been a virgin and it appeared that her seduction was consensual, half of the property belonging to both parties would be confiscated for good. If she could prove rape, which then as now was a very big "if," only the male would be penalized. Murder was also a common Roman punishment for premarital sexual transgressions. High-caste fathers, in fact, retained the right to murder their daughters for adultery even after their daughters were married, and killing their daughters' adulterous lovers fell within their legal rights as well.

In Greece, too, murder was not an uncommon response to a daughter's unauthorized virginity loss—Giulia Sissa, in her monograph *Greek Virginity*, mentions a case in which an Athenian archon, upon discovering that his daughter had been "ruined," fed her to a hunger-crazed horse. Additionally, the law provided for a punishment even more socially radical than the economic sanctions that penalized *stuprum* in Rome. Under Solon, Athenian fathers who discovered that their unmarried daughters had been seduced or impregnated were obligated to disown them, to treat them as "a body that had become foreign," revoking their daughters' citizen status and making them slaves. It was the single circumstance in all of Solon's legal code in which a freeborn Athenian could be forced into slavery.

To an Athenian of that period, this punishment would have made sense. A daughter's premarital loss of virginity, in the explicitly patriarchal ancient world, constituted both a shameful lapse of control on the part of the family and of the girl herself, and a property crime against her father. As a part of the paternal household, daughters literally belonged to their fathers, just as wives belonged to their husbands and slaves to their masters.

Unlike slaves, however, daughters and wives could not be sold. A daughter's primary worth, both to the paterfamilias and the society at large, was that she could be given in marriage. The right of the father to give his daughter away was not the metaphorical handing over we understand it to be today, a role for a beaming dad sharing a special day with his daughter. It was very real and legally binding. A great deal might hinge on a marriage: power, land, reputation, and riches, perhaps even war and peace. A daughter's marriageability itself hinged on virginity. Without it, the rest was out of the question. No longer reproductively pristine, her body was no longer of use in the exchanges of the social economy of the elite. Her value became literally whatever her body was worth as utilitarian human clay.

But what of the women who started out as utilitarian clay—the slaves, serfs, and servants? We might well wonder whether, without the issue of dynastic marriage to make virginity seem so vital, the virginity of these women was still perceived as having value. The answer is a qualified yes. We have little to no direct evidence from these women themselves, but what we do have is a legal paper trail. Rape laws have often drawn distinctions between the rapes of virgin and nonvirgin women, as well as between the rapes of women of high status and women of low status. It is to these laws that we must look to find out how the virginity of low-caste women compared to that of their elite sisters in the eyes of the ancient world.

What the laws tell us comes as no real surprise. In the ancient world, virginity was considered primarily as a commodity and only secondarily as a metaphysical quality. A Cretan legal code dating from circa 450 B.C.E. stated separate penalties for the rapes of virgins versus nonvirgins: the rapist of a female household serf would be fined at two *staters* if the serf in question had been a virgin, and only one *obol*, essentially a slap on the wrist, if she had not. These payments, made not to the raped woman but to her owner or master, were clearly token restitution for property damage, not punishment for a personal assault.

Virginity, then, was a well-known quantity to the ancient world. Depending on whose virginity it was, and where a person lived, losing it (or stealing it) might be a matter of anything from parting with some pocket change to losing one's life. And yet at the same time, we have considerable evidence that at least in some cases, being a *virgo* (in Latin) or a *parthenos* (in Greek) might not have meant what we now take it to mean: there were virgins who could, and did, have sex.

Virgins and the Sons of Virgins

The idea of a virgin with a sex life may appear to be a paradox, but really it is only a problem of language. Neither *virgo* nor *parthenos*, nor the Hebrew equivalent *betulah*, in their dictionary meanings, denotes an exclusively sexual status. They could be used to indicate sexual inexperience, but the commonest meaning of either word was roughly equivalent to "girl" or "unmarried female."

Just as a maiden becomes a wife in English, a Roman *virgo* became *uxor* (wife), and later *matrona* (matron) after bearing children. In Greece one went to one's wedding chamber a *parthenos* and left it a *gyne*, a wife, or, more literally translated, a woman. Marriage and its sexual consummation were what socially and linguistically transformed a girl into a woman, a virgin into a wife. German is among the modern languages that retain this linguistic shift. German for "girl" or "young woman" is *Mädchen*; the word for "virgin" in the specifically sexual context is *Jungfrau*; but the word for "wife" and the word for "woman" are one and the same, *Frau*. A female of sufficient age can be called *eine Frau* (a woman), without being married, but to call her *Frau* So-and-so is to call her someone's wife.

In the ancient world just as now, a woman's first experience of sex did not necessarily coincide with her wedding night. Although we assume that premarital sex was uncommon for women then, the very existence of laws that penalized it tells us that it did in fact take place. So do accounts of premarital pregnancies discovered and bastards born, which are sufficiently frequent that we know premarital sex was not so very rare as all that. At the same time, though, the terminology used to categorize women's status was firmly bound to the estate of marriage. The inevitable result was that *parthenia*, the state of being a *parthenos*, could and sometimes did describe women who were sexually experienced and even some who had borne children.

This apparent paradox is the nucleus of a fascinating mytho-literary tradition. Clearly it should be impossible for a virgin to give birth, and the Greeks particularly found this contradiction to be symbolically rich and useful. An extraordinary person should, they felt, have extraordinary origins, and in Greek legend they often did: many of Greece's most beloved heroes and heroines, including Helen of Troy, were described as *parthenios*, the "sons of virgins." In Helen's case, her father Zeus famously seduced her mother, Leda, while he was in the form of a swan. Atalanta's son Parthenopaeus was *parthenios*, too, along with fellow Homeric heroes Asclepius (fathered by Apollo), Heracles, and Perseus (both fathered by Zeus). Some *parthenios* children went on to repeat their mothers' performances: Evadne, daughter of mortal Iphis and immortal Poseidon, was herself the mother of a *parthenios* son, Iamus, by Apollo. Often these *parthenioi* have a single mother and two fathers, a divine one who is the child's real father and a human one who marries the woman after the child is born and adopts her child as his own.

Not, of course, that every real-life *parthenios* was a hero. Many of them were probably born and abandoned by their desperate mothers to die on the slopes of the Parthenion, the mountain of virgin births reputed to lie on the border between Argolis and Arcadia. But the term for "virgin-born" existed, and so did the precedent of the legends. There is little doubt that at least a few rank-and-file women and their families took advantage of the trope to blame an inconvenient pregnancy on a *hieros gamos*, a marriage (in this case a euphemism for "bedded by") between a human and a god.

Claiming that a *hieros gamos* had occurred seems silly to us today, but in its day it would have represented what we would now call a "harm-reduction strategy." If such a claim were accepted, the status of the woman and her child might remain relatively intact within their community and the mother could even honorably be taken to wife. Who, after all, can do anything about what the gods decide to do? Certainly we can see evidence of all these patterns in the stories told about the most famous *parthenios* of them all, Jesus of Nazareth. Undeniably heroic, Jesus, too, is presented as having been the dually fathered son of a virgin, his human father having been persuaded to marry his mother by the reassurance that the baby she bore was of divine paternity.

Sacred Virgins

Unlike the Virgin Mary, or at least the version of the Virgin Mary that has come down to us today, the average *parthenos, betulah,* or *virgo* of the ancient world was literally the girl next door, no holier or more worthy of veneration than any other adolescent. Nor was her virginity anything particularly spectacular. It would end whenever her wedding night arrived, a date which, in the ancient world, was probably destined to be sooner rather than later . . . unless she was one of a small cadre of women who were the exception that proved the rule, the consecrated virgins of antiquity.

The idea of consecrated virginity is now indissolubly linked in our minds to the Roman Catholic Church, but like many of the Church's other practices, it existed long before the Church. Sacred virgins dedicated to the service of the Divine were just another of the myriad aspects of pre-Christian religions that later found a home under the vast syncretist umbrella of Christian practice. Some pre-Christian sacred virgins, like the Greek Leucippides, female virgins who served Apollo's sisters, were primarily servants of the temples. But save the absence of marriage and children, the life they had in the temples may not have been much different from the life they would have had outside of them. Temples, too, after all, required people to clean, cook, sew clothing, weave cloth, and tend the hearths and gardens. Others, like the well-known vestal virgins of Rome, might be figures of enormous sacred and secular influence, and led lives that were so far outside the normal trajectory as to be of near-mythic proportions.

Becoming a priestess was not, however, an easy out for those who weren't interested in marrying. A woman couldn't choose that path just because she wanted it. Consecrated virgins were typically handpicked by religious officials and were often drawn from the ranks of the elite. Moreover, consecration as a sacred virgin did not necessarily mean permanent virginity. The term of service rendered by consecrated virgins was usually limited, in some cases beginning in childhood and ending around the time that a girl reached marriageable age. Even the vestals served only thirty years, at which point (though precious few of them exercised the option) they were free to marry if they wished.

Vestal Virgins

The tomb, or rather a small underground cell near the Colline Gate, beneath the packed earth of Rome's Campus Sceleratus, was a constant specter in the lives of the vestal virgins. For them, it symbolized not their daily lives, but rather what they could expect should they break their virginal vows. Plutarch describes the punishment of a seduced vestal in chilling detail:

A Virgin who is seduced is buried alive . . . they prepare a small room, with an entrance from above. In it there is a bed with a cover, a lighted lamp, and some of the basic necessities of life, such as bread, water in a bucket, milk, oil, because they consider it impious to allow a body that is consecrated to the most holy rites to die of starvation. They put the woman who is being punished on a litter, which they cover over from outside and bind down with straps, so that not even her voice can be heard, and they take her through the Forum . . . When the litter is borne to the special place, the attendants unfasten her chains and the chief priest says certain secret prayers and lifts his hands to the gods because he is required to carry out the execution, and he leads the victim out veiled and settles her on the ladder that carries her down to the room. Then he, along with the other priests, turns away. The ladder is removed from the entrance and a great pile of earth is placed over the room to hide it, so that the place is on a level with the rest of the earth. That is how those who abandon their sacred virginity are punished.

This merciless penalty was not used often (only ten vestals are documented to have been put to death), but it was used. Sometimes the charges made against the vestal in question were legitimate, but many were not. Occasionally, as in 215, when the Emperor Caracalla himself seduced or raped one of three vestals he wished to remove from office (he had her buried alive along with the other two in a gruesome trifecta), the "punishment" of a fallen vestal was in reality nothing more or less than a politically motivated murder.

None of this would make sense if the vestals had been nothing more than giggling sorority girls who spent their days lounging around the Atrium Vestae. But it makes perfect sense when we realize who and what the vestals really were: the most powerful women in Rome, a fiercely elite and autonomous cadre, privileged at an even higher level than most men. The vestals were guardians of the sacred flame that symbolized the hearth of Rome's patron goddess, Vesta, housekeeper to the Roman pantheon, and were thus nothing less than the protectors of Rome's most important connection to the gods. Consecrated to the goddess, the vestals were almost alone among Roman women in not being required to have male legal guardians. When a vestal finished her thirty years' service, she was well provided for financially by means of an impressive dowry from the imperial treasury, set aside for each vestal when she became a priestess. Those who survived their thirty years' service retired to a wealthy civilian existence of rarely paralleled freedom.

A vestal's power and autonomy were not merely symbolic, nor were they limited to matters of religion. Vestals enjoyed privileges at the level of magistrates (their personal bodyguards were lictors, normally assigned to judges) and in some cases even at the level of the emperor himself: vestals had the prerogative to pardon any condemned criminal who crossed their paths, provided the meeting was not prearranged. Given that, now as then, executions might be ordered for political reasons, anyone with the power to commute a death sentence held not just the power of life and death but potentially considerably more. Vestals were also the guardians of important military and treasury records, could testify in courts of law without having to take an oath, and were the executors of the emperors' wills. It was quite an extraordinary life for women who, under normal circumstances, would probably never even have been legal persons in their own right. As it has for many other women throughout history, consecrated virginity bought the vestals a great deal.

If the vestals wielded enormous power, which they did until the adamantly Christian emperor Theodosius abolished the institution in 394, a whopping eighty-one years after the Roman Empire became officially Christian, we should not imagine that they were somehow unfit for the task. On the contrary, these women were to the manor born. When a vestal died or left the temple, the daughters of the Roman elite between the ages of six and ten would be assembled, and twenty of these girls would be chosen as the pool from which the next initiate would be picked. Their bodies had to be completely sound, with no deformities or faults, their hearing and speech perfect, and each girl's parents, whose pedigrees had to be suitably upper-caste, both had to be living. These twenty little girls would be brought before the pontifex maximus, Rome's chief priest, who would choose one by lottery, then take her by the hand and recite the formula "I take you, beloved, to be a Vestal priestess."

As of that moment, she no longer belonged to her family, and could not even inherit property from them: she belonged to Vesta and to Rome. The girl would then be led away and her long hair cut short (shearing the hair is a common symbolic gesture in virginity-consecration and sex-renunciation rituals). The priestess-to-be would be dressed in the white robes and decorated metal headband of her new order, and, no doubt somewhat dazed and grieving the loss of her childhood home and family, she would take the vows that would pledge her to thirty years' virginal service. She was no longer anybody's daughter, but instead the most junior of six women who would be her only family for what would likely be the rest of her life.

Then the work began. The vestals tended the sacred fire, of course, but they also baked special ritual salt cakes for Vesta and sacrificial cakes for various holidays, fetched water from a sacred spring and carried it back to the Atrium Vestae (the home of the vestals) or to the Aedes Vestae (the temple itself), kept the temple clean, and guarded certain sacrifices. Naturally, they also dealt daily with one another as mentors, mothers, daughters, sisters, and, undoubtedly at times, as in any group of people living in close quarters, as rivals and enemies.

The vestals were dedicated channels, state-sponsored consecrated bodies whose carefully protected virginity was the conduit between the human and the divine, dedicated quite literally to direct intercession between a people and its gods. Their virginity was not meant as a sacrifice to the gods, nor was it making them more moral or exalted. Instead, human virginity functioned in relation to the gods in much the same way as it functioned in relationship to marriage, as a guarantee of an uncontaminated channel. The vestals were virgins so that their loyalties remained undivided.

Celibates in the Desert

If this classical version of virginity seems simultaneously familiar and yet incomplete, there are good reasons why. The ideology of virginity has accumulated for millennia in much the same way as coral forms a reef. Certainly some aspects of ancient ideologies of virginity, for example that a virgin provides an uncompromised vessel, are still with us. But at the same time ancient-world virginity did not include several elements that later became critical to the way the West grew to think about the subject. The addition of these elements—the spiritualization, personalization, and egalitarianizing of virginity—utterly transformed the way the Western world would think, feel, and behave in regard to virginity.

This shift only seems to have happened suddenly because we look back on it from such a distance. In reality, it happened slowly, and it certainly did not happen without resistance. It represented a sea change in the way the body was understood to function in society as well as a profound rearrangement of the way people thought about their roles in the world and their relationships to the divine. These changes were what made virginity, and all that it symbolized and implied, into a foundational tenet of a new religion that went on to govern much of the world for the better part of two thousand years.

Ironically, the topic of virginity itself was one on which Jesus of Nazareth, the nominal founder of that new religion, spoke scarcely at all. Jesus had literally nothing to say (that we know of) about virginity. Christians, on the other hand, had a great deal to say about it, derived from the philosophies of Jesus's teachings as they understood them but just as influenced by other emerging ideologies and philosophies of the time. A specifically Christian approach to virginity began to coalesce about half a century after Jesus's death, but required most of the next five centuries to mature. None of it, however, would have been possible without the presence of philosophical and religious precursors that laid the groundwork for Christianity's radical new take on sexuality, the body, and virginity.

Around a century before the birth of Jesus, on the shore of Lake Mareotis, south of Alexandria, Egypt, just far enough outside the city walls to feel quite isolated, a community lived at the edge of civilization. This was the largest community of the religious movement known as the Theraputae, literally "the healers," celibate men and women who lived together in simplicity and deep religious contemplation. Many of them were nominally Jews, or at least Judaeans (the two were at that time synonymous), but regardless of their origins or the faith traditions from which they had come, they were all Gnostics, people who believed that the individual soul was capable of *gnosis*, the literal personal experience of God.

The path to *gnosis* was not for everybody. It represented the choice to live a life that was truly set apart from family, home, and everything in which one had learned to take comfort. Joining a sect such as the Theraputae would have meant the assumption of an entirely new social existence. As is true of Buddhism, renunciation of the material world formed an important component of the struggle to know God. This appears to have been, at least at its core, a practical asceticism. Renouncing things like family, personal wealth, or sexual activity did not automatically generate holiness but did reduce the number of distractions one had in the world of the flesh.

Not all of the Gnostic sects in the pre-Christian world admitted women. In fact, the Theraputae are the only ones we know of that did. It is primarily thanks to the writings of Philo of Alexandria, a Jew who flourished from roughly 20 B.C.E. to 50 C.E., that we have so much information about the Theraputae. In their quiet and simple celibacy, female and male renunciates living side by side and referring to one another as "brother" and "sister," the Theraputae certainly prefigure the celibate Christian households, compounds, and monasteries that came later.

Celibacy for the sake of God, however, was not a practice limited to the Gnostics. There were also groups of Jews—like those living at Wadi Qumran, the writers of the Dead Sea Scrolls—who donned spiritual armor in the form of celibacy as a way to prepare for holy war. For these men, celibacy appears to have been a way for them to realize the words of the prophet Ezekiel (Ez.

36:6), in removing something that was an obstacle to opening themselves completely to God. They did this at the expense of extant Jewish law that called, as Jewish law still does today, for the maintenance of household, marriage, and family in a sanctified and religiously regulated fashion, but to them, it was justified.

With such renunciate communities as a backdrop, it makes perfect sense that, as Peter Brown writes, "the fact that Jesus himself had not married by the age of thirty occasioned no comment." There was no shortage of radical young spiritual seekers who had added celibacy, even lifelong celibacy, to their spiritual practice. A long tradition within Judaism held that prophets were often unmarried and sexually abstinent: Moses himself was held to have found his sexual appetites permanently removed from him following the forty days he spent in the presence of God. Pliny the Elder, a slightly younger contemporary of Jesus's, commented on the paradoxical vigor of the celibate Essene community at Engeddi, noting that it managed to stay vibrant and well populated despite having made an end run around the usual cycle of marriage, sex, and birth. It should thus come as no surprise that, in the Bible, more is not made of Jesus' apparent virginity. In the sort of religious circles in which a man like him would have traveled, it would have been quite ordinary.

Eunuchs for the Sake of the Kingdom of Heaven: Jesus

These ordinary celibates were the men of whom Jesus likely spoke when he so famously said "there are eunuchs who have been so from birth, and there are eunuchs who have been made eunuchs by others, and there are eunuchs who have made themselves eunuchs for the sake of the kingdom of heaven. Let anyone accept this who can" (Matt. 19:12). Sexual renunciation was seen as an essential aspect of an aggressively individual relationship with God, and it is little wonder that Jesus promoted it. It seems likely, given both the Jewish abhorrence for bodily modification and the widespread association, in the ancient world, between castration and pagan priests (such as the *galli* of the cult of Cybele), that the word "eunuch" was intended to be taken metaphorically, not literally.

Rather, this metaphorical self-castration was a physical gesture of separation,

placing one's self entirely outside of the normal life cycle and refusing to participate in the sexual acts that the ancient world considered not only an intrinsic part
of human nature but also a necessary aspect of the functioning of the human or-
ganism. In refusing to take part in the socially critical processes of marriage
and fathering children, one dealt a slap to near-universal social priorities. For a
radical preacher and prophet, these rejections were simultaneously heartfelt and
strategic. The effort to create a new society where belief, not heredity or wealth,
formed the basis for inclusion, glory, and salvation required no small amount of
tearing down extant societal structures.

The rebellious preacher from Nazareth set a good example in this department, peripatetic, celibate, neither owning nor working land, wifeless (as far as
we know from the canonical Gospels) and childless. Like the Essenes waiting
for God's angelic armies out in the desert, he surrounded himself with like-
minded men who shared his willingness to reject everything they had ever
known in favor of existing for a while in close rapport with the Divine, sure
that a new and better world was close at hand. Like the Theraputae, he helped
and healed the sick and the lame. Most of all he preached, spreading a liberation theology of radical autonomy and rejection of worldly privilege that
could not have been better calculated to anger the Roman forces that occupied
and subjugated his homeland.

What is odd about this is not that Jesus would have exhorted his immediate
followers to celibacy. That was psychologically and politically strategic, as
well as au courant. What is odd is that this exhortation to a very small group of
people living in a very specific and embattled moment in time was taken up
with such fervor, expanded upon so enormously, and implemented with such
unhesitating enthusiasm. In Paul's first letter to the Corinthians, he admits that
he has no specific instructions from Jesus in regard to virgins (1 Cor. 7:25), and
yet not only he, but generations of writers after him (only a few of whom are
discussed here), elaborated the concept and requirements of Christian virginity to an extent that would scarcely be believable if they hadn't gone to such
pains to write it all down. Virginity's metamorphosis within monotheism,
from a matter of tactical guerrilla celibacy to the highest of moral virtues (and
not coincidentally the subject of dozens of deeply misogynist and erotophobic
treatises), is not something we owe to Jesus. It is his followers who deserve all
the credit—and all the blame.

The Menacing Flesh: Paul

Paul of Tarsus was, in some ways, the very model of a cosmopolitan Diaspora Jew. A well-traveled polyglot who wrote excellent Greek and was apparently at one point made a Roman citizen, he spent years at a time in the greatest cities of the Aegean, including Phillippi, Ephesus, Thessalonica, and Corinth. Less typically Jewish, he was an evangelist and a missionary. Prior to being put to death in Rome around the year 64, he had spent the lion's share of his life pursuing the missionary work of establishing Christian communities throughout the Greek-speaking world and attempting to provide long-distance guidance for those communities after leaving for his next port of call.

This is the exact context in which the first letter to the Corinthians was written. As the man who helped to found their community, Paul was the spiritual father to whom they turned in times of trouble. And trouble there was. We do not have the letter or letters to which Paul's epistle is a response, but we do not need them. Between the lines of Paul's reply, written around the year 54, we can figure out exactly what kinds of trouble the Corinthians were having among their ranks: strife and jealousy, people patronizing prostitutes, gluttony, Christians partaking of the meat of animals that had been offered as pagan sacrifices, uppity women wanting a voice and a presence in church, and what seems a generalized lack of focus.

By turns patronizing and avuncular, severe and accommodating, Paul's letter begins with a striking reminder of one of the things Paul, and Christianity, offered the Corinthians to begin with. This was a profound personalizing and egalitarianizing of the experience of the Divine, the notion that each individual body was a temple of God, that all people had the potential to experience God within themselves (1 Cor. 3:16).

This was a complete departure from the classical model of human contact with the Divine, which was generally accomplished through at least two layers of intercessors. One of these layers was the human layer, the priests and/or priestesses whose job it was to be in direct contact with the Divine. The other layer was the layer of material sacrifice. Sacrifices, then a primary mode of worship, demanded goods that could be sacrificed. A spotless kid or lamb or even a dove for the altar of the great temple in Jerusalem, or even a loaf of ritual bread for one's local altar to Artemis or Apollo, represented a not insignificant expenditure. The wealthier one was, it almost goes without saying, the greater one's ability to curry favor with the gods.

By locating God within the individual, even within the individual body, Christianity upset this applecart. It completely transformed the socioeconomics of religion as it then existed, as well as essentially eradicating the need for the hierarchies of priestly professionals on which pre-Christian worship depended. In a single sweeping move, the nature of the human-divine relationship went from being predominantly external to being decidedly interior. Objects of sacrifice were no longer inanimate objects or dumb animals but actual human bodies, offered up in the hopes that individuals would not only become instruments of the Divine, but also literally be adopted as dwelling places for God.

The way in which believers constructed and organized their ideologies of ritual purity began to migrate inward. Formerly, ritual purity might have consisted partially of hereditary caste—the vestals were daughters of the elite, for example, and the *kohanim*, or priestly class, of the temple at Jerusalem were all descended from a specific lineage. Ritual purity had also consisted of the observance of numerous vows and taboos concerning, for example, ejaculation or contact with dead bodies.

Now, with the integrity and purity of the individual self at such a premium, having sex likewise raised a number of problems. As the occasion during which the physical and psychological boundaries of the self seemed most permeable, sexual activity seemed fraught with peril. Paul wrote that when one had sex with a whore, one became "one flesh" with her (1 Cor. 6:16), that the boundaries of one's body and one's self were compromised. The result of such compromise could only be impurity.

For Paul, and for Christians generally, sexuality was also symbolic of the struggle between desire and will, the flesh and the spirit. In what it was hoped would be a brief interval between the miraculous resurrection of Jesus and the time when he would return to Earth to take his followers with him "into the air," the concern of his most ardent followers was to become undivided in their hearts, able to open themselves unstintingly to God in anticipation of that ultimate and permanent *gnosis*. Everywhere a Christian turned, though, his flesh threw up obstacles to this complete and selfless dedication. Reading between the lines of 1 Corinthians produces a laundry list of the problems that resulted. Paul's task, at his writing desk in Ephesus, was to help his parishioners in Corinth to resist their ids and egos, erect penises and salivating mouths not only with greater individual force of will but in ways that would contribute to the success and cohesion of the group.

This is why, when it came to sexuality, Paul did not simply write "Flee fornication" (1 Cor. 6:18) and leave it at that. A totally celibate community would have been in keeping with his feelings on sex and with the goals of his Christianity, but it would not have been sustainable. Inevitably, individuals would be unable to toe the line, and would either leave, be punished, or, worst of all from the perspective of developing a completely undivided heart, lie. Nor would universal celibacy have helped to keep the community stable. The Corinthians had always lived in a world of married households. Life without marriage and households would have felt anarchic and confusing to the Christians and their pagan neighbors alike. Insisting on universal celibacy would have been a horrendous tactical error.

Thus the fateful words of 1 Corinthians 7:9, "But if they do not have self-control, let them marry, for it is better to marry than to burn." The burning to which Paul referred was not, as is occasionally suggested, a burning in the fires of Hell, but rather the burning of sexual desire. In essence, what Paul was saying was that not every person will be able to resist sexual impulses, and if one cannot, it is better to give in lawfully than to be constantly tormented and distracted by it. Extant Jewish law provided for the establishment of sanctified households through marriage, and while Paul made it clear that this was definitely second best, he was equally clear (as was Jesus) about stating that not everyone had been granted the knack of sexual continence. This being so, marriage was the preferred, and religiously kosher, alternative: "he who gives in marriage does well, he who does not does better" (1 Cor. 7:38).

Such a moderating strategy is emblematic of Paul. We can see the direction in which the Christian dogma of sexuality and human relationships would soon take off, and at the same time we can see how vital the married household remained. The critical change, in Paul, is that the body is no longer something which can be treated, as it was in classical Judaism and throughout the ancient world, with a combination of indulgence and discipline. In the penultimate chapter of 1 Corinthians, Paul makes explicit the fact that all flesh is always already corrupt: "And I say this, brothers, that flesh and blood is not able to inherit the kingdom of God, nor does corruption inherit incorruption" (1 Cor. 15:50).

In a single intellectual move, one that Paul made many times and in various contexts, we see what H. D. Betz and Peter Brown characterize as "a particularly fateful 'theological abbreviation.' " Flesh is equated with corruption. For Christianity and Western culture generally, there was no turning back. Thus it is ultimately unsurprising that Paul says virtually nothing about virginity in 1 Corinthians. He doesn't have to. Even allowing for the fact that, as Paul admits, Jesus gave no specific instructions in regard to virgins, the course that virginity would take within the developing church was already evident, for, as Paul put it, "he who does not does better."

Boycotting the Womb, Emulating Eden

As Paul's example demonstrates, Christianity's early philosophers and theologians had their work cut out for them. Justifying, explaining, and expanding the teachings of Jesus was only part of the job. The growing Church had needs of its own. The presence of an increasingly large and varied flock meant that, among other things, there was an immediate need for doctrine regarding the physical body, including the arena of sex.

It should be stressed that the generalized misogyny of early Christianity is only coincidentally Christian. From our twenty-first-century vantage point, seeing how the treatises and diatribes of the church Fathers mounted up, we may get the impression of a deeply misogynist Christian conspiracy. This is only partly true. Early Christianity's attitudes toward sex and women were indeed deeply misogynist, but they were neither new nor a conspiracy. What we often perceive as being all of a single monolithic piece, driven by a single overt agenda, was a much more gradual and far less uniform accretion of ideological sediment. While Christian misogyny did develop its own specific tendencies, in its association of the female body and female sexuality with sin and Satan, that kind of thinking in relation to women would have seemed only slightly unusual to any first- or second-century Greek, Roman, Syrian, or Jew.

One of the thick early layers in the bedrock of Christian virginity was a philosophy known as encratism, from the Greek *enkrateia*, or continence. Heavily influenced by the *Diatessaron*, the first version of the Gospels that combined the four canonical Gospels into a single text, encratism explored the question of the appropriate place of sex in the lives of Christians from the perspective of the promised second coming of Jesus. Tatian, the *Diatessaron*'s compiler, and the anonymous author(s) of the apocryphal *Acts of Judas Thomas* felt that there was no place for sin among the people of God as they waited for the end of life as they knew it.

Christians wanted fervently to live out their principles as the second coming drew nigh. For several reasons, renouncing sexuality was part of that. It was considered advantageous not to have a human relationship that might interfere with the relationship between the individual and the Divine. Additionally, the Christian had the challenge of making one's human self as close to the angels as possible. It was believed that the *vita angelica*, the angelic life, was one of *apatheia*, a Greek Stoic concept meaning passionlessness or desirelessness. The ideal life was the life of the spirit, the life promised to believers by the doctrine of the second coming and the "world to come" in which communion with God was constant. The physical body, on the other hand, served only to anchor humans to the cycle of birth, death, and decay, the daily demands of keeping the body alive and perpetuating the species serving only to further distance them from their destiny with God.

The most ethical and productive thing to do, as a Christian, was literally to go on strike. The phrase "boycotting the womb" has often been applied to this sit-down strike against human biological imperative, and it is apt. "The works of women," namely birth and its inevitable result, death, were on the short list for elimination, since they had no place in the "world to come." This meant celibacy.

Ghosts in the Machine: Clement and Origen

In the era of Clement of Alexandria (late second century and early third) just as in Paul's day, however, celibacy just wasn't that simple. Not everyone could sustain celibacy, and it was a troublesome truth that fervent insistence upon celibacy tended to reduce the numbers of well-off householders likely to participate at high levels in the Church. For a church that had traditionally drawn many of its most effective clergy from the ranks of married male heads of household, this inevitably caused friction. Besides, as Clement pointed out, grumbling that the encratites "set their hopes on their private parts," there was more to being a Christian than just being celibate.

A moderate man, Clement's notion of the ideal relationship of the Christian to his penis was essentially Greek. The body need not be entirely renounced, he believed, if one could retain a conscious, rational control of it. *Orexis*, the biological urges that were the unavoidable "ghosts in the machine" of a physical body, were untidy and annoying, but not overpowering. There was a place for sex in Clement's Christianity, but such carefully passionless sex proved even more difficult than encratism.

We find some echoes of this rationalist, Greek approach to sex much later, in the works of another African, Augustine of Hippo. But in the hundred-odd years between Clement's era and Augustine's lay a figure whose approach to virginity, sexuality, and the body was so dramatic, drastic, and, in its vivid misanthropy, so popular that Clement's moderation didn't stand a chance.

This celebrity extremist was Origen, son of a martyred Alexandrian Christian. The body, for third-century Origen, was worth nothing unless it was used as a tool for spiritual transformation. It is accepted as being probably true, for example, that Origen had himself castrated in the name of his faith. The body, he believed, was what the spirit had fallen into when it lost its unity with God. The distance between the body and the spirit constituted an unbridgeable and tragic gap that only widened as the body succumbed to the proddings of its *logismoi*.

Like Clement's *orexis*, Origen's *logismoi* were the various appetites of the flesh; unlike Clement's version, they were not essentially benign. Coupled with an ardent belief that Adam did not "know" Eve in the Garden of Eden, and thus human origins could confidently be said not to include sex of any kind, Origen felt quite sanguine about presenting virginity as the fitting ornament of a disciplined, earnest, and above all successful Christianity. *Adunatio* in action, virginity was simultaneously a sign of moving toward oneness with God and a principled resistance to the temptations of the flesh. When Origen beckoned "I beseech you, therefore, be transformed. Resolve to know that in you there is a capacity to be transformed," it was a literal and fundamental transformation of human instinct and social reality that he had in mind, and nothing short of entirely abolishing the libido would do.

Never Satisfied: Jerome

Despite his immense learning, erudite and prolific writings, and immaculate intellectual and spiritual heritage—he was fluent in several languages including

Greek, had traveled widely, spent two years living the hermit life in the desert at Chalcis, studied at the knee of Gregory Nazianzen, and, among other things, produced the first Latin version of the Bible—Jerome never did learn to play by the unwritten rules of what was fast becoming the old boys' club of the Church. A man of spectacularly irritable temper and infinitesimally small tolerance for deviation from what he perceived as being the right way to do things, Jerome's enormous influence on the Church was achieved partly in spite of himself. He was a harsh and constant critic of what he saw as inappropriate actions on the part of the Church and its clergy, and was literally run out of town (in this case Rome) after his protector, Pope Damasus I, died in 384. Despite the efforts of some of his friends to save Jerome from his own caustic extremism, Jerome managed in the space of a scant three years to alienate the Roman clergy to the point that he was compelled to live out the rest of his life in exile in Bethlehem.

Unwelcome among his fellow clerics, whom Jerome frequently castigated in classic do-what-I-say-not-what-I-do fashion for practices including the maintenance of intimate spiritual friendships with monied Christian matrons, Jerome himself spent the bulk of his adult life supported and surrounded by rich Roman women. Marcella, his patron in Rome, was a chaste widow of many decades' standing. Paula, who became his patron and established him in his own Bethlehem monastery after his exile (she herself maintained a parallel convent of sorts for expatriate Christian women), was a thirty-something widow recently devastated by the loss of her husband and raising a daughter, Eustochium, who had been consecrated as a Christian virgin. Jerome would have been horrified to think of himself as a family man, but it would not be entirely incorrect to say that, in some respects at least, he was. A part of Paula's extended household until his death, and a friend and confidant to Paula herself, he was also in a way a paternal figure to the young Eustochium.

Deeply influenced by Origen, Jerome felt the heavy weight of the flesh as a very real and evidently terrible insult. Writing of his experiences of the solitary renunciate's life in the desert, he described the horrifying discovery that no matter how he fasted and deprived himself, he still felt the bonfire of lust within. The metaphor served him well: if lust could survive the snuffing-out of other material yearnings (represented by the emaciated, nearly dead flesh of the desert hermit), then sexuality truly represented the most intractable aspect of the human animal.

This disgust of the body, and particularly to any feminine or erotic aspects of it, appears throughout Jerome's writing, but nowhere quite so vividly as in his letters to Eustochium. He encouraged her to fast and to shun the lushness of her own nubile body, saying "the one who mortifies her bodily members . . . is not afraid to say, 'I have become like a wineskin in the frost, whatever moisture there was in me has been dried up." He advised that Eustochium's "hot little body" should be secluded from the world and from all manner of potential excesses, including wine and heavy foods, clothes that were either too stylish or too deliberately slovenly, and affected speech. It was all part and parcel of preventing the onslaught of desire, whether Eustochium's own or that of those with whom she might come into contact. For, as Jerome warned her, "if those whose bodies are eroded can still be assailed by such thoughts, what must a girl endure, who is exposed to the thrills of easy living?"

The text of Jerome's controversial *Adversus Jovinianum* (Against Jovinian) makes Jerome's black-and-white views on virginity even clearer. Virginity, he stated, should be a priority not only for the individual but for the whole of the Church. For Jerome, marriage was barely acceptable (he told Eustochium that he could only praise it because it produced virgins), despite the fact that the Church officially embraced it. Second marriages for widows or widowers, in their transparent pursuit of the carnal, were to Jerome scarcely distinguishable from whoredom. Further, Jerome felt the clergy should be made up solely of virgins. Married clergy, who at that time were in the vast majority, were to be regarded as only temporary substitutes until such time as the requisite number of virgin clergy, their Christianity tempered in the forge of sexual asceticism, could come forward to take over the Church.

With attitudes like these, it is no wonder that Jerome did not last long in the resolutely worldly milieu of Rome. As the age of the great Latin fathers drew to a close, the man who would leave the most striking stamp on Christian virginity turned out to be a rather more politically suave and philosophically moderate man, one with whom Jerome, at the end of his life, would dismissively refuse to engage. This last and greatest synthesist of the Patristic era was none other than Augustine of Hippo, whose own early ambivalence toward sex was summed up in his notorious cry, "Lord, give me chastity . . . but not yet!"

Triumph of the Will: Augustine

A man of the world and a man of his time—the late fourth and early fifth centuries—Augustine was no virgin. Although he forswore sexuality when he became a Christian at the age of thirty-two, Augustine's younger manhood, which included a thirteen-year relationship with a concubine and the birth of a son (who died shortly thereafter), was unapologetically carnal. Extensively educated, he was the pride and joy of his mother, Monica, a devout Christian. Prior to becoming a Christian himself, Augustine spent considerable time studying the principles of the ascetic Manichaean movement, but never became part of its rigorously celibate elect.

It was only after his career as a rhetorician took him from his home in Africa to the Imperial residence in Milan that things began to change for Augustine. Ambitious, he planned a marriage to the much younger daughter of a prominent local family. When he did so, the concubine who had been his romantic and sexual partner for over a decade went back to Africa as custom dictated. Without a concubine, and with his wife-to-be not yet old enough to marry, Augustine took a mistress, a move which revealed to him the crassness of his sexual needs. Shattered and bereft, mired in what we might think of as a sort of post-divorce crisis, Augustine looked inward, to his own soul, and outward, to the rich intellectual and religious world of Christian Milan.

The experience changed his life. The nourishing intensity of the spiritual joy Augustine found in Christianity made connubial bliss pale by comparison. His connection to his new religion was immediate, his conversion swift, and his rise to prominence breathtaking. Baptized at the hands of his teacher Ambrose, a scant five years later he was back in Africa in Hippo (in what is today Algeria) founding a monastery. In 400, he became the city's bishop.

Looking across the Mediterranean toward Rome and across the gulf of his own conversion at his former life, Augustine was able to bring a distinctive and sympathetic synthesis to the questions of sexuality, continence, chastity, and virginity that had for so long been central problems to Christianity. Reordering a time-honored hierarchy that put virgins first, widows second, and married people last in line for the favors of heaven, Augustine put martyrs first and foremost and virgins second, a move which would have appealed to Origen. Jerome, though his admiration would no doubt have been grudging, would have agreed with Augustine's judgment that sexual desire was no mere physical stirring of *calor genitalis*, genital heat, that could be dried up by fasting and mortifications of the flesh, but rather the manifestation of an inborn and lifelong psychological phenomenon he called *concupiscentia carnis*, carnal concupiscence, that knew no master but the will.

Sin, argued Augustine, was what happened when the will was disobedient to God. In the wet dreams that plagued him and reminded him of his sexually active past Augustine felt the distance between his will, which desired only God, and his fleshly self, which had other things in mind. That this dark, prideful, disobedient heart could be so powerful as to overwhelm the will was a source of deep sadness for Augustine. Developing the will and schooling it in Christian virtue became the key to successful management of this indwelling foe. "The virtue which governs a good life controls from the seat of the soul every member of the body, and the body is rendered holy by the act of a holy will," he wrote in the first book of *De civitate Dei*.

This philosophy gave rise not only to Augustine's veneration of Mary, who in her submissive obedience during Jesus's conception replicated the utterly libido-free sexuality of Eden, but to his notion that virginity resided not so much in the body as in the mind. In the wake of the horrifying Gothic invasion of Rome in 410, this allowed Augustine to provide some small comfort, personal and doctrinal, for the consecrated virgins raped by the invading Goths as an act of war. "No matter what anyone else does with the body or in the body that a person has no power to avoid without sin on his own part, no blame attaches to the one who suffers it," he wrote. (A double-edged sword to be sure; the phrase "the power to avoid" can damn as well as reprieve.) But Augustine also wrote that the holiness of the body did not lie in the integrity of its parts, "*enim eo corpus sanctum est, quod eius membra sunt integra.*" A raped virgin was not necessarily ruined in the eyes of either the Church or God: it was ultimately the integrity of her soul that mattered.

The relocation of virginity from the body to the soul was an imperfect solution to the problems of either rape or virginity, but it was a brilliant stroke of philosophy. After Augustine, both libido and virginity were matters of the conscious self at least as much as they were matters of the body. How one dealt with them spoke volumes about one's morality, one's Christianity. Making sexuality and its control a matter of individual motivation took away the easy excuse of being overpowered by the body's appetites. Virginity was no longer just a marker of a pure and empty vessel. It was more than just the boycott of the womb or the distrust of the motives of the pleasure-seeking flesh. It was all those things and more: a test that measured moral commitment, spiritual purity, and personal strength. Augustine's ingenious and adept synthesis created an ideology of virginity that has remained central to Western thought for millennia. In it, virginity is a triumph over more than just the imperatives of the body. It is, in every way, a triumph of the will.

CHAPTER 9

Heaven and Earth

Valde durum est contradiciere quod habet gustus pomi.
It is so hard to deny things that taste of the apple.
—Saint Hildegard of Bingen

THE VIKING FORCES that landed on the North Sea coast of Scotland in 870 swept south with a vengeance, leaving utter devastation in their wake. The only thing that traveled faster than the Vikings was the news that they were on the way.

When word of the approaching berserks reached Ebba the Younger, abbess of Coldingham Abbey, a convent located just north of the present-day border between England and Scotland, she gathered the sisters together, knowing that they had no greater strength than the community they shared. Warning her community of virgins of the probability that they would all be raped by the invaders when the convent was sacked, Ebba took a razor and sliced off her own nose and upper lip, making a bloody, mutilated spectacle of her face that she hoped would repel the invaders. One after the other, the nuns followed suit, fearlessly carving into their own flesh with cold steel in the hopes that it might forestall their having to endure a violation of their bodies that these consecrated virgins perceived as far worse than the ones to their faces.

According to the legend, it worked. The Vikings took one look at the ruined faces of the nuns who appeared at the convent gate, and burned the place to the ground. Trapped inside the inferno of their cloister, Ebba and all her nuns died a horrifying death. But in death they found victory: the women of Coldingham died virgin martyrs, guaranteed a place in Heaven.

Gruesome, coldly practical, and yet oddly transcendent, the story of the nuns of Coldingham Abbey provides a useful snapshot of the often extreme nature of the medieval world. In this era a retreat into the monastery did not reprieve one from having to face the realities of invasion or war, nor did it in any way protect women from the threat of rape. Although this was the heyday of the great scholar-theologians, the golden age of monasticism, and the period during which the Roman Catholic Church achieved an unprecedented hold over virtually all of western Europe, it was also an era dominated by seemingly perpetual war, budding class struggle, devastating epidemics, internecine politics, Crusades and Inquisitions, a slowly but surely metamorphosing economy, and, at different times and places, the very real problem of armed invasion. A great deal of medieval culture was necessarily preoccupied with the difficult task of negotiating and maintaining the perpetually uneasy balance between the mandates of heaven and those of earth. Virginity was central to that struggle because of its own critical role in the dominant institution of the Middle Ages, the Catholic Church.

As the Catholic Church matured, its influence spread wherever the Roman Empire's roads preceded it. With the northward and westward migration of Roman Catholicism went its singular philosophy of sexual renunciation, asceticism, and sacrifice. To the farmers, hunters, and craftsmen of early medieval northern Europe, the idea that their sons, daughters, and perhaps even wives might try to secede from the household in the name of God must have seemed radical and unsettling. In the subsistence economies of premodern Europe, a childless woman was a tragic figure, more often mocked and reviled than pitied. Spinsters and bachelors were as rare as hen's teeth. Remaining unmarried was not an option many would, or could, choose. Economic survival meant participation in the economy of the larger household and community, both in terms of labor and of the reproduction of human beings who would labor in turn.

In any case, the majority of people, living as vassals, serfs, villeins, and in other various forms of tenancy on lands owned by feudal aristocrats, did not have the right (or for that matter the financial resources) to remove themselves or their labor contribution from their lord's holdings if they had wanted to. Given these issues, it comes as no surprise that throughout most of the Middle

Ages the bulk of those who assumed the profession of consecrated virgin were daughters of the aristocracy.

The Origins of a Vocation

Within Christianity, the elite already had a long tradition of being first in line to step into the rarefied space between earth and heaven. A great deal of the operating capital behind the first several centuries of Christian development had come directly from wealthy women. As Christianity became officially recognized within the Roman Empire, bishops and other churchmen with the ability to pull strings within the secular power structure helped these women and their virgin heiress daughters to remain free agents who were legally able to dispose of their property at will. Thus money and power flowed in mutually beneficial currents between unmarried (or no longer married) women and the Church. Wealthy women in early Christianity not only had the ear of powerful bishops and archbishops, but they could sometimes also wield limited ecclesiastical power themselves. Women deacons called *diaconissae* catechized converts, meditated on religious principles and shared the benefit of their insights, led prayers, taught, and were central in providing aid to the sick and poor.

The first religious vows made available to women represented an effort to formalize these relationships with the Church. In the first century an informal division of three orders of widows became customary, with two groups devoted to meditative prayer and teaching and the third devoted to the care of the needy. The establishment of institutional roles for women took a decisive step forward in the third century with the new role of the *sponsa Christi*, the spouse of Christ. There was not yet a distinct category of religious called "nuns" or a system of monastic rule under which they could live. But the *sponsa Christi* role gave shape to what would become the iconic role of the virgin within the Christianity. The lives of these "spouses of Christ" revolved around a nucleus made up of devotion, service, the renunciation of sexuality, and the dedication of their worldly goods to their heavenly spouse. It was not exactly like an earthly marriage, but it was recognizably similar.

Standing apart not only from the families they had left behind but also from the hierarchy of a Church headed primarily by married men, the early religious virgins provided a bold contrast indeed. The *sponsa Christi*'s life was lived at a more stringent level of sanctity than that of most priests. Priestly celibacy, although encouraged from the earliest days of Christianity, did not become doctrine until the Lateran Councils of the early twelfth century. Long before then, however, virgins and virginity were central to the Christian mission. Representing the New Covenant in their bodies by physically symbolizing the superiority of spiritual kinship over worldly family, virgins also provided the Church with critical capital, skill, labor, and, of course, their spiritual and mystical gifts. Perceived as being closer both to God and to God's design for ideal human existence, Christian virgins possessed a unique form of holiness that, like the sacred virginity of their forerunners in the pre-Christian world, was believed to provide a dedicated and uncompromised conduit between heaven and earth.

Daughters of Jerusalem

The spread of European monasticism, and that of female monasteries in particular, was due almost exclusively to the combination of heavenly devotion and earthly wealth. Wealthy women who dedicated their lives to the Church were the vehicles by which the earliest women's monasteries were formed. One of the earliest female monasteries in Europe, Saint-Croix at Poitiers, France, was established by the sixth-century queen Radegund, daughter of Thuringian king Berthaire, who walked out on her husband and used the income from various lands that had been given to her as part of her wedding gifts to found her abbey. Populated almost exclusively by other women of rank and wealth who brought additional endowments to the abbey, Sainte-Croix was notable in that Radegund required that all the sisters be able to read and write. The abbey's scriptorium, just like the ones in the male monasteries, produced many skilled copies of religious books and manuscripts.

Women like Radegund were behind the foundation of most of Europe's convents, and those in the British Isles as well. The great dual monastery of Ely, for example, was founded by Queen Aethelthrith, who left her second husband, the King of Northumbria, in order to found Ely on land left to her by her first husband. In founding or merely joining religious communities, even married aristocratic women were able to choose their own path at a level and with a degree of control to which they otherwise could not aspire. Remarkably, the Church welcomed these wealthy wayward wives with open arms.

The entrance of a marriage partner into a monastery was considered legitimate grounds for annulment of the marriage by the Church, even if the partner had not consented to his or her spouse's actions.

This did not mean, however, that husbands and families just stood there waving good-bye when their womenfolk wandered off to found convents. On the contrary, women's efforts to devote themselves to a religious life were often thwarted at every step. But for the women who either had familial support or managed to shame, outwit, or just outrun their opposition, consecration was the one respectable ticket out of the various miseries of a married woman's life. Women who freely entered the monastic life as never-married virgins, like the aristocratic Ethelburga, who, courtesy of her brother (the Bishop of London), went from being a member of the family of the King of Wessex to being foundress of Barking Abbey, knew very well how fortunate and unusual they were.

This is an important concept. To most people today, the life of a nun, with its vows of chastity, poverty, and obedience; regular obligations of the monastic rule; and restrictions on personal liberties, seems shockingly limiting. We often assume that such a lifestyle must represent an enormous personal sacrifice. But limitation is not necessarily synonymous with loss.

For medieval women, the regulations of the monastic life were often very welcome, not only because of the opportunity they offered for real religious devotion but because despite their strictness, they still offered more freedom and opportunity than the married state. Destined to act as the human glue that cemented dynastic relationships between aristocratic clans by producing offspring of august and verifiable paternity, women who did not successfully lobby for the religious life could expect their lives to be quite literally ruled by marriage. Elite marriages might take place as early as a girl's twelfth birthday, and betrothals even earlier.* These women's lives were so thoroughly oriented

---

*It should be noted that we know that the sexual consummation of these marriages was sometimes but not always postponed for several years due to the youth of the brides. For example, although Edmund Plantagenet, second son of Henry III of England, was married to the ten-year-old Aveline de Forz at Westminster Abbey in 1269, the marriage was not consummated until 1273, when the groom was a robust twenty-eight and the bride had finally turned fourteen.

toward expedient marriages that sometimes they were sent away as little girls to be raised in the households of the courts over which they would later preside. A case in point is Matilda, daughter of King Henry I of England, sent at the age of seven to be reared in the court of Holy Roman Emperor Heinrich V so that upon her marriage to the emperor five years later when she was twelve (and he was twenty-eight), she was already conversant with the language, customs, and politics of his court into which she married and able to immediately take up her duties.

Women without religious vocations existed quite literally in the service of men. Used as bargaining chips in the politically and socially vital marriage market by their fathers or guardians, elite women almost inevitably wed. Often they were married off to men who were decades older, and it was more the exception than the rule for a woman to actually know her husband socially when she found herself standing beside him at the altar. Sexual submission to one's husband was both socially and legally mandated, and the difficult, dangerous, and frequently fatal prospect of childbearing was all but inescapable.

All this was absolutely normal and expected, but it was also quite understandably distasteful to many. Choosing to take Christ as a spouse was not merely an emblem of devotion, it was perhaps the only means a woman had of exercising any choice whatsoever in the matter of what would form the core of her adult life. In the texts left to us by some of the great literary nuns of the High Middle Ages, like Hildegard of Bingen and Elisabeth of Schönau, marriage is described in terms nearly identical with slavery. It was partially the daunting physical demands of married life—submitting to men's sexual demands, bearing children, wiping bottoms, running a household—that women found undesirable. Marriage simply used women up. By contrast, in the words of the thirteenth-century *Hali Meiðhad*, "Virginity is the blossom which, if it is once completely cut off, will never grow again, but though it may wither sometimes through indecent thoughts it can grow green again nevertheless." Virgins not only got to escape the perils and inconveniences of earthly marital life, but additionally they would always (at least metaphorically) remain in the eternal blossom of youth.

These were not the only benefits awaiting those who chose the monastery. The monastic life also promised the opportunity to devote time to charity (convents often included poorhouses, hospitals, and leprosaria), to live in a community of like-minded people, and to be genuinely useful. Nuns also enjoyed spiritual communion and the joys of being in a position to help others through intercessory prayer: nuns' prayers could, among other things, help to free souls trapped in Purgatory.

Virginity also held the promise of education. Monasteries were renowned as places where women became literate. Years of singing or listening to a relatively limited collection of familiar texts while looking at books like psalters and missals would eventually result in women figuring out how to match what they heard to what they saw. But that was not the way most nuns who became literate this way understood their experience of "spontaneous" literacy. To them, it was a miracle bestowed upon the deserving, pure-hearted virgin by God: when the gift of literacy bloomed in the mind of Hedwig von Regensburg, the entire choir of sisters saw her heart shine through her body and habit "like the sun through glass."

As for the sexual continence expected of nuns, it seems that relatively few among those who voluntarily entered orders seem to have found it a particular difficulty, although there is evidence that a few nuns were troubled by lust in a manner similar to the way it so often tormented male monastics. Allegorical stories of the period allude to the difficulties some nuns may have had in successfully obeying the rules. One describes how a nun and a monk, in love with one another, arrange a nighttime rendezvous, but when the nun tries to sneak out of her convent to meet her monk, she finds the way barred by thickets of crucifixes. In one version of the story, the nun fetches an ax to chop the crosses down, only to find that when she hoists the ax it miraculously becomes stuck to her shoulder, which jolts her into realizing the error of her ways. In another version of the same story, the nun prays to the Virgin Mary to remove the crosses instead, which makes the Virgin so angry that she slaps the errant nun across the face, knocking her unconscious. Unsurprisingly, she is mightily repentant when she comes to.

Many women, however, not least the numerous widows who only had a chance to take the veil after their husbands' deaths, were relieved to enter the convent. But neither women nor men would have entered the monastic life under the misapprehension that they were giving up some nonexistent no-holds-barred carnal cornucopia. Regular required abstinence from sex was a way of life for virtually all medieval married couples. Many followed a (originally Jewish) custom of abstaining from sex during a woman's menses. Sex might similarly be avoided during pregnancy or while a woman was still nursing an infant. It was also a common teaching that couples were to abstain from sex during the penitential season of Lent, during Pentecost, and for the four weeks of Advent, as well as refraining on Wednesdays (in memory of Christ's arrest), Fridays (in memory of Christ's death), and Saturdays (in memory of Mary). Significant sexual restraint was an unremarkable commonplace for those on the outside of the monastery walls as well as for those within them.

Such a constant and deep relationship between sexuality and religion helps, in some ways, to explain some of the mystical eroticism we find in writings by medieval nuns. Mystical meditation was the mode of choice through which medieval women interacted with religious subjects. The mystical writings and teachings of women like Hildegard of Bingen, Elisabeth of Schönau, Catherine of Siena, Margery Kempe, and Birgitta of Sweden were not only well known during their own time—Hildegard's visions were so famous and highly regarded that she received dispensation to make four separate tours as a preacher during a period when women's preaching was technically outlawed by the Church—but have endured, coming down to us across the ages as important documents of women's literature and Christian thought.

Looking at these women's writings, as well as at the stories of other medieval women saints, we often find them describing intensely bodily and intimate interactions with the Divine. Saint Ita, an eighth-century Irish saint, was one of many women who had visions of "heaven's King who every night / Is infant Jesus at my breast." Women rejoiced passionately in visions of being embraced by their heavenly spouse, or in touching their lips to his wounds. Famous English mystic Margery Kempe sometimes fell to the ground crying out and writhing in bodily ecstasies when she meditated on the sufferings of Christ on the cross, and described a vision of Jesus in which he gave Margery permission to "boldly take me in the arms of thy soul and kiss my mouth, my head, and my feet as sweetly as thou wilt."

As tempting as it may be to think of these kinds of things as nothing more than the neurotic projections of erotically deprived virgins, this would be both inaccurate and unfair. A more accurate way to think about it is in terms of the overall dynamic that made sexuality an important aspect of Christian spirituality in the first place: the relationship between heaven and earth. If controlling one's bodily sexuality could help to engage the spiritual self and transform it into a zone of joyous communion with God, it only makes sense that communion with God might engage the earthly body, too, transforming the experience of the physical and even the erotic into something quite transcendent.

This is certainly the impression one gets from the writings of Hildegard of Bingen. As abbess, she sometimes dressed her well-born nuns in beautiful crowns and elegant silk veils, put golden rings on their fingers, and permitted them to sing in church with their hair unbound because of her belief that the requirements of modesty "do not apply to the virgin, for she stands forth beautiful in the simplicity and integrity of paradise." For Hildegard, there could be no shame for a nun in being beautifully female, because virginity transformed flawed femaleness into embodied spiritual perfection.

To the medieval mind, virginity was by no means just a state of not having had sex. It was a state of mind, a form of spiritual practice, a key with which to gain access to the divine and its mysteries, and an assurance of sanctity. Additionally, it was a means of transcending rigid gender roles and a scaffolding that allowed women to ascend to heights of intellect and earthly power that they were otherwise rarely permitted to contemplate. Virginity permitted some abbesses to enjoy power and wealth on a level with bishops and kings.

In some cases virgins simultaneously held enormous ecclesiastical and secular power. Tenth-century abbess Mathilda of Quedlinburg, daughter of Saxon emperor Henry I, not only wielded bishop-level power in nonsacramental matters, but acted for a time as empress regent. Other abbesses, like those of Shaftesbury, Barking, and Nunnaminster in England, controlled sufficient territory that they were summoned to serve in parliaments. Only queens regularly exercised similar levels of power, and for them to do so usually required extenuating circumstances that removed their husbands or fathers from the picture. To be sure, abbesses were almost always of aristocratic stock, but where their married sisters only rarely had the chance to take the reins of power, virgins might well become old hands in the saddle.

Sex and the Sacred Virgin

Women entered convents to escape from the demands of the world, only to discover that the world followed them in, willy-nilly. The most personal, and in some ways the most insidious, of the ways that the world entered the convent was through sex.

Consecrated virgins have always had to defend their right to their own sexual decisions. If a family had pinned its hopes on good marriages for its daughters, having a daughter devote herself to virginity could seem disastrous. Family resistance could be substantial. Some vowed virgins, like Christina of Markyate, had to contend with their families actually instructing men to seduce or rape them (she escaped), or were forced into unwanted marriages (she convinced her husband to accept a celibate marriage).

But entering holy orders, even with the blessing of one's family, did not grant medieval virgins a reprieve from the threat of sexual violence. The medieval crime known as *raptus* is usually translated as "rape" today, but its literal meaning was something closer to "the theft of a woman." *Raptus* typically included kidnapping, the literal physical removal of a woman from her convent, as in the case of Gerberga, a ninth-century aristocratic nun from northern Spain who was kidnapped by her brother's enemies, charged with witchcraft, and murdered. More commonly, the *raptus* of a nun was followed by forced marriage, since that was the most common legal remedy for rape at the time. For aristocratic men who had little to bring to the marriage market—younger sons, for example, who could not expect to inherit in the same measure as their elder brothers—this could make the prospect of simply snatching a wellborn bride out of the local convent quite appealing. The "sporting" aspect of abducting a nun from her cloister also contributed to convent *raptus*. At various places, at various times, wellborn rakes apparently considered it a fine challenge to see if they could make off with a young virgin from a convent.

Between the voluntary and involuntary comings and goings of nuns, the well-known phenomenon of the disaffected nun placed in a convent by her parents, and the many ways in which the all-female world of the convent seemed a strange and exotic alternate universe, it is little wonder that many an outside observer felt entitled to assume that whatever went on behind the mysterious doors of convents had to be sexy stuff indeed, leavened as it was presumed to be with the yearnings of repressed virgins. Urban legends about nuns and convents are so common as to be stereotypical, but few appear to have had any basis in fact.

In truth, nuns were the objects of constant suspicion. If they went out from the cloister to do the economically necessary work of visiting and administering lands and properties, seeing to the provisioning of the convent and the sale of its various products, and interacting with merchants and guildsmen, they were tainted by worldliness and suspected of unlawful dalliances with the men with whom they had contact. Unfortunately for the nuns, economic survival depended on such "suspicious" activities. Attempts to force the various religious orders to which individual convents belonged to provide for their material support were only sporadically successful. Monastic orders, with the notable exception of the Franciscans, openly resented the responsibility and the financial outlay of the *cura mulierum*, the care of women: the Carthusians referred to their five convents as "the five wounds of our order." The installation of monks who would act as the nuns' business agents only proved that these monks had few scruples about skimming a convent's profits.

Of course, having even these men in contact with convent virgins was also considered suspicious. According to the medical wisdom of the day, women were inherently lustful and liable to give in to their base natures at any time. Even if they succeeded in staying completely chaste, they were still women and thus an attractive nuisance for men. As resentment of nuns increased, veiled virgins were frequently depicted as being so enticing that their presence might compel even a pure man to commit rape. Popular literature, song, and legend provided convent-abduction and disgraced-nun stories galore, producing what passed for "proof " of these supposedly incontrovertible facts.

There is certainly sufficient mention of convent *raptus* in the medieval legal literature, including Gratian's *Decretum*, that we know it was a real and relatively significant problem. But the degree to which vowed virgins might have willingly engaged in illicit activities is significantly harder to gauge. Despite the sardonic use of the term "brothel" to mean convent and "nunnery" to mean brothel—as in the notoriously double-edged line Shakespeare has Hamlet spit at poor Ophelia—the odds are quite against it having been an apt comparison. Neither father confessors nor abbesses typically kept detailed records of nunly transgressions, and overall we have relatively few logs of such things even in civil criminal records. In the few cases where historians have been able to compare female and male monastery records in regard to sexual transgressions, however, it does not appear that women were any worse than men.

Women's sexual misconduct, however, has always been seen as being worse than men's. The whole ideology of virginity that underpins the female monastic system means that even the slightest breach is unforgivable, whereas male unchastity is merely "incontinence" and usually easily swept under the rug or explained away as an instance of "boys will be boys."

Stories of genuinely dissolute convents (like the Venetian abbey of Sant' Angelo di Contorto, where nuns not only received lovers in their cells but were also, with their paramours, sometimes taken out on picnics by the abbess) were, as in a game of "telephone," widely repeated as well as distorted and inflated. This happened regardless of whether or not the tale was actually true. It seems probable that a great many of the stories told about naughty nuns, wayward abbesses, and vicious virgins were nothing more than fiction. But like today's urban legends about rock stars or big corporations, they were also frequently accepted as figuratively true.

As eminent scholar JoAnn MacNamara points out in her works on convent history, however, it does not make practical sense for it to have been possible for frequent transgression, and particularly sexual transgression, to have been commonplace among female monastics. The reason for this is simple: the continued existence of female monastics depended upon the public's impression of the reliability of their sanctity and intercessory prayers, and the reliability of women's sanctity and prayers depended directly upon their virginity. Virginity, again, functioned as a bridge between heaven and earth.

Unlike sacraments given by priests, who receive an official imprimatur (ordination) that renders their sacraments uniformly effective, nuns' prayers are not guaranteed by the Church. What gives weight to a nun's spiritual efforts is her personal holiness and the sanctity of her community. A patron who supported convents would have been unlikely to support nuns whose spiritual interventions on the patron's behalf seemed likely to fail. Pilgrims would scarcely bring offerings to a shrine whose nuns' reputations had been tarnished. Women who valued their own ability to participate in monastic life were not likely to be tolerant of having other women put their vocations at risk. Indeed, judging from what hard evidence we do have on the subject, such as convent rules that prohibited nuns from spending time alone together, required them to sleep in barrackslike communal dormitories, and forbade affectionate touch and hugging, most built careful fences around the law to avoid even the hint of sin.

Virgin Superstars

Cultivating the Christian cult of holy virginity meant cultivating holy virgin role models. The virgin martyr saints of the Catholic tradition filled that niche in many ways during the medieval period, both as top-down propaganda promoted by the Church and as beloved grassroots icons. As privileged friends of God who had been granted a special place in heaven, their physical remains were believed to partake of their holiness. They were (and still are) also believed to have the ability to transmit requests directly from the devout to the Divine. In terms of the history of virginity, though, the most important aspect of the cult of the saints wasn't what remained after they died or how those remains were venerated, it is their hagiographies, or life stories.

Like Jesus, although at a bit of a theological remove, saints are both human and holy. They look like us, they have mothers and fathers and sisters and brothers like us, they have aspirations to greatness like we do. Very much like we do, they face temptation, cope with obstacles, and get into trouble. We empathize with these people, and we look up to them. As we do with rock stars and movie divas, comic book heroes, or legendary martial artists, we look to saints as role models.

The retelling of saints' stories began in the early years of Christianity, when often-persecuted believers drew courage from the success stories of their belief community. That "success" was defined in somewhat unusual terms—death in the service of the religion—was part and parcel of the Christian message. A true Christian, looking forward to eternal life, would hardly fear losing his or her earthly one.

The classic stories of Saint Agatha and her spiritual descendant Saint Lucy are good cases in point. Both Sicilian saints, a generation or so apart in age, they are described as having been beautiful girls who became Christian when young and dedicated themselves body and soul to God.

Both reject male authority and are sent to brothels as a punishment. Lucy is brought to the attention of the authorities when she rejects the man who wants to marry her. Agatha, on the other hand, has no man to whom she is betrothed. Instead, the governor learns of her Christianity and decides to try to turn her away from her spiritual perversion before it can cause problems. In both stories, these women are sent to brothels in an attempt to break their wills, making it abundantly clear that their primary crime is not the spiritual disobedience of professing Christianity but instead the very secular disobedience of refusing to consent to marriage and sex. The message is clear: if these women will not voluntarily submit to sexual relations like normal women, then they are to be forced.

Neither woman, however, can be forced into sex, even in a brothel. In the thirteenth-century versions of their legends found in the English source known as the Katherine Group, both women are loudly unwilling to change their ways. After Agatha is sent to the brothel of Aphrodisia, the whores urge her to submit by describing a life of pleasure, but she responds by saying, "Shut up, bitches! You won't get anywhere with me. I've given my heart to the highest prince of all!" Lucy, for her part, responds to the judge who sentences her to the brothel by paraphrasing St. Augustine: "No woman can be deprived of her virginity, no matter what is done to her body, unless her heart consents. If you defile my body against my will, my virginity is all the purer and my reward all the greater." When the judge's henchmen try to take Lucy to the brothel, they discover that she has become miraculously immovable, and cannot be dragged off even with a team of oxen.

The consequences of persisting in holy virginity and not submitting to sexual intercourse are torture and death. The tortures are often specifically sexual. Agatha's iconic torture is having her breasts torn off with pincers, which is why paintings of Agatha often depict her proffering her mutilated breasts on a tray. Lucy, on the other hand, is stripped naked and has boiling pitch poured over her body in front of the assembled onlookers. Despite the torture, neither woman recants or repents. Instead, they display an extraordinary indifference to pain, which they credit to God.

Virgin martyrs continually and vocally reaffirm their commitment to Christ. No torment is sufficiently severe, and no torturer sufficiently sadistic, to stop them from preaching. Lucy is one of many virgin martyrs (another is the legendary Saint Reparata) whose throat is slit by her torturers simply because she refuses to shut up. Lucy is unstoppable. Eyeballs plucked out and throat slit, she goes right on preaching while she holds her bloody eyeballs in her hand.

When virgin martyrs do finally die, they die on their own terms. Agatha and Lucy both choose the moment of their deaths. Agatha prays to God to let her die and promptly does so. Lucy's legend variously has her welcoming the thrust of a dagger into her neck, or, in other versions, calling for her supporters and being given last rites, whereupon she permits herself to expire in time

with the final "amen." Even the anomalous Welsh saint Winifred, the only virgin martyr to survive her own beheading (a miraculous resurrection that
leaves her with a white scar around her neck for the rest of her life), chooses
her own demise, telling the nobleman who is also her would-be seducer that
she would rather he cut off her head than take her virginity.

The basic traits of virgin martyrs are remarkably consistent. They are
known for their beauty and attractiveness, and, as in the case of Saint Wilge-
fortis (also known as Uncumber), whose prayer to be delivered from an unwanted marriage was answered with the miraculous appearance of a beard
and mustache, for their pious vowed virginity. Their refusal to submit to sex
and to sexual gender norms forms the basis for the persecution. Finally, the
fervor of their belief induces God to grant them miraculous immunity to
public humiliation, sexual violation, and physical torment. Throughout, they
speak. Holy virginity gives them powers of speech that normal women do not
have, letting them alone among women baptize, preach, exorcise demons, and
banish Satan.

As spiritual superheroines, virgin martyrs have been phenomenally attractive
role models. Particularly prior to the tenth and eleventh centuries they rivaled the
Virgin Mary in popularity, their shrines, relics, and stories making up a vital
realm not just of medieval theology but also of education and popular culture.
Over time, however, as the culture changed and expectations of women's roles
changed along with it, the ways virgin martyr stories were told changed, too.
The disruptive, mouthy, dangerous, even deadly virgin rebels of the early
Church are harnessed and brought to heel as quiet, self-effacing lambs. The rebellious thirteenth-century version of Agatha cited earlier, with its fiery invec-
tive, became, over the centuries, the story of a rather undeveloped personality
discreetly described as having been taken to a brothel where she "refused to accept customers." Lucy no longer preaches throughout torture and has her throat
slit as a result, but instead is described mildly as having "prophesied against her
attackers" before dutifully baring her throat for the dagger.

These women, once so mad, bad, and dangerous to know, become women
whose only salient characteristic is their refusal of sex. This is often true of
modern-day saints as well. The twelve-year-old Maria Goretti, for example,
was sainted after her would-be rapist stabbed her to death in 1902. But she is
lauded for having suffered death rather than the loss of her chastity and for
granting forgiveness to her attacker on her deathbed, not for having fought

back against a vicious armed rapist. Canonized in 1950 with both her mother and her murderer in attendance, she is invoked as an example to young women that they should be prepared to preserve their virginity at any cost.

But even Maria Goretti's example, controversial for its implication that it is better for a woman to die than be sexually penetrated, appears to inspire its fair share of "grrl power." In October 2003 a group of young students at the all-female St. Maria Goretti High School in South Philadelphia, Pennsylvania, fought back against a twenty-five-year-old man who had been stalking several schoolgirls and had repeatedly flashed his bare genitals at them. The girls spotted the man one afternoon and, as a pack, dropped their book bags and chased him through the city streets, finally catching and beating him badly enough that he required hospital treatment. Although modern feminism undoubtedly contributed to these young women's willingness to fight back against a sexual predator, we cannot say the example of their school's patroness might not have had a role to play, too.

Desperately Seeking Mary

Although she is central to Christianity and was beyond question the most important female figure of the Middle Ages, we know virtually nothing about the woman who became immortalized as the Virgin Mary. Of the canonical Gospels that form the core of the New Testament, only Luke mentions her at any length. Mark, the earliest of the Gospels chronologically, mentions her a grand total of twice. John, the Gospel assigned the latest date of composition by historians, not only fails to mention her by name but doesn't mention most of the major Marian episodes that the other Gospels include. Out of the four articles of dogma that the Roman Catholic Church has articulated in regard to its most famous woman (and its second most important human figure after Jesus), only one, her having given birth to Jesus, can be substantiated by scripture. The other three, her virginity, her immaculate conception, and her assumption into heaven, were established by papal decree in the fourth century, 1854, and 1950, respectively. Even so, as of this writing, the Vatican remains undecided whether or not Mary's bodily virginity survived childbirth and beyond, as well as on the question of whether Mary actually experienced death or was translated bodily into heaven.

The historical Mary, whoever she may or may not have been in the literal, physical flesh, is still a work in progress. As for the literal version, we presume she existed, was a Judaean, got pregnant, had a baby boy who grew up to have a career as a radical preacher, and witnessed the political murder of her son at the hands of an imperialist army of occupation. Everything else that is "known" about her stems from sources that are either sufficiently improbable or uncorroborated as to be open to debate at the very least. We do not even know what Mary looked like. Unlike the virginal beauties whose good looks are detailed in so many virgin martyr legends, neither the four authors of the Gospels nor even Paul, who makes the earliest chronological reference to Mary (Gal. 4:4, circa 57 C.E.), describe her. There is virtually no information about her from people who might have ever personally seen her or spoken with her.

We simply cannot pretend to discuss Mary in any factually biographical way. Readers wanting to know if she was "really" a virgin will have to keep waiting. But we can look at how other people have described her and examine the roles she has played in Christianity and in Western culture, and specifically, we can look at the issue of her virginity and its importance to Christianity.

In the earliest canon sources that mention Mary—the four canonical Gospels—it is unclear whether all the authors of the Gospels felt that Mary's virginity was of major importance. Only in Luke and in Matthew, which, like Mark, is believed to have been written over a century after the events in question, do we find unequivocal statements in regard to Mary's virginity. Of Luke and Matthew, Luke's statements about Mary are the more famous. Luke depicts Mary in conversation with the angel Gabriel, responding to Gabriel's announcement that she is to bear a child with the famous words, "But how can this be, seeing as I know not a man?" In Matthew, virginity is established at more of a remove through a statement that Jesus was conceived of the Holy Ghost prior to the time that Mary and Joseph "came together." Otherwise, Mary's sexual status is not made explicit in the New Testament. Paul does not mention it. John, the last of the Gospel authors, writing at the end of the first century, begins his infancy narrative with the simple statement that the word was made flesh and proceeds from there.

We don't really know why some of the New Testament writers chose to mention Mary's virginity and others overlooked it. Perhaps Matthew emphasized the role of the Holy Ghost to forestall skeptics. There were certainly a number of alternate ancestries for Jesus that circulated during the earliest decades of Christianity. We know about them because the church fathers felt compelled to debunk them. One popular story held that Jesus's father was actually a Roman centurion named Pantherus. The sexual abuse and rape of women in occupied territories by the soldiers of occupying armies was no newer a phenomenon in the antique world than it is today, and this eminently believable rumor was quite popular. A more limited rumor, which apparently existed primarily in Alexandria, claimed that Jesus had been the product of an incestuous union between Mary and her brother.

Perhaps it simply took someone like Luke, who is definitely the most talented writer among the Gospel authors, to imagine the poignant confusion of a young unmarried woman who has never had sex but who is told that she is going to have a baby. Or maybe Luke, canny storyteller that he was, thought that invoking the popular literary device of the *parthenos* who bears a God-fathered *parthenios* would help to substantiate Jesus's claims to greatness. As historian Marina Warner points out, the similarities between the story of Jesus's conception and birth and the Greek pagan tradition of the *parthenios*, the half-human son of a god who goes on to become a great, even miracle-working man, were controversial in the early years of Christianity. Jesus was not, after all, the only historical figure for whom divine ancestry had been claimed. There was a real and pressing need to distinguish Jesus's birth from that of people like Plato or Alexander the Great, both of whom enjoyed similar reputations for being *parthenioi*.

Church fathers offered various explanations to explain the unique nature of Jesus' virgin birth. Justin Martyr maintained that Mary's conception of her child differed from, say, Leda's or Semele's because Mary was neither seduced nor coerced by God but rather accepted the Word freely and without any sensual pleasure whatsoever. Origen, for his part, argued that Mary's conception had been a sort of spontaneous generation. It was not until the end of the fourth century, when the Apostles' Creed was developed, that a uniform understanding that Jesus was "conceived of the Holy Ghost through the Virgin Mary"—*conceptus est de Spirito Sancto, ex Maria Virgine*—began to become the accepted party line. Even so, the Creed was not formally drawn up as a document within the Church for another four centuries after that, which gives some indication of just how long it could take for even such a seemingly fundamental element of Marian theology as the manner in which she conceived Jesus to become set in stone.

The long, drawn-out process of establishing stable dogma in regard to Mary's conception of Jesus is an excellent illustration of the way that the personality we think of as Mary developed over time. By the end of the fourth century, a more or less consistent, if not yet complete, image of her had coalesced. Specific events, like Pope Siricius's 390 proclamation of Mary's inviolate virginity both during pregnancy and throughout her labor (*in partu*), signaled key points in the solidification of Mary's public image.

Lurking behind the scenes of these papal bulls and council proclamations, and contributing enormously to them, were a number of now-obscure sources of information, opinion, and imagination. One of the most important of these sources is the document called the *Protoevangelion*, the "pre-Gospel," attributed to James, the "brother" of Jesus.* Given the date of its likely composition, which would have been approximately a hundred years after Jesus' birth, it seems rather unlikely that the author was a direct contemporary of Jesus, much less an actual brother. Nonetheless, well-read Christians of the second century knew this document and believed it to be accurate: both Origen and Clement of Alexandria cite it as proof of the virgin birth.

This enormously influential piece of writing, the earliest version of which exists in Syriac (other copies exist in Greek and Ethiopic), was not fully translated into Latin until the sixteenth century. Parts of it, however, were combined with parts of the likewise apocryphal *Gospel According to Thomas* and issued in Latin in the eighth or ninth century under the titles *The Gospel According to the Pseudo-Matthew* and *The Story of the Birth of Mary*. This timing is probably partially responsible for the enormous increase in Marian veneration in the centuries just following, because what the *Protoevangelion* provided above all else was a fleshed-out life of Mary, including an elaborately fanciful justification of her pure, unsullied, ritually ensured virginity.

The *Protoevangelion*, according to historian of ancient literature Helen Foskett, is the only piece in the early Christian literature that goes into any detail at all regarding the ancestry and upbringing of a female protagonist. This is

---

*The nature of the relationship between the author of the document and Jesus himself has been the subject of long controversy. Explanations that allow for the existence of Jesus's brothers and sisters, mentioned in the Bible, but that also allow for Mary's perpetual virginity have been many and varied.

HEAVEN AND EARTH 165

not because it is the only one that has a female protagonist. Rather, it seems that its author felt that Mary needed a very specific kind of background, one which could immunize her against skeptics and firmly situate her as a woman without peer.

The *Protoevangelion* begins with the story of Mary's parents, Anna and Joachim. Anna is barren, and has, like several miraculous Old Testament mothers, reached a fairly advanced age without being able to have children. Then, as happened to Sarah and Abraham (the Old Testament parallelism is detailed and clearly intentional), an angel brings word that Anna and Joachim are to have a child. Anna and Joachim embrace when they hear this happy news. This bear hug of joy, a popular subject for paintings throughout the Middle Ages, transfers the spark of life to Anna's womb. This coitus-free beginning for Mary is an obvious harbinger of things to come.

The baby is born, and her parents raise the child in a cloistered bedchamber. Anna, respecting what she somehow understands are the needs of this late-life miracle baby, does not offer the child her breast until after she has undergone the ritual purification that all Jewish mothers undergo following the several-week-long *niddah yoledet*, a period of ritual impurity caused by childbirth and postpartum bleeding. While Mary is at home as a small child, her feet are not permitted to touch the ground, so she literally never comes into contact with the earth. Her companions are "the undefiled daughters of the Hebrews." Then, at the age of three, Mary is taken to live at the temple, where the high priest greets the toddler with the phrase "the Lord has exalted your name among all generations." Little Mary is allowed to run around freely in the temple, even dancing on the steps of the altar. She is fed "from the hand of an angel." She only leaves the temple at the age of twelve, when the priests raise the issue that she is now about to become a woman (the age of legal autonomy for women under Jewish law is twelve and a half). The implication that she would present a threat of ritual defilement should she start to menstruate and thus become *niddah* while in the temple is not elaborated, but clearly the author understood the nature of the menstrual taboo. After an elaborate process in which Joseph is chosen as the best and holiest possible guardian for her, the priests entrust Mary to his care and turn her out into the world.

This is a unique upbringing, to be sure, rather holier than the way Jesus' own is described. It's also demonstrably fictional. Although it is conceivable that a baby might be coaxed to suck milk from a wet rag (an alternative to baby

bottles in the days before they existed) for the minimum of fourteen days during which Anna would have been *niddah yoledet*, the refusal to breastfeed the
child during this period is unprecedented, and not in any way required by Jewish law. And on the point of Jewish law, we might well wonder by what unprecedented exception Mary would have been raised in the temple, where such
fostering of children was not practiced and from the inner reaches of which females were categorically prohibited. It seems impossible that such a radical departure from a centuries-old norm could have gone unnoted in the copious
writings of the Rabbis.

Very probably, Anna (or whatever Mary's actual mother's name might have
been) didn't really wait two weeks or more to feed her baby. We can take as writ
that no little girl was ever raised in the presence of the Holy of Holies like some
aberrant Jewish vestal. In all likelihood Mary wasn't raised in a sanctuary-like
bedchamber with a retinue of virgins as playmates, either, except perhaps insofar
as she might possibly have been raised around a lot of other little girls in a family
compound of the sort that were reasonably common in the antique Mediterranean region. The *Protoevangelion* makes a fine story, but it bears only glancing
resemblance to anything remotely historically likely.

Not that this mattered to those who read it. The vividly detailed life of a
very special little girl growing up in unprecedented circumstances formed a
compelling chunk of backstory predisposing the reader to accept the special
circumstances attached to a known event: the birth of Jesus.

As the story winds closer and closer to the Nativity, this preparatory agenda
becomes more and more overt. After Mary leaves the temple and goes to live
under Joseph's protection, she is given the task of spinning the thread for the
temple hangings, which is described as being performed only by "true virgins
of the lineage of David." This again emphasizes Mary's sexual status as well as
giving her an ancestry that puts her in line with Old Testament prophecy concerning the messiah, without having to supply an actual family tree.

Joseph is out of town on business when an angel comes to Mary and announces to her that she has found Divine favor and will conceive by the word of
God. Mary accepts this, and wonders if this means she will give birth like other
women do, or in some other manner, a question that goes unanswered. Mary
then goes to visit her cousin Elizabeth (as in the canonical Gospels), who recognizes Mary's divine pregnancy. After her visit Mary returns home to Joseph,
by now visibly pregnant. Joseph is furious, and presumes that the pregnancy is

illegitimate, a reasonable deduction given that Mary has been away from home for a while. He gives Mary (who should know better, what with her upbringing) a thorough tongue-lashing for having done something so stupid as defiling herself by getting pregnant out of wedlock. Mary's response is bizarre. She maintains that she is still a virgin, but at the same time, she does not know how she became pregnant. One would not think that the Annunciation would be something a girl would just forget.

Joseph takes Mary to the temple to have the matter addressed legally and religiously. The high priest decrees that both of them will undergo the trial by ordeal described in Numbers 5:17–28. This is the trial of the *sotah*, the woman who is suspected of adultery by her husband, a frightful ordeal with permanent consequences. In it, the priest mixes a potion, curses it, and gives it to the woman to drink. If she is guilty, her belly bloats and sags, her genitals become grotesque, and she becomes infertile. If she is innocent, however, she is made fertile (some interpretations understand this to mean that the innocent wife will then conceive her husband's child).

The implication of the *sotah* trial applied to Mary is obvious: the rabbis of the temple believe that she may have fornicated. It is a little harder to determine why Joseph would also be made to undergo this trial, but it seems possible that the author of the *Protoevangelion* wanted to make sure to remove any suspicion from Joseph as well. Both of them are vindicated by the test, and the story proceeds, with the reader and Joseph redundantly reassured of Mary's virginity.

The next substantial episode in the *Protoevangelion* is the Nativity sequence itself. Mary and Joseph travel to Bethlehem so that Joseph and his household can be counted in the imperial census, although Joseph notes that he is somewhat confused as to how to categorize Mary as a relation for official purposes, since she is neither his wife nor his daughter. Mary begins labor en route, and Joseph leaves her in a roadside cave and rushes off in search of a Jewish midwife. He returns with a midwife just in time to witness a cloud of light hovering at the mouth of the cave, which both he and the midwife recognize as a sign of God's presence. The midwife announces that the savior of Israel has been born. As they enter the cave she announces, using the explicit word "*parthenos*," that a baby has been born to a virgin.

Although her presence is not explained, another woman (whom some have identified as a second midwife) is also on the scene. This woman, named Salome, is no relation to the more familiar Herodian Salome who requests and receives John the Baptist's head, but she is nonetheless portrayed as being a bit on the wicked side: she is suspicious and refuses to believe the trusting midwife's claim that Mary remains a virgin. Salome begins a manual virginity test, reaching between Mary's legs as any midwife might, but on touching Mary's genitals Salome's hand is instantly burned to a withered crisp. "I am damned for not believing and for my transgression!" Salome yelps. "I put the living God on trial!" An angel (some versions claim that it is Gabriel) tells Salome to pick up the baby, and when she does, she is miraculously healed. Loud praises of the infant savior finish out the episode. A more dramatic or colorful Nativity scene is hard to imagine. Little wonder that it was a favorite subject for religious art—Salome's hand and all—for hundreds of years.

Every aspect of the *Protoevangelion* is crafted to hammer home the message that Mary was a virgin. From her sex-free conception and her strange "boy in the bubble" upbringing to her calm acceptance of the Annunciation and her apparently unattended and, we are given the impression, effortless childbirth of Jesus, Mary's life is abnormal in every particular. Even the virginity tests she is subjected to are bizarre. Astute observers have remarked that the Salome episode of the *Protoevangelion* is actually about the presence or absence of belief in Mary's virginity, and not about virginity itself. This insight applies equally well to the *Protoevangelion* as a whole. Who could come away from such a meticulously interwoven tapestry of purity, innocence, otherworldliness, submission, and virginity with anything resembling doubt?

Certainly not the medieval Christians who encountered aspects of this story beginning around the ninth century. Although it isn't really possible to pinpoint a precise date on which general interest in Mary began to increase, the emergence of the Latin versions of the *Protoevangelion* stories coincided with a sharp rise in her popularity across western Europe. The story arrived at the right time. Politically, culturally, aesthetically, and theologically, the time was ripe for the Virgin Mary to become more popular than ever before.

After Jerusalem fell to the Ottoman Empire in 638, many Christians felt that the very origins of Christendom were under siege. Because of Mary's association with Bethlehem and Jerusalem, anything that aroused interest in the Holy Land—very much including the ongoing Crusades—tended to arouse interest in Mary, and vice versa. There was a strong sense among Christians that they deserved to have a real political presence in the country that had produced the mother of the human embodiment of their God.

Culturally and aesthetically, too, the Virgin Mary was figured in ways that made her iconic to the Middle Ages. She was, for example, elevated to the rank of queen. If the world was governed by kings and queens, it only made sense that heaven should have a queen, too. Many of the greatest churches and cathedrals of Europe, like the great Notre Dame of Paris and the monumental cathedral at Chartres, both built at the height of the Middle Ages, specifically honor Mary's queenship. Within these churches and thousands of others, statues and paintings of Mary show her draped in silk, gold, and pearls, just like a well-dressed earthly queen. Of the four Marian antiphons of the Catholic liturgy, all of which date from the period between the tenth and twelfth centuries, three are dedicated to Mary in her queenly aspect, the *Regina Caeli* (Queen of Heaven), *Ave Regina Caelorum* (Hail, Queen of the Heavens), and the *Ave Regina* (Hail, Queen). They invoke her as the lady of heaven and the queen of paradise, her royalty inseparable from the perception of her as "*o clemens, o pia, o dulcis Virgo Maria*" ("o clement, o loving, o sweet Virgin Mary").

When the Virgin Mary is the subject, the lines between heaven and earth blur. As much as the Church shaped Mary into a model for women, who have been admonished to follow her example of virginity, submission, and humility ever since the fourth-century Council of Nicaea, rank-and-file believers have also shaped Mary. By writing her stories, painting her picture, and in the process of everyday invocation and prayer, Mary's devotees have created an entity whose personality and virginity are developing to this day. Of the myriad examples of this process—literally hundreds have been documented by historians like Jaroslav Pelikan and Marina Warner—many have, unsurprisingly, revolved around Mary's virginity.

Medieval Christians felt that the majesty of Mary's virginity would be enhanced if, according to the priorities of the feudal age, it were given an illustrious lineage. Medieval stories explained how God prepared the virginity of Mary by singling out not only Mary's parents but even her grandparents with signs and miracles. In one fifteenth-century tale, Anna's mother Esmeria—Mary's maternal grandmother—was said to have joined the Carmelite order only to leave it because the other monastics recognized that she was supposed to be progenitor of the Messiah and was thus intended to marry. She not only married, she did it five times. But each time she married, Satan struck down her new husband in an effort to prevent the Messiah's grandmother from being born. Finally, Esmeria managed to find a man named Stollanus who was made of sturdier stuff than her first four husbands. From this union, Anna was born.

Attempts·to give a lineage to Mary's virginity also happened on the institutional level. The doctrine of the immaculate conception—the notion that Mary was without the taint of original sin and thus empty of sinfulness from the moment of her conception—was not officially enshrined as dogma until 1854 when Pope Pius IX proclaimed the bull *Ineffabilis Deus*, but it had its roots in the work of scholastic theologians like twelfth-century Peter Lombard. The history of this particular doctrine is a labyrinthine journey through the niceties of Catholic theology, but the influence of Mary's existence as the only fully human being who could ever claim sinlessness was far reaching.

The Virgin Mary is both a major medieval legacy and a complicated, messy mixed bag. She is a gleaming example, the highest and most revered woman of all, a queen whose queendom, based as it is equally on both virginity and motherhood, lends its regal honor to all women. Countless Christians have drawn strength and comfort from belief in her imperturbable sanctity. The example of her humility, compassion, and submission has been a motivating force in countless acts of grace, charity, and aid. She has inspired great art, music, architecture, and literature. At the same time, the very perfection of her sinlessness and submission can only make everyone else seem that much more sinful and willful by comparison. Because virginity was the outward symbol of Mary's spiritual perfection, the same standard has been applied to all women, with predictable results. Only one woman can possibly maintain Mary's standard perfectly. The rest are forever condemned to judgment.

Finishing School

As vital as the Church was to the Middle Ages and as vital as virginity was to the Church, virginity mattered to medieval culture in secular ways as well. Medically, magically, and of course socially, virginity was at issue in everyday medieval life. The power of virginity reflected in Mary's miracles or saintly legends was an indication of what people believed about virgins. Impervious to sin and all things demonic or satanic, virginity's supernatural properties came from its holiness. Virgin magic was the work not of the devil but of God. A whole realm of more or less magical practices involving virginity, ranging from the innocuous to the evil, existed in medieval Europe.

The use of herbs, both medicinally and magically, was an everyday part of medieval life. Major European herbals deal frequently in virginity and virginity references. In them, for example, one often finds mention of an herb called "virgin's comfort," otherwise known as cicely (*Myrrhis odorata*), a hardy plant native to northwestern Europe and Scandinavia whose leaves and seeds taste of anise. Commonly recommended as a tonic for adolescent girls, it was supposed to ease menstrual discomforts and other "female problems." A different kind of female problem entirely could be alleviated by St. John's wort (*Hypericum perforatum*). On August 20, St. John's day, virgin girls were supposed to hang sprigs of St. John's wort over their doors and tuck them under their pillows when they went to bed so that St. John would show them visions of their husbands-to-be in their dreams. The herb would additionally protect them from any demons that might attempt to take their virginities in the night. Some herbals also counseled that a virgin who worried about finding a mate should eat a bowlful of St. John's wort as a salad, dressed in oil, to ease her anxiety. Given what is now known about St. John's wort's effectiveness as an antidepressant, this seems like good advice.

Alchemists likewise invoked the mystical properties of virginity to various ends. Sometimes virgins were involved as the source of an ingredient, as in the many alchemical recipes that call for the ashes of a virgin's burnt hair or which incorporate the urine of a virgin boy as a critical ingredient in a chemical reaction (urine was a common source for salts and ammonia in early chemical industries generally speaking). Other times the word "virgin" was applied to a compound that actually had nothing to do with virgins at all, appropriating the mystical power of virginity through naming the compound for it. One example is the frequently utilized "virgin's milk," in reality a solution of benzoin and water. Added to malt and gold powder, it made an ointment used in treating gout. If properly mixed with semen it would also supposedly generate homunculi, and was considered critical to the understanding of the Philosopher's Stone.

The mystical virginal principle also holds an iconic place in the lore of the mythical unicorn, a staple of the medieval imaginary bestiary. A white horse-like quadruped with a single pointed spiral horn, the unicorn was a fearsome beast capable of running would-be hunters through with a single toss of its terrible head. England's royal coat of arms featured a lion and a unicorn well before the accession of the Virgin Queen; two unicorns hold the crown in Scotland's. Evasive and fleet of foot, the unicorn was believed to be an unattainable quarry unless one had a virgin handy. Only a virgin's mystical purity could tame the creature's ferocious tendencies, and it would approach her and lay its head in her lap or upon her bosom with perfect gentleness. Legend has it that virgins were used as bait for unicorn traps. Seated in the middle of a circular fenced enclosure, the untouched feminine principle acted as bait for the untouchable masculine principle, the wild and deadly creature whose phallic sword emerges from his head. Trying to use a false virgin would end in either a fruitless hunt or in horror, for the unicorn was supposed to be able to tell, and would drive his horn through the heart of a woman who was only feigning virginity. Somehow, no unicorn was ever captured, though narwhal tusks brought home by sailors sometimes furnished "proof" that some had been in the past. The inability to catch them now could only have to do with a lack of properly virtuous virgins in such a corrupted age, and not, of course, with myth.

Not all magical contexts for virginity were as symbolic or figurative as a vial of virgin's milk or stories of the unicorn hunt. The quality of invulnerability associated with virgins, including their supposed immunity (often repeated in saints' legends) to attacks by the devil and other dark forces, was "borrowed" by using the body parts of virgins in various applications. In accounts of thieves' magic dating from the fourteenth to the nineteenth century, outlaws from Germany east to Russia were said to make magical candles that incorporated the rendered fat of dead virgins. By burning the fat of virgins—whether the virginal bodies in question were to be obtained by violence or merely grave robbery is not mentioned—the thieves would generate a variety of magical effects. Some reports say that these were "soporitic" candles, guaranteed to put everyone who was in the household being robbed to sleep so that the thieves could work undisturbed. Other writers claim that thieves used these candles to render themselves invisible, especially when robbing churches. A related bit of thieves' magic involved using the severed hand of a virgin as a candleholder to produce similar effects, although not everyone insisted upon a virginal hand as their "hand of glory," since the hands of hanged men were also used in the same way.

Because virginity was indissolubly linked with the body, the bodies of virgins were believed to be indissolubly permeated with the power of their virginity in much the same way as the bodies of saints were believed to be repositories of sanctity. This was even true of virgins' blood, and it is in a wash of virgins' blood that we find the story of what is probably the grisliest verifiable medieval virgin magic: the all-too-literal bloodbaths of the mad Hungarian countess Erzsébet Báthory. Báthory was born in 1560, well over the chronological border into the Renaissance, but her obsession with virgin magic was sufficiently savage, feudal, and arcane as to make a fitting capstone to a list of medieval virgin magics.

The daughter of a powerful aristocrat, Báthory was reputedly a casually cruel person even as a young woman, and particularly vain. At fifteen she was married off to a wellborn professional warrior and installed as the mistress of the castle at Cséjthe, an isolated keep in the rural Carpathian mountains in what is now Romanian territory. A bored teenager with a husband who spent the better part of the year off fighting wars, she had a penchant for the occult and the sadistic, and a reasonable sum of money to burn. As the years went on she developed a reputation for entertaining guests who were learned in arcane disciplines like alchemy and, some sources say, sorcery as well. Reports that she had developed a taste for torturing peasants imprisoned for debt surfaced even before her husband died in 1604, but it was only after that date that Báthory's sadism reached its virginal nadir.

In a vain attempt to restore her lost youth and beauty, she latched on to the idea that bathing her skin with the blood of virgins would make her young again. The first victim, or so the legend has it, was Báthory's own chamber-maid. Many more followed, hung upside-down from rafters by their ankles just as butchers hang animals for bleeding, before their throats were slit. Báthory bathed in and sometimes drank the blood of her victims, continually desperate for the renewed youth that somehow never arrived. Stories of dubi-ous veracity and thoroughly rococo detail—a golden goblet from which Báthory was supposed to have drunk blood, the silver talons she used as a tor-ture device, her opulent bathtubs for blood bathing, and quite a bit more besides—have accompanied her legend. Supposedly they also fill the pages of her notoriously inaccessible diaries, which are the property of the Hungarian government and are reputed to be stored in state archives in Budapest.

The countess, with a small handful of accomplices, supposedly killed six hundred virgins by the time they were caught and brought to justice in 1611. Before that, however, they operated without interference. Initially preying on the region's female peasants, they later set themselves up as a (fatally literal) finishing school for the daughters of the aristocracy as a means of luring in new victims. The finishing school approach brought them under investigation, and soon the matter was taken to regional authorities.

Following two Royal tribunals, two of Báthory's female accomplices were burned at the stake and her male accomplice was beheaded. Báthory herself, by reason of her aristocracy (and perhaps due to the fact that her cousin Stefan had become king of Poland), was instead sentenced to house arrest. She died in custody aged fifty-four, looking every minute of it.

The Lord's First Night

Báthory's example was both ghastly and unique, but it was by no means unheard of for a noble to have an interest in the virginity of those he or she ruled. This was never a matter of the nobility attempting to impose a code of morality upon the peasantry. There was an entire Church for that. Aristocratic concern for the virginity of peasants was economic. The people who lived on and worked a noble's land were an economic resource whose productivity was of vital concern. Part of that productivity involved their own reproduction: sex, marriages, and the resultant babies who would form the next generation of workers all came into the purview of the noble who managed a given territory.

For this reason, the nobility in many regions developed systems of imposing fines or taxes on sexual activity that put the economic interests of the lord at risk. Canon (church) law and the institution of confession and penance existed to punish lapses in morality. Secular punishments, such as the type of fine known in middle Welsh as *amobr* and in middle English as *leyrwite*, on the other hand, were leveled against serfs who had disobeyed sexual rules concerning things like premarital and extramarital liaisons. In addition to fines imposed on sexual miscreants, taxes were also levied on marriages, especially those that involved a marriage between serfs of two different landowners. Like other feudal laws, these were rarely implemented uniformly, and while some nobles were more than fair about them, others used them abusively.

It is here, at the intersection of marriage, sexuality, and the economic exploitation of peasants by the nobility, that we find the roots of one of the most enduring virgin-related myths of Western history, the myth of the *jus primae noctis,* or "right of the first night," also referred to as the *droit du seigneur* (right of the lord) and sometimes as the *droit du cuissage* (right of the leg) or the *jus cunni* (the right of the cunt). The myth of the *jus primae noctis* holds that it was the automatic right and privilege of a feudal lord to take the virginity of any woman living in his domain, and specifically to deflower virgin brides. As described, it is the ultimate in symbolic theft, and a violation not only of secular law but church law as well. One would be hard-pressed to come up with a single act that could more effectively give an impression of a corrupt, exploitive, cruel, and callously selfish nobility. Perhaps that's why people had to invent the *jus primae noctis.*

This is by no means to say that aristocrats never laid claim, either consensually or by rape, to the virginity of women beneath them. Saying that the *jus primae noctis* was a myth is not the same as denying that sexual abuses of power took place. But acknowledging that sexual abuse took place is a very different thing from claiming that a particular sexually abusive practice was either customary or, as the word *jus* (law) implies, an aspect of the formal and legally extenuated rights of the nobility as a class. The former is a given. The latter is a myth.

Given how important virginity was to medieval culture, it seems likely that had the practice of the lord of the manor deflowering every virgin on her wedding night actually existed, someone would have recorded it somewhere. As it stands, the earliest reference we have to any form of this supposed custom dates from 1526, in a text that attributes it as having been practiced by a medieval Scottish king. Unfortunately, the king in question is nowhere to be found in any records that date from earlier than 1526: he was apparently invented because someone wanted a bogeyman.

The market for aristocratic bogeymen has been rather brisk since the 1500s, given the number of *jus primae noctis* tall tales that appeared since that time. Take for example the story related throughout the eighteenth and nineteenth centuries about the formation of the free town of Montauban, a city in the Toulouse region of France. The story related how monks of the Abbey of Saint-Théodard, located in Montauriol, adjacent to the territory that became Montauban, had become greedy and power-mad, going so far as to enforce the *droit du seigneur* over the women of Montauriol. Montauriol's serfs eventually rebelled against this treatment, the story goes, by fleeing the abbey's lands and founding the free town of Montauban.

In reality, nothing of the kind ever happened. A charter of foundation for the free town of Montauban exists, dated 11 October 1144. In it, one Alphonse Jourdain, comte de Toulouse, established the city and charged its inhabitants with the responsibility of building a bridge over the River Tarn. Jourdain wanted a bridge, some of his serfs wanted independence. The deal was straightforward and honest.

Not all the fictions that have reinscribed this myth pretend to historical truth, however. Many, in fact, were intended as entertainment. From the seventeenth century to the present, the idea of the *jus primae noctis* has been used as a brilliantly engaging plot device. In the drama and opera of the eighteenth century, in fact, the motif became a literal classic through the successes of both Beaumarchais's play *Le mariage du Figaro* (1775–1778) and the opera *Le nozze di Figaro*, which Wolfgang Amadeus Mozart composed in 1786 to an Italian libretto adapted from the Beaumarchais original by the inimitably witty Italian Lorenzo da Ponte. These two works, probably the apogee of the *jus primae noctis* theme, are merely the best known.

It is no coincidence that the best-known dramas featuring the *jus primae noctis* date from the late eighteenth century. The rising tide of anti-aristocratic and anti-imperial sentiment in Enlightenment France all but demanded it. To invoke the *jus primae noctis* was to invoke a recollection of every unrighteous imposition or abuse from above, no matter how small. As a rallying cry it was hugely effective. Almost any hardworking but impoverished *paysan* could imagine himself a defenseless virgin whose only personal treasure had ruthlessly been taken by some greedy aristocrat, and so the myth of the *jus primae noctis* fanned the flames of revolution. In historical fact, however, the "lord's first night" never existed save in the minds of those who believed it did.

CHAPTER 10

To Go Where No Man
Has Gone Before

The "Flos Virginis," so much coveted by the Europeans,
is never valued by these savages.
—John Lawson

I N THE NATURAL COURSE of events the Queen is of an age where she
should in reason and as is woman's way, be eager to marry and be provided
for," wrote Baron Pollweiler, a negotiator visiting the court of the twenty-six-
year-old Queen Elizabeth I in 1559. Pollweiler was in England attempting to
broker a marriage agreement between Elizabeth and the heir to the Austro-
Hungarian Empire, Archduke Charles of Austria. "The natural and necessary
inference from all this is," he continued, "either that she has married secretly,
or that she has already made up her mind to marry someone in England or out
of it and . . . is postponing matters under the cloak of Your Imperial Majesty's
son, my gracious master. For that she should wish to remain a maid and never
marry is inconceivable."

For all intents and purposes, the Baron was right. In a country whose
monasteries and convents had been abolished by Elizabeth's father Henry VIII
in 1539, and in which she herself had firmly reestablished Protestantism as the
state religion, it was indeed inconceivable that a woman should wish never to
marry. Yet, as we know, Elizabeth remained unmarried to the end. By dint of

savvy political maneuvering, a blend of sincere and Machiavellian religiosity, and simply being beyond the reach of too much secular or religious strong-arming, she reigned for forty-five years as that most inconceivable thing—a public, powerful, and thoroughly secular virgin.

Despite the legion biographies, films, and fictions about her, the documentable facts of Elizabeth's anomalous life make her a difficult subject for the historian of virginity. We do not know and cannot say, for example, whether she was "really" a virgin in the sense of never having sexual relations with any partner at any time. There were as many rumors that she was in some way physically deformed and unable to engage in intercourse as there were that she had borne bastards by her longtime confidant Robert Dudley, Master of the Queen's Horse and later Earl of Leicester. No evidence of any of this has been found; indeed there is no documentary evidence of her sexual existence at all. What there is to work with is her enormous and often self-conscious legacy. It is more than slightly ironic that, despite the gallons of ink that have been spilled on the subject, what is known about the virginity of the Virgin Queen is little more than what she herself said in 1559: "in the end this shalbe for me sufficient that a marble stone shall declare that a Queene, having reygned such a time, lyved and dyed a virgin."

Elizabeth's odd-woman-out example does, however, shed some useful light on what the culture of Western virginity was like from the sixteenth through the eighteenth centuries: a tumultuous time, rife with discovery and reform. Recall that Vesalius had only finally isolated the hymen in the mid–sixteenth century, and scientific approaches to virginity were undergoing a general renovation. In the realm of religion, Reformationists and Counterreformationists, with Protestant and Catholic versions of sexual law, grappled for the minds and bodies of believers. Even the globe was changing, as explorers traversed the world and discovered "virgin" continents where the maps had formerly said "here there be dragons." Those engaged with the iconography, the ideology, and the physical reality of virginity were all alike obliged to go where no one had gone before.

Perhaps more than any other single force, Protestantism had changed the face of virginity in Europe. Putting marriage first and abandoning monasticism and celibate clergy, Protestantism flipped the Roman Catholic Church's emphasis on virginity neatly on its head. Where Roman Catholic doctrine had stated that virgins received 100 percent of heaven's rewards, while the married could expect only 30, Protestant theology set forth the principle that all godly believers would partake equally in heaven regardless of their sexual or marital status. Martin Luther was particularly vociferous on the subject of marriage, pointing out that neither lifelong virginity nor clerical celibacy was called for in the Bible, claiming that few people were naturally inclined toward either one, and contending that the result of requiring celibacy of people who were not inherently given to it was to encourage illicit sexual relations. Even the Pope, Luther claimed, had "as many concubines as Solomon." Himself a former Augustinian monk married to a former nun, Katharina von Bora, and the father of six children, Luther practiced what he preached when it came to placing a high priority on marriage and family.

Protestant enthusiasm for marriage and family was contagious among all Christian rank and file, including Catholics, the lion's share of whom were, of course, married. Unsurprisingly, this met with stern disapproval from Rome. As part of the Council of Trent (1545–1563), the Roman Catholic Church's Counterreformation assembly called in response to the emergence of Protestantism, the Church issued the treatise *De sancti matrimonii*. *De sancti matrimonii* stood as the central Catholic document on marriage and sexuality until the Vatican II assembly of the mid–twentieth century. Among its other doctrinal points, it threatened with excommunication any Catholic who claimed, à la Luther, Calvin, and other Protestant thinkers, the heresy that marriage was preferable to virginity.

In the Council of Trent's reminder of virginity's supremacy we see a Christian laity whose worldview had been thoroughly scrambled by the sudden appearance of Protestantism, and a Catholic establishment that was struggling to cope with the blow. It is difficult, from our vantage point in a world where Protestant denominations are as numerous as ice cream flavors, to empathize with the degree to which the Reformation transformed Christianity. With a nod to the preceding chapter, however, it may help to consider the nature and the magnitude of the differences between Protestantism and Catholicism, at least in regard to virginity.

The Fall of the Sacred Virgin

Protestantism had no place for consecrated virginity and thus no place for nuns or convents. Some priests, monks, and nuns abandoned their positions, their celibacy, and their Catholicism as Protestantism gained presence and power, but neither Luther nor his early followers had anything close to the clout it required to actually close down monasteries or convents. Some later closed their doors due to attrition or the Protestantization of the territory in which they stood, and the presence of nuns and convents shrank dramatically in the parts of Europe that became majority Protestant. Only in England, where Henry VIII single-handedly forced the conversion of the entire country to an Anglican church not beholden to Rome, were monastic institutions abolished outright.

But even in places where convents still stood, and in some cases even before Luther posted his ninety-five theses in 1517, various reform-minded Catholics had already begun to embrace marriage. In some ways this was the result of economic and social change more than religious reform. As feudal and manorial arrangements declined, individual wage-earning, goods-producing households became the new lowest common denominator of the burgeoning new capitalist cash economy. With nonaristocratic families gaining visibility as self-supporting entities, marriage among non-nobles started to have economic meaning that it had not possessed under intensive feudal or manorial systems. Marriage and reproduction gradually became as tightly yoked to the economic, social, and political interests of the non-noble family as they had always been for the dynastic clans of the nobility.

As economic autonomy became strongly linked to marriage, it led to a new way of conceptualizing the family and household. In Protestant and particularly Calvinist circles, the married household came to be seen as a closed system, each family replicating within its own members the kind of relationship that existed between governor and countrymen, a microcosmic version of the larger "family" of the secular state with the paterfamilias as ruler. By 1622 William Gouge, minister of Blackfriars Church, London, could write in his *Of Domesticall Duties* that "A familie is a little Church, and a little commonwealth, at least a lively representation thereof, whereby triall may be made of such as are fit for any place of authoritie, or of subjection in Church or commonwealth. Or rather it is as a schoole wherein the first principles and grounds of government and subjection are learned: whereby men are fitted to greater matters in Church or commonwealth." This pocket-sized vision of society positioned marriage as a vital tool that produced and trained men and women who would be fit to participate in the modern, secular state.

What this meant to virginity was that it became, almost by definition, brief and transitional. In the Protestant mind, there was no place for the convent, nor for any behavior that smacked of it. The cultural category of the spinster or old maid became prominent in English culture around this time, for there was no longer a functional niche in the society for women who either did not wish to marry or could not find husbands. Indeed, the assumption in regard to women was that, as a 1632 pamphlet entitled *The Lawes Resolution of Women's Rights* put it, "all of them are understood either married or to be married." Virginity was a commodity with a limited shelf life. Well into the 1830s, even writers like the relatively progressive British freethinker journalist Richard Carlile could say with a straight face that spinsters were "a sort of sub-animal class" and that "It is a fact that can hardly have escaped the notice of anyone that women who have never had sexual commerce begin to droop when about twenty-five years of age . . . their forms degenerate, their features sink, and the peculiar character of the old maid becomes apparent."

Just as it was considered "natural" for women to marry and have children, it was considered "natural" that they be virgins before they did. Virginity was a brief moment through which women passed on their way from being children to being wives. This naturalizing and trivializing of virginity had the effect of homogenizing the various forms of female chastity, as demonstrated in these lines from Diana Primrose's 1630 *A Chaine of Pearle, Or, A Memoriall of the peerles Graces, and heroick Vertues of Queene Elizabeth, of Glorious Memory*:

For whether it be termed Virginall
In virgins, or in Wives stil'd Conjugall,
Or viduall in Widdowes, God respects
All equally, and all a-like affects.

This scrap of verse serves as an eloquent summary of the fall of virginity in Protestant Europe. If all forms of chastity are equal in God's eyes, then there was no reason to draw distinctions between them. The virginity a woman took to the altar was of a piece with the monogamy she was expected to embody after she left it. Virginity itself, to the Protestant mind-set, no longer signified anything particularly special. It was something that could be expected of any reasonable, respectable unmarried woman. This way of thinking, argues literary historian Theodora Jankowski, created a subtle but important association: while chastity was a virtue of which a Protestant could be proud, the word "virginity" acquired specifically Catholic overtones.

Probably the single most striking way in which the Catholic mode of virginity was effaced from Protestantism was in regard to the praise and veneration of the Virgin Mary. While no Protestant ever denied Mary's virginity or that it was perpetual, all of them agreed that the way she was worshipped within Catholicism was not what they felt was appropriate for Christians. The Protestant Mary is no longer the quasi-goddess intercessor who reigns as queen of heaven, but instead a wholly human woman who happened to have had the honor of being Jesus' mother. The demotion was tangible: icons and statues of Mary do not exist in Protestant houses of worship in the way that they do in Catholic churches, nor are there Protestant equivalents of anthems like the Catholic *Salve Regina* or *Sub Tuum Praesidium* specifically praising Mary above all other women. Protestant insistence on the authority of scripture, and not the accumulated centuries of extracanonical literature, removed all but the essentials of Mary's identity.

The Virgin Mary's demotion within Protestantism led to some dramatic and curious historical moments. During the systematic restoration of Anglicanism that attended Elizabeth I's early reign (she had had to reinstitute it following her half-sister Mary's abortive attempt to restore Catholicism), among the striking anti-Catholic measures taken by the state were search-and-destroy missions aimed at finding and eradicating icons and statues of the Virgin Mary. Various scholars, including the incisive Helen Hackett, have looked at these anti-Marian campaigns as being part of a complex rearrangement of virginal power. It is difficult not to see the destruction of icons and statues of Mary as a way of destroying the old Catholic virgin so that she could be replaced with a new Protestant model—the queen herself.

The Making of the Virgin Queen

Elizabeth Tudor, daughter of Henry VIII and his second wife, Anne Boleyn, was never literally compared to the Virgin Mary during her lifetime. It would have been sacrilegious from the scripture-centered Anglican viewpoint. Also, it would not have made sense from the perspective of the Virgin Mary's role within the Gospels: according to the terms of the Thirty-nine Articles of Religion of 1563, the bearer of the crown also stood as head of the Church of England. It is difficult to imagine a role less congruent with the Virgin Mary's timeless and much-vaunted passivity to God's will than running a nation and a state religion. Nonetheless, Elizabeth's reign was nothing if not a lengthy process of creating a virginal persona that has proven to be very nearly on a par, in terms of its iconic popularity, with the Virgin Mary's own.

How much of this was deliberate, and how much the coincidental accretion of attention that accompanies a long-reigning and beloved monarch, is hard to say. Elizabeth's savvy in regard to managing and manipulating public opinion was substantial. She spent lavishly on gowns, jewels, portraits, and royal progresses, whistle-stop horseback tours of her domain that let her see and be seen. Her skill with rhetoric, both visual and verbal, was undisputed, as in the legendary speech delivered to her troops on the eve of the Spanish Armada. The queen, dressed in an Athenalike white gown and silver breastplate, told her men, "I have the body of a weak, feeble woman, but the heart and stomach of a king—and of a King of England too."

Elizabeth's kingly attitude toward her role as ruler played a significant part in her controversial, wily virginity. Twenty-five years old when she was crowned, Elizabeth had already declared a preference for virginity, having asked for permission to remain unmarried during the time that her younger half-brother, Edward VI, briefly occupied the throne. She had reiterated her desire "to remayne in that estate I was, which of all others best lyked me or pleased me" again, during the period when her half-sister Mary was queen, when several continental potentates made offers of marriage to the young princess. But what had been acceptable, if eccentric, behavior coming from a third-place princess whose (hypothetical) children might constitute potential competitors for any children her half-siblings had became unthinkable once Elizabeth was queen.

The third and last of Henry VIII's children to be crowned, Elizabeth was, in light of her brother and sister's ultimate failure to leave any heirs, also the last Tudor standing. Elizabeth could either marry and have children or let the Tudor line die with her. Domestic and international politics added to the marriage pressure. England was a small and isolated country in need of allies on the Continent, and the person next in line for the throne was the staunchly Catholic Mary, Queen of Scots, the granddaughter of Henry VIII's sister Margaret. Mary had the backing of France and other powerful Catholic countries on the Continent (her son, James VI, ultimately succeeded Elizabeth upon her death in 1603). But the notion of another Catholic queen on the throne, particularly in the wake of Bloody Mary's gruesome persecutions during the Catholic interregnum, sat exceedingly poorly with English Protestants for whom those persecutions were a still-ragged wound. When Elizabeth's first Parliament convened in 1559, they lost little time in formally petitioning the queen to marry.

Elizabeth responded with a statement on 10 February, in which she very carefully failed to refuse the prospect of marriage outright, but failed to welcome it either. The newly crowned queen said that if it pleased God to continue to maintain her in her sentiment that it was best she continue to remain unmarried, she would do so with pleasure. On the other hand, she said that she hoped that God would provide "in convenient tyme wherby the realme shal not remayne destitute of an heir that may be fitt to governe and peradventure more beneficiall to the realm then such an offspring as may come of me." Leaving the whole issue in God's hands was the most politic way of refusing to say either yes or no.

This was the first of two parliamentary petitions that exhorted Elizabeth to marry, and the first of three corresponding statements from the queen. Over the course of the two petitions and the three responses—1559, 1563, and 1569—we can trace a fascinating evolution in Elizabeth's apparent attitudes toward marriage. The brash young queen ducking the will of the Parliament in 1559 had become a bit wiser and cagier by the time her second Parliament issued a similar petition to the now thirty-year-old queen in 1563. Somewhat more forthcoming now, although having in the interim rejected the suits not only of her own subject (and probable love of her life) Robert Dudley, but also of some of the most powerful men in Europe, including Archduke Charles of Austria, King Erik XIV of Sweden, and even her own half-sister Mary's widower, Philip II of Spain,* Elizabeth appeared to take the question of an heir at least somewhat seriously.

---

*Although Philip was eager to renew his strategic alliance with England, the marriage was not a prospect Elizabeth was prepared to entertain seriously for a host of reasons, not least of which were Philip's Catholicism and the legacy of British hatred for Mary's Spanish marriage.

In the first of two responses to this petition, she reminded Parliament of the story of the biblical Elizabeth, whom God had blessed with a miraculous late-life pregnancy. Drawing the parallel between herself and her New Testament namesake, she told Parliament that she had heard and understood their request, even if she might appear to be waiting for divine intervention on the matter. The second response to this petition, in November 1566, shows further softening of Elizabeth's antimarriage stance. For the first time, the thirty-three-year-old queen avowed that she would marry as soon as she could conveniently do so, "yf God take not hym awaye with whom I mynde to marrye." Her reasons for wanting to do so were clear: "I hope to have chylderne, otheryse I wolde never marrie." But she was equally clear, and absolutely unabashed, about the fact that the people who most encouraged the marriage would be the first to declare their disapproval of anyone she chose as a husband. Furthermore, she revealed with arch disdain that there had been some who had told her that "they never requyred more then that theye myght ones here me saye I wold marrie," condemning such facile sentiments with a scathing "there was never so great a treason but myght be coveryde under as fayre a pretence."

This was, perhaps, not so much genuine reconciliation to the idea of marriage as it was sheer strategy. Having eluded marriage as long as she had, there was little chance, barring some unprecedented unanimous agreement on the parts of Parliament and the Privy Council as to an appropriate choice of husband, that she would be required to marry. Elizabeth may also have felt that she could finally allow herself to verbally placate Parliament because her subjects were increasingly likely, for political reasons, to back her desire to remain unattached. The queen had many powerful friends among her subjects who treasured her deep commitment to Protestantism. Some of them had begun to realize that given the options available to her in terms of suitable husbands, a married queen might ironically be even less advantageous to the Protestant cause than a virgin queen without an heir.

This was dramatically demonstrated during Elizabeth's last courtship. It would have been a most unusual pairing even by today's standards, let alone by those of the time: in 1579 Elizabeth was forty-six; the Duke of Alençon twenty-five. The intent was clearly political, since a marriage between Elizabeth and Alençon would have destroyed the looming potential of an anti-English alliance between France and Spain. But the English were having none of it. They had become accustomed to their spinster queen, had little love for the French, and, with Mary and Philip still very much in the collective memory, remained disinclined to entertain the idea of another marriage between any English queen and a foreigner. John Stubbs, an anti-Alençon writer whose tract *Discoverie of a gaping Gulf whereinto England is like to be Swallowed by an other French mariage* appeared in September 1579, earned swift Royal retribution. For his temerity in questioning the queen's right to decide her own affairs, and not at all coincidentally for having been sufficiently impolitic to raise the question of Elizabeth's ability to bear a child in her forties, Stubbs and his publisher were both permanently relieved of their right hands.

The rapidly abandoned Alençon courtship was the turning point for Elizabeth's career as virgin queen. Before it, there had been the lingering possibility, however slight, that she might at long last marry. After it, the idea was no longer seriously raised: Elizabeth was past the point where she could reasonably be assumed to be fertile. From that point on, writes Helen Hackett, "the Queen would be unequivocally celebrated as ever-virgin."

From 1582 until her death in 1603, Elizabeth's virginity became superhuman. Portrayed as Cynthia, Selene, Diana, Vesta, or Athena, Elizabeth and her virginity were poeticized, glorified, and abstracted. Her virginity was no longer a matter affecting a mundane human body and its reproductive functionings but a metaphysical aura attached to a larger-than-life persona. The doctrine of the King's Two Bodies, which held that the king (or queen, if she ruled independently) had a "body naturall" of flesh and blood and a metaphorical "body politicke" the abilities and role of which transcended whatever infirmities might inhere to the physical body, had been invoked at the beginning of Elizabeth's reign to argue that the intrinsic instability and lesser worth of her female "body naturall" were not as important as the intrinsic stability and value of kingship. During the last twenty years of her reign, though, the public image of Elizabeth's, and England's, "body politicke" had become enhanced by the overlay of her hard-won and ultimately mythicized virginity. Prior to Elizabeth's reign, this attribute could have been understood only as belonging to the feminine and frangible physical body that temporarily occupied the throne. Now it stood for something far larger, grander, and much more formidable: virginity as bulwark, standard, and shield.

"Her Treasures Having Never Been Opened"

During Elizabeth's reign, new vistas opened in more areas than just the queen's reputation. For over a century, voyagers and explorers had been returning from fantastic sea journeys with tales of unthinkably profitable lands far beyond Europe's shores. Elizabeth herself, well aware of the trading opportunities such remote locales represented, chartered the East India Company into existence in late 1600 to help her country take advantage of what lay beyond the horizon. Aside from her political and economic interest in efforts of discovery, exploration, and settlement, the queen also shared an unexpected similarity with these exotic locales: a reputation for opulent and well-endowed virginity. Indeed Virginia Colony, the first English settlement in North America, founded in 1607, was named for the recently deceased queen via her most celebrated attribute.

To many, the effulgent virginity rhetoric of the European expansion—Sir Walter Raleigh's characterization of Guiana as "a country that hath yet her maydenhead, never sackt, turned, nor wrought," for example—comes as a bit of a shock. Elizabeth's virginity may have been the elegant stuff of classical allusion, but the virginity of the New World was usually the nudge-nudge-wink-wink of the brothel. The soil of the New World was seen as being, as Robert Johnson's *Nova Britannia* (1609) put it, "strong and lustie of its own natur." Even the rocky, difficult shores of the New England coast were praised as "Paradise with all her Virgin Beauties." Indeed, as Thomas Morton wrote in 1632, it seemed to the colonization-minded explorers as if these new territories yearned for the touch of European, Christian settlement "like a faire virgin, longing to be sped / and meete her lover in a Nuptiall bed."

This seductively idyllic vision of eager, fecund virginity was a powerful motif. In illustrations of the era of colonial expansion, the New World is often depicted as a naked or at least bare-breasted woman, her hair loose, her posture unashamed. These female embodiments of the land beckon, sometimes even from a relaxing hammock, just another specimen of the tame-looking game that gambols in lushly fruited forests. The Americas, and by implication the indigenous peoples who lived there, were clearly understood as desirable, forthcoming, and, most important, unspoiled partners who not only failed to resist but indeed received with interest the advances of European men.

Partly this was wishful thinking: Europe and the British Isles had become crowded, arable land was pushed to its limits, and the reward of incessant backbreaking work was often poverty, disease, and, in bad years, famine. The idea of a place where one scarcely had to lift a finger to provide for one's self was understandably tantalizing. What better symbol for such an environment than a welcoming, sexually ready woman?

Indeed the New World did contain vast unsettled land as well as other resources that appeared to be wholly unexploited and ripe for the picking, so the vision was not an empty promise. Not only that, but as explorers began to return from the New World and publish tales of their adventures on the other side of the ocean, they produced a steady stream of stories of sexual encounters with virgin women who, it seemed, yielded to the Europeans as willingly as did the land. In accounts like Carolina explorer John Lawson's, published in 1709, we find goatish and doubtless hyperbolic descriptions of sexual interludes not just with indigenous women and girls, but *eager*, "naturally" promiscuous indigenous women and girls, who began their sexual lives "as soon as Nature prompts them." Even better, Lawson claimed, these were females whose reputations or lives could not possibly be ruined if a horny colonist happened to indulge his desires, "A Multiplicity of Gallants never being a Stain to a Female's Reputation, or the least Hindrance of her Advancement, but the more Whorish, the more Honourable."

There is a strong stench of what we might now call "sex tourism" in some of these descriptions. Virginia planter and chronicler Robert Beverley described a sort of prodigal aboriginal harem of which visiting "Strangers of Condition" were invited by their hosts to partake. "A Brace of young Beautiful Virgins" would be chosen for the European visitor to the native camp, to serve him, undress him, and be his bedmates, one woman to either side of him. It was, Beverley promised, no platonic gesture, for the women would "esteem it a breach of Hospitality not to submit to every thing he [the visitor] desires of them."

Accounts like these stirred multiple reactions both on the ground in North America and back home in Europe. On the one hand, they strengthened the resolve of the religious to send missionaries to try to civilize and Christianize the New World's apparently habitually wanton indigenes. On the other, they represented an alluring prospect for the numerous single men who went to the North American colonies (Virginia, Maryland, and the Carolinas particularly) to seek their fortunes. These tales were so influential that when some white Europeans, like Virginian planter-statesman William Byrd, visited with Amerind tribes and did not find themselves the recipients of the sort of hot two-girl action promised by accounts like Beverley's, they reacted quite peevishly at not receiving what they obviously thought was their due.

To what extent such stories and claims might have been true is almost impossible to assess at this historical remove. It is likely that at least some of the indigenous peoples intended the sharing of their women to forge reciprocal alliances between the European newcomers and the people already living there. Barriers of language, culture, and custom, on the other hand, assured that such intent would easily (and perhaps sometimes willfully) have gone unperceived by the Europeans. In any event, most European men would not have considered such "savages" as serious partners, despite the fact that numerous early male settlers depended on their indigenous common-law wives to translate, navigate, and help them feed themselves in an unfamiliar land. But as the titillated response to John Rolfe's 1614 marriage to Pocahontas (and their subsequent celebrity when they traveled, sponsored by the Virginia Company, to England) proved, a fully recognized marriage between a European and an indigenous American was a curiosity with few parallels.

The Puritans

In the United States, the iconic image of settlers in the New World is that of the Puritans of Massachusetts Bay Colony. Resolute members of a profoundly Calvinist version of Protestantism, their resistance to the state religion, their passionate devotion to their own version of moral and spiritual purity, and their militancy created tension and eventually contributed to the outbreak of outright war (the English Civil War) in England. Before the war and especially after it, Puritan believers, and particularly the more hard-line, often sought refuge in places either more congenial to their beliefs or at least less likely to oppose them.

One of these places was the East Coast of North America. Both the Virginia Colony and the Massachusetts Bay Colony were founded by Puritans on the principle that they would attempt to establish in the New World the Holy Commonwealth they had failed to institute in England. In Massachusetts, this plan prospered. In 1648, four Massachusetts communities adopted the Cambridge Platform, instituting a form of government where authority was centered in the "elect," the most upstanding and pious male members of Puritan congregations. The elect served as paterfamilias to their communities just as they did to their own households. The "little Commonwealth" of the Calvinist Protestant family was therefore the essential building block of the larger commonwealth then being carved from Massachusetts's stony soil.

Virginity was a serious issue in both literal and figurative commonwealths. It was part of the proper life pattern for women, as well as a determining factor in the reputation a woman and her family had within these close-knit communities. If an unmarried woman lost her virginity it was a socioeconomic crisis, because it made it unlikely that she would marry. A female-headed household was anathema; only a man could master a household or represent his household within the congregation.

A lost virginity was also an ideological and dogmatic crisis. Puritans believed that just as a wrongdoing on the part of one member of a family might reflect poorly upon the rest, a sin on the part of any member of the commonwealth could draw down God's wrath upon the entire community. Punishment and repentance were necessary in order to escape this fate, for example to have the wrongdoer stand, possibly in stocks, in a public place while wearing a sign that identified the nature of his or her particular sin. Although Puritan punishments often seem unnecessarily humiliating to our modern eyes, the fact that they were public and shaming was precisely the point: justice had to be seen to be done in order to alleviate fears that adequate reparations might not have been made to God.

The very public ways Puritan women were prosecuted for sexual transgressions have led some historians to assume that premarital sex was epidemic in the Massachusetts Bay Colony. The truth, however, appears to have been rather different. The work of historian Else Hambleton has revealed that the numbers of women representing known violations of premarital virginity taboos as either unwed mothers or pregnant brides were fairly small. Additionally, the numbers were, at least in the seventeenth century, typically about equal for unwed mothers and pregnant brides: in Essex County, Massachusetts, between 1641 and 1685, 135 married and 131 unmarried women were cited for fornication evinced by the birth of a child.

There were a few important differences between those who managed to marry while pregnant with a child conceived out of wedlock and those who did not. It was not that some were prosecuted and others were not: unmarried women who bore children and married women whose babies were born within eight months of their weddings were prosecuted alike. Nor was it a difference in the nature of the penalty, since fines, whippings, and other punishments were dispensed without regard to marital status. The difference was also not age, since most women involved in fornication prosecutions were under the age of twenty-five and over half were between the ages of fifteen and twenty. Rather, the differences had to do with the ways in which the women had become pregnant in the first place and what this meant for their lives down the line.

Women who were married by the time their babies were born were much more likely to be fully reintegrated into the community, in part because they married the men with whom they shared their regrettable lapse of conduct. As many as three-quarters of unmarried women convicted of fornication, on the other hand, would never find husbands. In this marriage-centric culture, this left them stuck on the fringes socially, economically, and religiously for the rest of their lives. These unmarried mothers were highly likely to have borne children fathered by men who were already married to other women and were far higher in the social and economic hierarchy. They were also significantly older. Approximately 60 percent of the men fined in Essex County fornication proceedings involving unmarried young women were at least twenty-seven years old. These disparities of age and status, to Hambleton, are "evidence not of an affective bond but of a predatory relationship."

Only rarely were any of these men, by definition more important to the community than the girls they impregnated, punished for their behavior. This led to a subclass of women in Puritan New England who lost their virginities to older, more powerful, and, frequently, predatory men, then ended up paying for it for the rest of their lives. Despite the superficial egalitarianism of the way this moral offense was punished in the Holy Commonwealth, with unmarried and married fornicators punished equally under the law, genuine redemption of a virginity lost outside of marriage was reserved for parties of two.

CHAPTER 11

The Erotic Virgin

A virginity taken by a street boy of sixteen is a pearl cast to a swine.
—Walter, anonymous author of *My Secret Life*

REGARDING ONLY WHAT IS BELOW THE GIRDLE, it is impossible of two Women to know an old from a young one. And as in the dark all Cats are grey, the Pleasure of corporal Enjoyment with an Old Woman is at least equal, and frequently superior, every Knack being by Practice capable of Improvement," Benjamin Franklin wrote in a 1745 letter to a friend. In this famous missive, he pointed out that from the male perspective, sex with older and more experienced women had a great deal to recommend it. Recognizing that "the debauching of a Virgin may be her Ruin, and make her for Life unhappy," and "having made a young Girl miserable may give you frequent bitter Reflections," Franklin concludes that any man is likely to be better served by a woman of some experience than he is by a virgin.

Franklin's opinions on the subject were doubtless a matter of considerable reflection and experience: he was well known as a lifelong ladies' man. For much of Western history, though, those sharing Franklin's sentiments have been in the distinct minority. For several hundred years—and possibly longer, although it is difficult to document these things in the West prior to the late-Renaissance flowering of pornography—the virgin has been touted as the ultimate erotic experience, a sort of sexual Holy Grail.

In this case as in so many other instances where we appear to be talking about virgins, what we're really discussing isn't virgins at all but what other people believe is true about them. (The erotic experiences and attitudes of actual virgins are virtually never taken into account for the simple, if inaccurate, reason that virgins are assumed not to have erotic experiences or attitudes to discuss.) When we talk about "the erotic virgin," we are not talking about virgins' subjective experiences but about how virgins have been experienced and imagined *as* erotic objects.

Pleasure, Power, and Projection

Why should virginity ever be perceived as sexy? A woman who has not been sexually active is a valuable commodity for genetic, and thus socioeconomic, reasons. In cultures where paternity is the underlying principle of social and economic organization, this is critical. But verifiable paternity itself is much too abstract to be sexy. One might argue that virginity is perceived as sexy because virgins are sexually appealing. But everyone alive, whether ugly or lovely, graceful or lumpen, is at some point a virgin. Nor can we make a reasonable claim that all virgins possess some physical quality that makes them more gratifying sex partners. This is particularly untrue in regard to virginal genitalia, which vary every bit as much as the nonvirginal variety except insofar as the specifics of their experience are concerned.

We come a bit closer to understanding what makes virginity sexy when we consider that virgins are often referred to as being "untouched." What is sexy about virgins is, in a very real way, their unknownness. Any virgin's body can be *believed* to possess specific appealing qualities. There is, after all, no evidence to the contrary. A virgin is a blank screen upon which to project one's fantasies of sex and of virginity itself. No matter how much we intellectually grasp that virgins and virginities are far from uniform, the fact that no one has yet proven *this* virgin to be one thing or the other means that we can fantasize that she is the way virgins are "supposed to be," whatever *that* may be in our minds.

A number of the things we believe virgins are supposed to be sexually are the very same things that are used as evidence in virginity tests. The Talmud, romance novelists, theologians, and pornographers all wax obsessive about the portentous and supposedly invariable tightness of the virgin vagina; it makes perfect sense that medical texts and sex toy catalogues alike offer means of generating said vaginal tightness through methods as diverse as exercises, irritants, and surgery. It is no coincidence that the demurely downcast eyes, chaste demeanor, and earnest ignorance that "prove" a virgin to Tertullian, Albertus Magnus, or William Acton are the very things that arouse the narrator of the nineteenth-century sex memoir *My Secret Life* to bribery, blackmail, and even self-acknowledged, outright rape. The bloody bedclothes demanded in the book of Deuteronomy are a critical part of the attraction for Mr. Norbert, the jaded *Fanny Hill* brothel patron who purchases Fanny's elaborately artificial "virginity" for an extravagant sum.

In fetishizing virginity just as in "proving" it, what counts most is whatever can be made outward and visible, because the thing itself remains eternally elusive. The elusiveness and evanescence of virginity, too, is part of the attraction for some virgin chasers. After all, how much more thrilling the hunt when the quarry is so tricky and fragile? Virginity has long been invested with magic powers. Faith in traditional virginity magic having become at least as rare, these days, as unicorns, it is little wonder that we are inclined to believe that virginity has magic powers in one of the only realms of human experience in which we still acknowledge transcendent experiences: eroticism.

The erotic specialness of virginity is not unlike the emperor's famous clothes. Few people have both the perspective and the temerity to question the nature, much less the existence, of something virtually everyone has agreed not only exists but is fabulously special. Therefore it does exist, and to the victor belong the spoils. And "spoils" is precisely the right word. Virgins as a class are a renewable resource—recall Jerome's comment that he could praise marriage because it produced virgins—but it was also Jerome who noted that not even God could raise up a virgin who had fallen. At the same time, because the body itself is notoriously silent on such matters, no one but God can accurately know whether a virgin has "fallen" or not. For the rest of us, and for virginity fetishists as for virginity testers, there is a constant search for tangible signs and the perpetual reiteration, in story after story, of what those signs mean.

The virginity fetishist's bounty consists of stories. Particularly popular among these stories is the tale of the skilled "conversion" of resistant virgin into willing wench. In these conversion stories, vanquished virginity is the key to sexual "realness" and mastery: it takes a "real man" to convert a virginal "little girl" into a sexually eager "real woman," and she is appropriately grateful. By being the first to have sex with her, the man literally makes the woman. A woman who does not like sex or who is lesbian is often snidely said to have "never had the right man," implying that if she had, she, too, would naturally have been converted—*abracadabra!*—by the magic of the "right" male wand.

Men also are "made" when they lose their virginity, but in a very different way. A woman who loses her virginity loses her mastery over access to her own person: she has been had. A man who loses his virginity, on the other hand, gains mastery. Our slang reflects it: a man "pops her cherry," but a woman "gives it up to him," a man "breaks her in," a woman "gets her hymen busted." Sex makes both men and women "real," but the subtext that the real male masters, while the real woman *is* mastered, remains.

Beyond mastery lies connoisseurship. Virginity, or so numerous sources assure us, is a proper object of such an approach. Indeed, some writers have insisted that sex with a virgin is quite lost on the average uneducated slob. "Few of the tens of thousands of whores in London gave their virginities either to gentlemen, or to young or old men—or to men at all," writes the upper-class narrator of the remarkable four-thousand-page sexual diary *My Secret Life*. "Their own low class lads had them. The street boys' dirty pricks went up their little cunts first. This is greatly to be regretted, for street boys cannot appreciate the treasures they destroy. A virginity taken by a street boy of sixteen is a pearl cast to a swine. Any cunt is good enough for such inexperience. To such an animal, a matron of fifty or sixty would give him as much, if not more pleasure than a virgin." This is an erotic outlook that depends in every way on a strict ideology of class and merit among men, and an even stricter ideology of the erotic value of virgin women.

All this begs the question: why? What's the attraction? What, for instance, is the sex tourist negotiating for the services of a child prostitute in a Patpong bar—or an Atlanta back room—really buying? What are the people who purchase a membership to Sexhymen.com getting for their money that they couldn't get from any other pornographic Web site? Is there something that can be gotten from virgins that genuinely cannot be obtained from a nonvirginal source? Medicine, science, sociology, and a not inconsiderable body of anecdotal evidence argue that there isn't. But perhaps all we need to know is that the most important sexual organ of all is found not between our legs but between our ears. To look for external proof of the erotic superiority of virgins is to put the cart before the horse: all we really need to know is whether one believes that it is true.

Épater le Bourgeois?

The end of virginity is no simple, tidy ending. It cannot be. Virginity drags too much history behind it. To interact sexually with a virgin is to interact sexually in a larger sense with parents, the law, maybe even God. It creates tension and changes social roles. It invokes vulnerability, breakage, and injury as well as validation, transformation, and completion. At the same time, it is often an occasion of demystification and disillusion. Holiness and sin are bound up in it, as are purity and pollution, fetish and taboo, anxiety and fear. Transgression seems inevitable, and unsurprisingly it is one of the primary fuels on which the erotic virgin mythos runs. Of all the motifs that flourish in virginity-related pornography, the most popular are invasion, possession, and destruction. But ultimately, such transgression is not truly transgressive at all. It is in fact terrifically socially conservative, and serves only to reinforce the system that holds virginity up as something that can be transgressed against in the first place.

The erotics of virginity are the priorities of patriarchal sexuality writ large. In eroticizing virginity, youth, physical nubility, ignorance, inexperience, fragility, and vulnerability are objectified from the perspective of someone who, by definition, is none of these things. The erotic charge of sex with a virgin rests on the interplay of the sexual aggression of an experienced partner and the sexual submission of a virginal one. It champions sex as a vehicle for completion and transformation, and it insists that a person who has sexual access to a woman automatically claims or colonizes her, body and soul. It likewise demands that no woman may be considered sexually real by herself, that it is only through the sexual action of a male partner that her sexuality is truly summoned into being.

Virginity porn imagery underscores these patriarchal priorities. It does so in a very specific way, intensely focused on giving the impression of newness, artlessness, and natural beauty. The women whose images make up so much of virginity porn have skin that is youthfully flawless and fair. Their makeup is subtle or nonexistent. There is a particular avoidance of the exaggerated lipstick and mouth gestures so common to the rest of the porn industry. A darkly painted, O-shaped mouth is too overtly a sexual performance, and this is a context where it is crucial that we be allowed to believe that there is no artifice, that whatever sexuality we see is the real McCoy.

There is a definite tendency, in this pornography, to visually recall early puberty. There is an emphasis on small breasts, slim hips, and pert buttocks. Models' hair is usually worn long but in styles typical of childhood, either left hanging and unadorned or, in what has become a virgin-porn cliché, schoolgirl styles like pigtails, ponytails, or braids. When virgin men are involved—which they are both in male-on-male pornography and in scenarios depicting mutual heterosexual virginity loss—they are likewise visibly young and fair, with little or no facial or body hair, and slim and lightly muscled, with dewy, plump skin. Their hair also may be tousled or slightly clumsy in cut, again a bid to showcase the supposed artlessness of youth.

These trends are extended with impeccable thoroughness to the genitals. Pubic hair is generally trimmed or shaven, both by porn industry standard and because there appears to be an expectation, well reflected in the prose pornography featuring virgins, that the virgin, perhaps because she is not a "real woman" yet, will have only a sparse growth of the stuff. The genitals themselves have the same attributes as the bodies overall. Plump, pink, and healthy, they never show any sign of droopiness. Labia majora are pert and smooth, labia minora small and symmetrical. Scrotums and breasts alike are firm, high, and taut, never pendulous. It is rare for genitals to display normal variation in skin texture or color, and typically they are pale.

In the extreme gynecological close-up, which is a staple of virginity porn whether in prose or picture, vaginas are inevitably depicted as both tight and tiny. Paradoxically, vaginal size is one of the things written pornography can describe more convincingly than photographs can show, because so little of the vagina is visible from the outside. But to ensure that a "tight" impression is given in photos, virginity-porn vaginas generally appear in isolation, disabling size comparisons. Some photographic close-ups purporting to show a "tiny virgin vagina" do not show the vagina at all, but rather the significantly smaller opening of the urethra. This sleight-of-hand goes completely unnoticed by the average porn consumer, who lacks the background to know the difference and who has, for that matter, already willingly suspended his disbelief in regard to what he is being shown.

Suspension of disbelief works in pornographers' favor not just in regard to urethral imposture, but in relation to the hymens of virginity porn. A popular focus object for virginity porn photos, they often appear retouched or perhaps even prosthetic, with strange skin tones and textures. But whether these hymens are fakes—and many of them transparently are—is only tangentially important. After all, how many viewers are in a position to be able to judge the authenticity of what they see, or will even care? They're much more concerned with the fact that they get to see it at all, whatever "it" is. What is important is not that the hymen is real but that it is really obvious. For the purposes of pornography, a hymen can be many things, even many improbable things, such as easily visible from across a room or an incongruous shade of Day-Glo pink. What it cannot be is ambiguous.

From hairdos to hymens, the message transmitted by the bodies of virginity porn is that of nubility and inexperience. They appear *ready* for experience, but they dare not show signs of having already had it. Breasts can never be allowed to sag. Elaborate hairstyles show too much sophistication and forethought. Stretch marks are out of the question. The bodies virginity porn offers to us are pristine, unmarked, and ready to be inscribed by the experience of being sexually claimed. Such carefully "natural" casualness, combined with the genre's standard stockpile of imagery of middle-class normalcy and iconic teen kitsch, bears an insistent, specific message. Magazines like *Hustler* subsidiary *Barely Legal* and its many porn-industry siblings depict their youthful beauties in contexts like suburban bedrooms, college dorms, locker rooms, school gym showers. The women are described as cheerleaders, students, babysitters, and sorority girls. Adult they may be, in the "all models are over eighteen" sense, but the immaturity symbolism is insistent.

The ultimate destination of virginity porn is defloration. Whether it is explicitly shown in a given piece of porn or is left for the reader or viewer to finish off in fantasy, the trajectory is unmistakable. When it is depicted, it must contain either penetration in action, one or more of the classic signs of lost virginity, or some combination. The hands-down favorite talisman of virginity-loss porn is blood. The Web site Ifitbleeds.com not only boasts an appropriately sanguinary name, but takes as its tagline not the journalistic truism "If it bleeds, it leads" (perhaps rejected as being too literary) but instead "If it bleeds, we can fuck it!" Virginity porn Web sites, films, and pictorials entice would-be viewers with copy like "Break their hymens!" and "You'll see their panties, their bedsheets, and more," and "You can see her bloody cherry." Never mind that much of the blood that is visible in photographic virginity porn is suspiciously copious and often appears artificial. This, too, has a long and honorable tradition.

Two other signature motifs of virginity porn are "proof" of the woman's enjoyment and the trope of transformation. There is often a special emphasis on the "realness" of the transformation inherent in first-time penetrative sex. Newvirginseveryday.com promises that the subscriber will see "the cocks that turned these little girls into real women," and furthermore tells us that "you can't afford to miss a second of their journey into REAL womanhood" (emphasis in the original). The "instant nymphomaniac," the virgin who becomes sexually voracious upon losing her virginity, is another of the images on offer. We also frequently find the virgin voyeur, who witnesses others having sex and thus becomes eager to have sex herself, or the virgin who is "sexually awakened" so that she will desire sex and willingly give up her virginity.

The motifs are often combined for greater effect. In the nineteenth-century *The Amatory Experiences of a Surgeon*, the surgeon of the title not only gradually awakens the inherent lust of a bedridden young patient to the point where she asks him to deflower her, but the defloration has "such a salubrious effect on my young patient that she eventually quite got the better of her spinal complaint, and was married at the age of eighteen." In virginity pornography, sex is a panacea. It cures immaturity by converting girls into women, transforms the ignorant into the knowledgeable, and turns the unwilling into the eager. It takes incapacitated girls and bestows upon them the capacity for wifehood. These fantasies transgress nothing. They are fantasies of male mastery and female conformity.

Bad Behavior and the Modern Man

The tendency to frame defloration as rebellion is in many ways only to be expected, given the time period in which eroticized virginity first came to the fore. Sexually explicit art and writing have been with us in various forms and modes since before the ancient Greeks, but the virgin as an erotic object really only comes into view beginning in what historians call the modern era, roughly from the sixteenth century forward.

Prior to the sixteenth century, pornography as we know it today did not truly exist. This was not because the sixteenth century represented a second Fall from some porn-free Eden, but because prior to the sixteenth century, the goal of obscenity was unlikely to be entirely prurient. Instead, obscenity might have ritual or mythological significance, as with the legions of phalluses that decorated ancient Rome. It could be an aspect of public entertainment (a lewd painting, joke, or song) or an advertisement for a brothel. It might sharpen the bite of satire, as in *Lysistrata*, the *Satyricon*, *Gargantua and Pantagruel*, *The Canterbury Tales*, or the paintings of Hieronymous Bosch. A lack of what we would now recognize as pornography did not mean a lack of obscenity or sexual content in the cultural waters of those times. Graphic sexual content has always been with us. It simply hasn't always been directed toward the same ends.

As a result of all this earthy art and prose, however, we have a reasonably good idea of what previous generations found smutty or sexy, and virginity seems not to have been much on their minds. In late-medieval Rabelais and Chaucer, for example, the classic erotically objectified woman is not a virgin but a young and lovely wife, like the saucy Alisoun of "The Miller's Tale" in *The Canterbury Tales*. Nor do we find the virgin in the book that arguably began the genre of modern, smut-for-smut's-sake pornography, Pietro Aretino's lavishly illustrated *Sonetti lussuriosi* of 1524. When we find her in Aretino's later *Ragionamenti* (two volumes, 1534–1536), she is not eroticized. Rather, she is a nun, established as one of the three types of women in Aretino's world: nun, wife, and whore.

When virginity does begin to appear in eroticized contexts in the High Renaissance, it is not particularly sexy. Classicized virgins, among them rather a lot of Artemises and Athenas (Queen Elizabeth I was frequently compared to Athena), were depicted as sexually attractive but also as inaccessible, and in fact opposed to carnality. As any reasonably well-educated member of the upper classes knew, those who tried to treat the virgin goddesses as erotic objects paid a hefty price: Actaeon was turned into a stag, Tiriesias was blinded. Conceptualizing well-born virgins as Athenas suited elite models of courtship. It supported the abstracted modes of public flirtation, such as the composition and performance of poems and songs, with which marriageable young people amused themselves while dynastic and political marriage negotiations were hammered out behind closed doors by their older relatives. Being an Athena was, to be sure, a limited-time offer, as virtually all of these young goddesses were destined for marriage. But as an archetype the Athena flourished, her virginity formally immune to sexual objectification.

Virgins of the lower classes, who began to emerge in literature and imagery shortly after the Athenas, had no such immunity. Like the Athena, the Servant Girl was also seen as sexually attractive and desirable. But where the Athena was protected by her rank and its corresponding veneer of classical otherworldliness, the Servant Girl's virginity was eminently worldly and vulnerable. Because it was vulnerable, it also became wily. If the Athena's virginity was notable because it was so lofty as to be untouchable, the Servant Girl's virginity was notable precisely because it was so accessible. Servant Girls, on the one hand, were held to be remarkable for the feistiness and skill with which they resisted would-be seducers. On the other, their poverty and lack of education was seen as making them unusually vulnerable to sexual predators.

Then as now, men's attempts on working-class women's virginity often became the site of pitched battles, such as the ones described in the popular early-eighteenth-century song "My Thing Is My Own."

A master of music came with intent
To give me a lesson on my instrument.
I thanked him for nothing, and bid him be gone,
For my little fiddle must not be played on.

Chorus: My thing is my own, and I'll keep it so still,
Other young lasses may do as they will,
My thing is my own, and I'll keep it apart
And no man shall have it 'til I have his heart.

A cunning clockmaker did court me as well,
And promised me riches if I'd ring his bell.
So I looked at his clockwork, and said with a shock,
"Your pendulum's far too small for my clock."

Written down by Thomas d'Urfey in his 1719 *Pills to Purge Melancholy*, this song speaks volumes about the nature of the working-class battle between the sexes. Conflict over material resources, relationship security, social acceptability, bodily safety, love, and men's right to expect women to fulfill their sexual desires are all in

the mix. Not coincidentally, so is the matter of female erotic pleasure, with unabashed comments about penis size. Neither classical allusion nor religious scruple
matters much here. Urban caginess, on the other hand, matters a great deal.

Town and Country

The eroticization of virginity is tied to the rise of capitalism and the growth of
cities. Beginning in the sixteenth century, the rise of capitalist economies and
the eventual prominence of an industrial, rather than an agricultural, economy
transformed both geography and culture. Over time, currency replaced land
as the primary vehicle for wealth. Working for wages, and commerce via currency, became the mode by which labor was done and trading carried out.
Cities, particularly those strategically sited for good transportation and ship-
ping, grew at exponential rates over a very short time. London was the biggest
of all, its population handily outstripping that of its nearest rival, Paris, to become the first Western city to hit the one million mark around 1835.

As cities grew ever larger and denser, and jobs within this new urban-
industrial world grew increasingly specific and specialized, there was inevitable
social fallout. All the daily needs of the people living in these huge cities had to
be handled: clothing, food, fuel, sanitation. Ever-larger numbers of support
staff, like cooks, maids, grooms, seamstresses, laundresses, peddlers, tailors,
porters, valets, and delivery boys, were required to fill these and other needs.
The moneymaking opportunities the big cities offered lured countless thousands of rural men, women, and children. They arrived by the wide-eyed cart-
load, and suddenly discovered that the big city had its own rules of engagement
about which they knew virtually nothing.

Which brings us back to our virginal Servant Girl. It is possible, were she
city born and bred, and a particularly quick and lucky study as well, that she
might have been the chary urbanite of "My Thing Is My Own." But far more
commonly she was a great deal more along the lines of the babe in the woods
we meet in the first chapter of *Fanny Hill*. Raised with the social expectations
of the village or rural community, where geographic stability and community
interdependence provided for a certain degree of honesty or at least accounta-
bility in regard to standards of behavior, these girls lost their safety nets when
they arrived in the cities.

Friendless and penniless, new arrivals had few options. And while these country girls might succeed in protecting their virginity through the rocky acclimation period, they also might not. There were, notoriously, brothel-keepers who might trick new arrivals into becoming new hires, and preda-tory employers who would prey sexually on recently arrived rural women who didn't have anywhere else to go. But a young woman also had to con-tend with her own perfectly normal desires for affection, comfort, and plea-sure. The poverty, hard work, and social isolation of migrant life left women vulnerable. Such vulnerabilities were well known and well exploited. As another tune in d'Urfey's *Pills* counsels, "would ye have a young Virgin of fifteen Years," one must merely "wittily, prettily talk her down . . . and all's your own."

Sophisticated, naive, or somewhere in between, the Servant Girl inevitably had to contend with the issue of sex. Reflecting this, stories of menaced vir-ginity became signature narratives of the eighteenth century. The opening chapters of *Fanny Hill* are one famous example of this (as they are of so many other things), but there are many more. The earlier of Samuel Richardson's two titanic morality-play novels on the theme, *Pamela* (1740), is an operatically proportioned version of this tale. *Pamela* ends victoriously with marriage, but Richardson's later *Clarissa* (1748) ends with its heroine falling victim to rape. The legendary Marquis de Sade wrote his own dramatically darker versions of the story, *Juliette* and *Justine*. Whether comic or tragic, the story of the men-aced lower-class virgin serving in a sexually threatening upper-class milieu re-mained a constant in books and plays partly because of the accuracy with which art imitated life.

Print, Protestants, and the Pox

Of the various things that contributed to the creation of a climate in which vir-ginity became a pronounced sexual obsession, one of the most influential was the emergence of a popular press. Books were crucial to the formation and dis-semination of the idea that virginity was something that could be objectified as a thing in and of itself, without real reference to the women who nominally possessed it. Popular books like Nicholas Venette's enormously influential *The Mysteries of Conjugal Love Reveal'd* and the anonymously authored *Aristotle's*

*Master-Piece** helped to transmit the idea of virginity as a physical object to a readership that was growing by leaps and bounds.

What readers learned about virginity from these books was that it was, as the anatomical description of the hymen in *Aristotle's Master-Piece* made clear, an object. To be sure, it was an object that gave rise to a great deal of anxiety: medical books like Venette's, as well as novels like *Fanny Hill* and *Moll Flanders*, exposed their readers not just to an objectified version of virginity but revealed the existence of age-old practices of "sophistication." The spiritual, moral, and psychological aspects of virginity preeminent in the minds of Augustine or Hildegard or even Aquinas had been shoved brusquely onto the back burner. Virginity was an object now, a thing in itself, something that could be discussed in isolation, as if it had no connection to the body of a living, thinking, feeling human being. This was a version of virginity that required no metaphysics whatsoever and indeed admitted none. Conquering the maiden could be considered a separate problem from the more straightforward task of conquering the maidenhead.

Maidenheads were there to be had, and at a disadvantage to boot. Whether a woman was a young girl arrived fresh from the countryside, a daughter of the working classes, or a spinster who had to make ends meet somehow, unmarried women were economically and personally vulnerable. The sexual exploitation of domestic workers was sufficiently widespread that Edmond and Jules de Goncourt, the elegantly acerbic literary lions of the French nineteenth century, defined a housemaid as "a girl who was ruined by the young man of a household." For really, what was to stop him? Differences of wealth, social status, and gender put the power on the male side. Most men felt little or no responsibility for whatever consequences might befall a woman with whom they had had a sexual liaison.

For men, the benefits of recreational sex easily outweighed its potential risks. Socially, it was often seen as proof of virility, an asset. As for venereal disease, the frequent affliction of the roué, it was merely another factor in favor of seeking sex with virgins. Both gonorrhea and syphilis were rampant in early

---

*Venette's book was reprinted in multiple editions and pressings from the time of the 1696 French original to the last British edition, which came out sometime after 1774; versions of *Aristotle's Master-Piece* appeared from the seventeenth to the nineteenth centuries and were in circulation well into the twentieth.

modern Europe, treatable but not yet curable. The cautious lothario would thus often seek virgins out on that basis alone. In his 1724 *A Modest Defence of Publick Stews* ("stew" being a term for "brothel"), Bernard Mandeville wrote of "epicures in venery," men who pursued sex exclusively with virgins. This erotic fixation on virginity is, however, defensible in Mandeville's eyes, for it is "chiefly for their own personal Safety." Escaping a "taint" or "the pox," Mandeville felt, was a good reason to prefer virginal women, for, as he wrote, "some Men are afraid of venturing even after themselves."

Overall there was a sensibility, among the early modern men who pursued sex with virgins, that the only damage they were really doing was mechanical and short-term. It was both natural and inevitable that a woman be penetrated by a man; every young woman would lose her virginity eventually. Men and procuresses might even congratulate themselves on having done the deflowered woman a favor, on the theory that the indignity were less if a woman were deflowered by a man of station than some member of the great unwashed. Combine these attitudes with a world in which cash had become king, cities swarmed with economic migrants, and the extended agricultural family gave way to fragmented groups of poor people dependent on whatever coin they could bring in, and the presence of a growing bourgeoisie with a well-established fascination for sex and a tendency to spend large sums on luxuries, and the development of a sizeable virginal sex industry should come as no surprise whatsoever.

Virtue and Vice

The sale of virginities as a commonplace branch of prostitution begins to appear in the historical record around the beginning of the eighteenth century. Mandeville's *Defence* makes the availability of virgins-for-hire clear, and there are occasional references in seventeenth-century brothel and entertainment guides to cities like London and Venice intended for wealthy travelers. Brussels was anecdotally claimed to be a hotbed of brothel deflorations as late as the turn of the twentieth century. Cleland's *Fanny Hill*, of course, is often pointed to as evidence of the trade in maidenheads, and it seems reasonable to take it as being at least representative if not documentary. The bulk of the evidence we have to work with on the question of the prostitution of virginity, however, comes from nineteenth-century England.

This was the time of the great surge of middle-class philanthropy, the era when urban poverty and its attendant problems had finally begun to draw attention from organized groups of private citizens. We know relatively little about the prostitution of virgins in the nineteenth century, and what we do know is available to us primarily because of the work done by those who were attempting to eradicate the practice. But using these records creates some problems for the historian.

The gulf between the philanthropists and the women they wanted to reform was huge. The world of prostitutes and the poor, as described in the accounts of these philanthropists, is routinely filtered through the pens of people who were neither and often looked down on both. There was continual, uneasy, mutual distrust between those who had realized that virtue alone rarely put bread in their mouths or clothes on their backs and those who, having no shortage of bread or clothes, had no reason to empathize with a shortage of virtue either.

For these reformers, the only conceivable reasons that a woman might enter into prostitution were either that she had been seduced or raped and abandoned, that she were facing starvation, or both. Anything else was scarcely imaginable to them. Prostitutes who seemed glad of the ability to keep a roof over their heads, dress themselves suitably for their needs, and eat regularly were characterized as dissolute and sinfully devoted to fashion and luxury. Women who openly enjoyed male company and sex were seen as wanton and essentially irredeemable. The very existence of unapologetic sex workers, particularly those who brought other women into the life or worked as brothel-keepers, abjectly contradicted the popular notion that there was an inborn female essence of purity, nurture, and virtue. In such perverted creatures, womanhood itself disappeared: no less an eminence than Dr. Elizabeth Blackwell wrote that such women became "human tigers who delight in destruction and torture." Indeed, prostitution was believed to make women disappear. There was a notion widely repeated among reformers (despite ample evidence in their own writings of women who had been involved with prostitution for decades) that three years of prostitution were enough to kill any woman.

The truth of the matter is that then as now, women of virtually every type and temperament existed within the sex industry. Many were genuinely victimized and hapless, and those stories are heartbreaking and horrible. But it is no more true that every prostitute was a victim of sexual predation than it is that career prostitutes dropped dead promptly upon spending three years in the business. Nor is it true, despite the vivid claims of many reformers, that every woman who fell into prostitution even once stayed there for good. Occasional casual prostitution was a relatively common means for poor women to supplement the skimpy wages they received for their regular work, and was sometimes done with the knowledge of husbands or parents.

In considering the prostitution of virgins, it's important to keep all this in mind, and also to remember that what the reformers were willing to show of the trade in maidenheads is as driven by its own agendas as any pornographic version. In fact, reformers' writings about virgin prostitution often sound dramatically like pornography on the same subject, except that where the pornographer writes in order to induce lust, the reformer writes to generate shock and disgust. The object of reform literature was never accuracy. It was emotion—in the interest of spurring political and social action.

What can be pried from philanthropists' writings about the sale of virginities reveals that while it was an acknowledged market, it was also considered a relatively risky one and existed mostly on the quiet. Along with sadism, masochism, bondage, and various less-exotic perversions like anal intercourse, a taste for virgins was just another of the variegated sexual tastes that could be catered to in the brothels if one knew the right people and had sufficiently deep pockets.

We also know some of what a virgin-hunter looked for, knowing as he did that brothelkeepers might try to pass off nonvirgins as the genuine article. There were a number of characteristics that were considered hallmarks of a genuine virgin, generally some combination of a rural background, naïveté, and youth. Rural life was seen as wholesome and clean, both literally and metaphorically, by comparison to the filth of the cities. Naïveté, such as a lack of awareness of what a "seduction" actually entailed or what was meant when a procuress offered money if a girl would go "play a game with a gentleman," was considered a sure sign that the young woman was not only physically inexperienced, but was too ignorant to recognize the value of her own virginity. Youth, of course, was the sine qua non.

The Maiden Tribute of Modern Babylon

Youth was also the sine qua non of the controversy over the prostitution of virgins, and of the special and concentrated efforts of reformers to end it. At stake in this controversy was nothing less than a redefinition of what it meant, both culturally and legally, to be a child. Passage of the Criminal Law Amendment Act in 1885 raised the age of sexual consent in England from twelve (prior to 1875) and thirteen (during the decade 1875–1885) to sixteen. Because it was the law, and because those engaged in legally risky practices have a remarkable tendency to know the letter of the laws to which they might be held, these ages formed a more or less functional bottom line for both brothel owners and their clients. What to our modern eyes looks like pedophilia was legally nothing of the sort, prior to 1885. By law, at that point, thirteen-year-olds were not girls but women, and therefore prostituting them was no particularly special crime.

But this would not be the case for long. The culture was changing, and with it, views on both childhood and sexuality were changing, too. Beliefs that children should be sheltered from the harsh realities of the world, that exposure to sexual images and ideas is injurious to children, that children should not be required to work, and that children are naturally innocent are all notions that rose to cultural prominence along with the nineteenth-century middle class from whose ranks the philanthropists came.

The poor could scarcely afford to be so high-minded about children and childhood. Thirteen, however young it may have been for sex, was not at all young to be earning a living. Child labor was endemic to the nineteenth century, and the children of the poor worked as a matter of course. Children of the poor were rarely schooled beyond rudiments, if they got even that much, for formal education took money their families did not have to spare. Instead, as soon as they were judged to be capable, most poor children worked. In rural areas, children labored alongside their parents and relatives in the home, in the fields, and in small family businesses. In the cities, they might help their parents at work, but were just as frequently employed elsewhere. Children as young as four or five worked in factories, mines, and sweatshops. Children also worked in the streets in massive numbers, selling matches and newspapers, hawking various wares, touting entertainments, running errands, and so forth. This was not exceptional. For better than half the population, it was the norm.

When we consider the plight of the nineteenth-century adolescent who sold her virginity for cash, we cannot afford the luxury of thinking of her according to our own contemporary standards. She was expected to do what she could to earn money in order to to help support her family or to provide for herself, and sexual labor was not necessarily out of the question. Indeed, her parents themselves may well have viewed their daughter's virginity as a realizable asset. Trading a daughter's virginity for a spot of cash rather than a strategic marriage is merely a testament to the exigencies of living hand-to-mouth, not evidence of an attitude about women that was fundamentally different from that of the upper classes.

Furthermore, the daughters of the poor were already considered worldly, to a certain extent, in the eyes of others, and were commonly assumed to dispose of their virginities at the first possible opportunity. How, when exposed to the interactions and enticements of the classically male public realms of commerce and the street, could they possibly stay pure?

In reality, they were often purer—or at least remarkably more ignorant in some respects—than one might expect. The carnal culture of the nineteenth century was a firmly double one, as revealed by historian Peter Gay in his landmark study *The Bourgeois Experience: Victoria to Freud*, in which an intimate familiarity with the grisly realities of life from the butchering of food animals to the squalor of urban poverty went hand in hand with a carefully maintained, strictly gendered, sexual ignorance. "Respectable" women were expected to have no awareness of matters sexual until such time as marriage forced the issue. In an 1843 letter to her half-brother, novelist George Sand summed up women's sexual lot in middle-class Victorian society: "We bring them up, as much as we can, as saints, and then we hand them over like fillies."

The taboo on sexual matters was hardly limited to bourgeois and upper-class families. Although it is probable that poor children would have been exposed to more sexually explicit scenes and information simply because their living spaces were likely to be quite crowded, it does not follow that they were more sexually self-aware as a result. Nor does it follow that they would have been better educated in regard to what their sexual futures might hold. Procuresses and reformers alike understood what all this meant: poor young women were likely to be an easy mark. The proceeds of a virginity sale did not have to be more than one or two pounds sterling to represent a lump sum greater than most of them had ever had to work with. Most had a limited understanding of what sexual intercourse was or meant, and procurers and johns were happy to reassure young women that everything would be fine. If such soothing failed, a young woman would simply be told that it was inevitable, that it happened to everyone sooner or later, and that she should simply keep a stiff upper lip.

Young women who sold their virginities did not have what we would today term a safety net. Their families could not offer them economic security. They did not have access to education or to jobs that paid well enough to make prostitution seem less appealing. Reformers struggled to find a way to help protect these young women. This meant finding a way to characterize them as a class deserving of state protection. To do so, they used the ingenious—if in some ways disingenuous—expedient of making virginity rhetorically synonymous with childhood.

This trump card was played to international effect in a series of thunderous, vividly sensational 1885 exposés collectively entitled "The Maiden Tribute of Modern Babylon." In them, *Pall Mall Gazette* editor William T. Stead used the image of the victimized child to crack the taboo that had kept the sale of virginity absent from respectable public discourse. Son of a Congregational minister, Stead was, in the fashion of many a pulpit-pounding preacher or favorite professor, an instinctive showman. On July 4, 1885, he set his stage, printing in his *Pall Mall Gazette* a "Notice to our Readers: A Frank Warning" that let the readers know that a "long, detailed report, dealing with those phases of sexual criminality which the Criminal Law Amendment Bill was framed to repress" was to appear in installments beginning the following day.

Titillated not only by the promise of "sexual criminality" but by allusions to "calculation in high quarters" by those who would prevent the Criminal Law Amendment Act from passing into law, readers could scarcely wait for the curtain to rise on what promised to be a cavalcade of scandal. They were not disappointed. In the name of "the most imperious sense of public duty," Stead set forth a thunderous, sensational stream of reportage, centering upon a seemingly ceaseless supply of young women who had either been victimized or narrowly escaped being victimized, each more pathetic than the last. Namechecking the myth of the *jus primae noctis* along the way, Stead created a vision of a world in which the "shameful abuse of the power of wealth" resulted in a situation where "princes and dukes, and ministers and judges, and the rich of all classes, are purchasing for damnation, temporal if not eternal, the as yet uncorrupted daughters of the poor."

Invariably, Stead describes these "as yet uncorrupted daughters" in infantilizing terms. They are "daughters," "girls," "maids," "maidens," "dainty morsels," and "little girls." A young woman may be described as "a frightened lamb," or simply as a child, as in the infamous line with which Stead ends the first lengthy section of his report: "For the child's sob in the darkness curseth deeper than the strong man in his wrath."

The possibility that any of the young women involved might genuinely be willing to participate in such a transaction is, both explicitly and implicitly, discarded out of hand. The actual age or degree of self-awareness or self-sufficiency of these young women seems to be of only incidental relevance to Stead. Young women of sixteen and eighteen, some with professional jobs (one is a cook in a first-class hotel), are discussed in terms identical to those used to describe penniless adolescents of thirteen or fourteen. A sixteen-year-old capable of stating articulately that given a choice between making a small sum of money and not giving up her virginity and giving up her virginity for a large amount of money, she would prefer the latter, is disregarded as incompetent: "Could any proof be more conclusive as to the absolute inability of this girl of sixteen to form an estimate of the value of the only commodity with which the law considers her amply able to deal the day after she is thirteen?" For Stead, any woman who willingly sells her virginity is a child, because only a child could be so ignorant as not to realize that virginity is beyond price.

Stead also takes repeated aim at the middlemen responsible for bringing together those with maidenheads to sell and those with means to buy them. On some levels, this was a wholly appropriate thing to do. But procuresses and their accomplices, no matter how satisfying a target their perverse maternalism made for Stead's outrage, were not the whole of the picture. As with similar modern-day exposés of the trade in illegal drugs, blaming the dealers only obscured the problem of demand.

This demand, Stead claimed, was staggering. Citing procurers who boasted of producing literally dozens of virgins for sale, Stead conjured an image of a rapacious and insatiable market both in England and abroad. He encouraged the impression that this was all a mechanical business, a virtual assembly line in which the bodies of "little girls" were systematically abused for profit and then spit out again at the other end, a nightmarish factory involved in the unfeeling conversion of raw virgin resource into profit.

It is impossible to say to what extent this might have been true. It is quite possible, on the other hand, to detail the extent to which Stead went out of his way to be sure he had a sufficiently spectacular tale to tell. As part of the research that went into "The Maiden Tribute," Stead himself purchased a thirteen-year-old named Eliza Armstrong, whom he called "Lily," for a paltry five pounds. With the help of retired procuress Rebecca Jarrett, whom Stead blackmailed out of retirement to do the dirty work of arranging his virgin-hunting caper, Stead took custody of the girl. He brought her to a midwife, who pronounced her *virgo intacta*. From there, Stead and Jarrett took "Lily" to a brothel in Poland Street, where Jarrett administered a dose of chloroform to the young woman, and after she passed out, left Stead alone with her. Stead waited with the young woman until she woke, then took her to be examined by a physician to certify that nothing sexual had transpired. Afterward, he packed young "Lily" off to Paris so that she was conveniently out of the way while Stead wrote and published "The Maiden Tribute." Without ever identifying himself, and alternately omitting and suggesting details, Stead described this salacious undertaking—although not his part in it or the exportation of its subject to France—to thunderous public furor.

It was a glorious moment for Stead. He was the talk of England, let alone London, unable to print copies of the *Gazette* fast enough. But Eliza Armstrong's mother had been reading the newspapers, too. She recognized her daughter in the descriptions Stead had given and went to the authorities. Aided by competing newspapers, she eventually brought a lawsuit against Stead. (Eliza herself was meanwhile quietly returned to England, none the worse for wear.) The eventual outcome, in November of 1885, was that Stead became the first man in England to be sentenced under the Criminal Law Amendment Act, the very piece of legislation for which his exposé had gathered such effective support. He served a three-month misdemeanor sentence. Cruelly, Rebecca Jarrett, though she had been blackmailed into participating in the scheme, was given a sentence twice as long, as was the midwife involved in the case.

Despite his conviction and prison sentence, and despite the fact that he was essentially ruined as a newspaperman once his journalistic fraud had been exposed, Stead remained convinced that he had not only done the right thing but that Eliza Armstrong, the "frightened lamb" of thirteen whom he had purchased, subjected to two gynecological examinations, drugged unconscious, and sent off to another country, had "experienced not the slightest inconvenience." Nor did Stead's conviction in any way hamper the cause of criminalizing sex with adolescents. "The Maiden Tribute of Modern Babylon" made an intense emotional and motivational impact in England and across the Atlantic as well. In the United States, numerous states revised their ages of consent as well as laws on prostitution and trafficking due to reform efforts prompted by

Stead's "Maiden Tribute" and the prominent "white slavery" activism that succeeded it. Illinois, for instance, raised its age of consent from ten to fourteen in 1887 (it was raised again in 1905, to sixteen). Likewise in 1887, New York's age of consent rose from ten to sixteen. Massachusetts made it illegal to have illicit (i.e., unmarried) intercourse with any person under the age of eighteen. Even notoriously laissez-faire Virginia changed its laws during this same time frame, criminalizing seduction and raising the age of consent from ten to twelve.

Stead's legacy, the canonization in law of the ideal of "female adolescence as a hiatus free from the burdens of adult sexual life," as historian Joan Jacobs Brumberg has aptly put it, probably would have pleased him a great deal. But much of what people took away from Stead's writing (and that of his imitators) is troublesome. In Stead's view, virgins were children not just at five or eleven but at sixteen and eighteen, and at any age they were hapless victims, completely unable to make sexual decisions for themselves. By failing to address the idea of virginity's erotic desirability itself, and harping on the numbers of men he claimed were willing to pay for it, he confirmed and indeed may have enhanced virginity's reputation as a transcendently desirable erotic object. Neither contention is necessarily true. But Stead made them so emotionally compelling that they were—and still frequently are—taken as writ.

The Virginity Void

This is not to say that Stead was necessarily wrong. As with most radical claims, there was certainly a core of truth to Stead's. Young women and children were, then as now, sold into prostitution, and then as now, it is difficult to imagine a more stomach-churning enterprise. Although it was all but lost in the wash of carefully cultivated sensationalism, Stead had a very worthwhile point: children and adolescents generally, and poor children and adolescents specifically, face a well-documented disproportionate risk of sexual exploitation.

This is saddening, maddening, and indisputably true. Youth plus economic and social powerlessness is a pancultural, panmillennial recipe for sexual exploitation and abuse. This was true for the sexually vulnerable slaves of the ancient Mediterranean whose stolen virginity could be repaid by the transfer of a small sum to their master. Cases like those of the "Blood Countess" Erzsébet Báthory; infamous fifteenth-century molester and murderer of boys Gilles de

Rais; and the Abbé Claudius Nicholas des Rues, convicted of having raped 133 virgins in Paris prior to 1726, prove that the same held true thousand of years later.* We have seen the role it played for the many European young women who headed to big cities like London in search of jobs and found themselves prey either to virgin-hunters or to the sexually predatory wiles of their employers. The same combination of youth and poverty plays a large part in the contemporary child sex trade in Asia and even here at home in the First World, where such things are often supposed not to happen. The sexual exploitation of the young has never been limited by time or place. The question, for the purposes of this book, is not whether children and adolescents are sexually abused and exploited—they are. The question is whether or not the sexual exploitation and abuse of children and adolescents has anything to do with the eroticization of virginity.

The answer to this question is far less clear. We simply do not know to what extent those whose sexual desires run toward children and adolescents are motivated by the eroticization of virginity. Bizarrely and tellingly, given how easy it is to come by examples of the desire for virginity and virgins at work, the erotic fascination with virginity has never been identified as its own discrete phenomenon by sexologists, sociologists, or psychiatrists. There is no word for it, and neither the term "parthenophilia" nor the word "virgophilia" is recognized by sexology or medicine.

It is an odd omission. During the formative decades of the disciplines of sexology, psychiatry, and psychoanalysis, terms were developed to describe erotic attractions to children ("pedophilia") or adolescents ("hebephilia" or "ephebephilia"). These terms are still used to describe the attractions of those who sought sex with young adolescents; the term "ephebephilia" is obscure today, but "pedophilia" is a household word.

As W. T. Stead's canny use of terms like "little girl" and "child" and "lamb" makes clear with such admirable economy, there is a significant degree of overlap between the population of virgins and the population of adolescents

---

*The case of the Abbé des Rues was so sensational and titillating that accounts of the trial were published and sold in several languages, demonstrating that the contemporary appetite for salacious true-crime stories as entertainment reading may not be so contemporary after all.

and children. Indeed, we would not bat an eyelash if Stead had referred to "pedophiles" instead of "virgin-hunters." Some portion of the men Stead wrote about may have been pedophiles. But this does not seem to have been the case for all of them. First, not all of the virgins about whom Stead wrote were children, and some were as old as eighteen or twenty. Additionally, some virgin-hunters were described as having a strong preference for postpubertal young women of fifteen, sixteen, or older—neither legally nor culturally children.

"Pedophilia" is not an accurate word to use to describe the erotic desire for virginity for the simple reason that not all virgin fanciers are interested in children and not all pedophiles particularly care about virginity. What I will call parthenophilia—a pronounced sexual interest in virginity or virgins—is a genuine, observable sexual predilection. The reason I propose we have for so long lacked a term for this particular erotic attraction is that unlike sexual interest in children, a sexual interest in virgins is something our culture considers entirely normal, acceptable, and ideologically correct.

No studies have been done on parthenophilia. We do not know how many people experience it. We do not know when the desire begins to be felt, whether those who feel it perceive it as an innate or learned preference. We have no idea how many people have pursued specific sexual encounters on account of this desire, or what kind of sexual encounters they have pursued. No research into its possible role in motivating sexual assault or abuse has been conducted. We do not know to what extent it does or does not play a role in child sexual abuse or child prostitution. Even Sigmund Freud did little more than glance at it.

This is the virginity void. Despite the strength and breadth of the erotic interest taken in virginity in our culture, the three centuries of virginity-related pornography, the China Shrink Creams and Lotus Blossum Pocket Pal masturbation sleeves for men (the package copy touts this particular pink plastic production as a "sleek, silky-soft pussy with intact hymen"), even in the face of all the young women's virginities sold around the world, the erotic desire for virginity has been continually avoided as a subject of intellectual and clinical inquiry, as if there were no reason to ask and nothing that could possibly be learned by asking.

The virginity void exists on the other side of the fence as well. As little as we know about the erotic desire for virginity, we know even less about the erotic lives of virgins. Specifically, we know very little about how virgins themselves might understand themselves to exist as erotic objects or how they might themselves be erotically affected by the mythology of the erotic virgin that so permeates the culture. Virgins are not exempt from the mythologies of their own sexual status, after all. A virgin may well be every bit as erotically caught up in the implications of her own sexual status as the man who fantasizes about popping her cherry, but she is even less likely than he to be asked about it. How strange, in a culture so often obsessed by virginity, that we have chosen to be so blind.

Virginity is not the opposite of sex. Rather, it is its own unique and uniquely troublesome sexual entity, and one we have largely avoided addressing. Our presumptions about virginity have been with us for a very long time and will require a great deal of time and effort to question, let alone change. If we are ever to fill the virginity void with something more realistic than propaganda and more accurate than pornographic fantasy, however, this work is a challenge we would do well to take up.

CHAPTER 12

The Day Virginity Died?

Virgin: teach your kids it's not a dirty word.
—billboard, Baltimore, Maryland, 2003

D ID YOU HEAR about the virgin parade they were going to have in Hollywood?" asked a popular Jazz Age joke. "One girl got sick and the other didn't want to march all alone." As this 1920s joke demonstrates, the liberalization of sexual culture in America started well before the so-called sexual revolution of the 1960s. During the twentieth century, our beliefs and expectations in regard to human nature, our economic lives, our experiences of the body and identity, and our relationships to religion have all undergone massive—and ongoing—change. It is small wonder that our ideals and expectations in regard to virginity have been shifting, too.

As often as magazine articles have lamented the "death of virginity" in the twentieth century, and as many jokes as have been made about virgins being an endangered species, virginity is hardly so fragile as all that. Still, it has been changing, its place in our lives and its role in our culture shifting with the tides of history. We can see the nature of this shift in a massive study conducted in the late 1980s among young adults in thirty-seven different countries around the globe. The study revealed that while for both males and females premarital chastity—virginity—still earned a place in a list of the eighteen characteristics considered most desirable in a potential mate, both men and women ranked it lower than most other traits. What was more, men and women assigned it nearly equal importance—sixteenth most important in the eyes of males and eighteenth most important to women. For men and women alike, virginity was significantly less important than things like "dependable character," "education and intelligence," and "emotional stability."

Clearly, virginity still matters. But just as clearly, it matters differently now than it did a hundred years ago, or five hundred, or a thousand. As the primary determining factor in perceptions of female virtue, honor, character, and worth, virginity is indeed on the decline. If we believe that reckoning intrinsic human value should be based on deeper and more substantive qualities than whether or not someone has once been sexually active, we should find this pleasing.

The Empirical Virgin

There is in any event little point to hysterical proclamations that virginity is vanishing. To paraphrase P. T. Barnum, there's a virgin born every minute. And as long as human beings have to negotiate the transition into adult-partnered sexuality, virginity will continue to be meaningful both personally and socially. The question we need to be asking is not *whether* the culture of virginity has been changing over the last century or so. It has. The questions we need to be asking are *how* and *why* it has changed and whether or not these changes are yet complete.

The primary way that we have done and continue to do this is through the scientific study of sexuality. Accustomed as we have become to having an empirically based medical establishment, it is sometimes difficult to appreciate how recently this mode of research became commonplace, but in truth we cannot begin to speak of a consistently scientific approach to either medicine or sexuality until the second half of the nineteenth century. Earlier research into sexuality typically depended more upon compelling anecdote than on reproducible data.

Sexology, the scientific study of sexuality, had its beginnings in the late-nineteenth-century work of psychologists and psychiatrists like Havelock Ellis and Richard von Krafft-Ebing. Although early sexologists were primarily concerned with abnormal and criminal sexuality, as in Krafft-Ebing's famous *Psychopathia Sexualis*, they soon began to study the parameters of "normal" sexual desires and activities as well. Surveys of sexual behavior and attitudes began to be conducted in the United States as early as the 1920s. Within a couple of decades, British and continental researchers had begun to follow suit. Still, the kinds of massive, quantitative sex surveys we now think of when we think of sex research did not come into being until after World War II, with Alfred Kinsey's monumental 1948 *Sexual Response in the Human Male*.

However one might be tempted to critique Kinsey's work (and some of the criticism is merited), it nonetheless transformed our expectations about what we could and should know about sex. Prior to Kinsey and Kinsey-influenced research efforts, such as the British Mass Observation surveys that followed close on Kinsey's heels, notions of what could be considered sexually "normal" or "average" were based mostly on hearsay and conjecture. After Kinsey, on the other hand, laypeople and experts alike could point to charts, graphs, and statistics and use them to determine what was and was not "typical." Attempts to take the behavioral and attitudinal measures of entire populations through statistics became a hallmark of sex research.

During the same time period, increasingly rigorous research methods helped to reduce the role that emotions and cultural prejudices played in how the medical establishment dealt with women's bodies. This did not, by any means, magically eradicate sexism within medicine, but it did provide for vastly improved levels of transparency and frankness. Many women eagerly embraced this more matter-of-fact approach to their own reproductive and sexual lives. Women like Stella Browne and Marie Stopes in England and Margaret Sanger in the United States, all of whom worked to educate women about sexual health and contraceptive options in the early years of the twentieth century, were often overwhelmed by the sheer numbers of women who wanted to learn what science had to teach them about their own bodies and sexualities. An unsqueamish and, above all, unsentimental approach to dealing with women's reproductive and sexual health rapidly became the expected standard for the medical profession.

Between 1890 and 1945 the West witnessed the rise of the birth control movement, the first commercially produced menstrual tampons, the establishment of the custom of the premarital gynecologist visit, the requirement (in some places) of venereal disease testing prior to the issue of a marriage license, the beginnings of a sexuality self-help literature written by women, and an increase in the popularity of hospital births.

This new frankness was by no means limited to doctors' offices and the family planning clinics that were beginning to crop up in larger cities. For example, at the phenomenally popular 1939 World's Fair display devoted to the new vaginal product known as Tampax (introduced to American markets in 1936), hundreds of women a day stopped to get information and ask questions of the nurses there to answer them. Topics gynecological were addressed in books, pamphlets, and in the new genre of magazines appealing to female audiences. Even in 1918, a young British couple might get advice on contraceptive devices and sexual compatibility from Marie Stopes's *Married Love*. By 1930 a book intended for similar audiences, Theodor van der Velde's *Ideal Marriage: Its Physiology and Technique*, quite unsqueamishly reassured its readers that many women did not enter married life as virgins. In 1940 books like Oliver Butterfield's *Sex Life in Marriage* provided readers access to clinical detail on topics as explicit as resistant hymens, vaginal lubrication, and "honeymoon" cystitis. Magazine advertisements for contraceptive devices and nostrums tended to remain back-of-the-book items along with other quasi-medical appliances, but advertisements hailing the convenience of tampons moved into the main pages of major women's magazines. Women increasingly felt entitled to take advantage of, and even to demand, no-nonsense, directly vaginal products like tampons that were both convenient and conducive to an active lifestyle. A large number of women clearly wanted to be able to deal with their sexual and reproductive lives in a practical, literally hands-on way. This was particularly true in the United States, where, as contraceptives historian Lara V. Marks has revealed, women were earlier and more fervent adopters of female-controlled intravaginal contraceptives like diaphragms and contraceptive jellies.

At first such products were marketed to and considered acceptable only for married, presumably nonvirginal, women. But this state of affairs did not last long. What mothers and big sisters used and liked in terms of managing their own needs, particularly in regard to menstruation, younger women eventually heard about. And while this "trickle down" effect took some time, it is clear that women of all ages quickly came to embrace tampon use. As early as the end of World War II, Dr. Robert Dickinson's medical assessment of tampon use appeared in both the *Journal of the American Medical Association* and, in a somewhat less technical version, in *Consumer Reports*. Dickinson specifically stated that tampons did not "impede standard anatomic virginity," thus paving the way for younger women to use them and for tampon manufacturers to feel justified in marketing to that demographic. Authors of late-1940s and 1950s office gynecology textbooks took it as a given that any woman of menstruating age might well use tampons.

By the 1980s, up to three-quarters of high school women used tampons regularly. While tampon manufacturers have occasionally felt moved to publicly allay fears that tampon usage threatens virginity, as in a 1990 Tampax ad that showed an introspective, white-shirted teenaged girl beneath the question "Are you sure I'll still be a virgin?" (the ad's text made it clear that the answer to that question was "yes"), on the whole it has become relatively rare for contemporary First World women to question the suitability of tampon use for any woman of menstruating age. The lesson of the tampon was that the vagina could be emotionally and sexually neutral territory. To learn to use tampons to absorb menstrual flow was also to learn that the insertion of an object into the vagina might be purely utilitarian, with no larger social meaning at all.

It is difficult to appreciate, from our current vantage point, just what a radical departure this was from the nineteenth-century view. As in the controversy over the use of the speculum, Victorian doctors and patients alike lived in fear of even the most stringently medical contact with the vulva, let alone vaginal penetration. This permeated the nineteenth century's attitudes toward women and their genitals to the point that Victorian girls and women were ideally not to be permitted to straddle anything, ever. Little girls were kept from riding on seesaws or hobbyhorses, and they were discouraged from running, jumping, or gymnastics, for, as historian of childhood Karin Calvert notes, it was believed that "playing the wrong game or with the wrong toys could prematurely awaken sexual feelings in children and destroy their natural purity." Ladies who rode horseback did so sidesaddle for the same reason. In this paranoid context, even bicycling constituted a terrifying threat. As two-wheelers became more and more popular among middle-class young people around the end of the nineteenth century, the medical journals revealed a feverish, sometimes pornographically detailed, concern that the pressure that the bicycle seat placed on the vulva and perineum not only held the menace of creating "arousing feelings hitherto unknown and unrealized by the young maiden" but might, the articles claimed, contribute to painful and debilitating disorders of the genitals as well.

Intriguingly enough, the idea that such spraddle-legged activities constitute a threat to virginity shows up in sex education texts to this day. Despite the lack of any actual studies in the literature regarding whether horseback riding, gymnastics, or riding bicycles might have a particularly high rate of damaging women's hymens, virtually every contemporary writing about virginity aimed at teen girls is duly equipped with a disclaimer that says something along the lines of "many girls tear or otherwise dilate their hymen while participating in sports like bicycling, horseback riding, or gymnastics." Other activities, like tampon use and masturbation, are sometimes added to the list. But astonishingly, given the near-complete lack of hard evidence to support their inclusion, the odd mantra "bicycling, horseback riding, and gymnastics" shows up again and again.

Today these three activities are invoked in a very different way than they were a hundred years ago. A century of liberalization of attitudes toward women—and sports and sexuality as well—has transformed bicycling, horseback riding, and gymnastics from looming bogeymen into a laundry-list reminder that not all women will have the same experience of virginity loss. Whether or not physical activity can actually damage the hymen is debatable; more debatable still is whether or not the hymen alone is a useful gauge of virginity anyhow. "Bicycling, horseback riding, and gymnastics" is now a placeholder for the idea that just because something happens to physically involve the genitals doesn't mean it's sex. Women's genitals, in other words, may finally be achieving the ability to simply be just another bit of the body, as essentially neutral and as variable as any other.

The New Woman

At the same time as empirical science was transforming attitudes about women's bodies, social and philosophical understandings of women were being transformed by progressivism, urbanization, and, perhaps most of all, by sheer economics. Urbanization, the rise of factory labor, and the accompanying surge of poor and working-class migration to the cities continued at a dizzying pace in the new century. The huge labor market meant that more and more women went to work, not merely as domestics (although many did) but also in sweatshops and factories. Regardless of whether the job was mechanized "women's work," as much sweatshop work still is to this day, or something quite different, women worked for a living and were paid in cash.

Working women worked because they had to earn money to survive. But it would be a mistake to imagine that these women were blind to what it meant that they were breadwinners and had the ability to pay their own way in the world. It would be a bigger error still to imagine that the culture in which this was becoming a more and more common state of affairs could possibly remain unchanged.

Prior to the industrial era, there were only two groups of women who were likely to be self-supporting, the very wealthy whose wealth was inherited and the extremely poor who scraped by on whatever they could earn. Most women married not merely because it was socially expected that they would do so, but because marriage was, as Jane Austen had written nearly a century earlier in *Pride and Prejudice*, the "pleasantest preservative from want." Women were expected to be economically dependent on their husbands, their domestic labor compensated only in kind, not in cash.

Over the course of a century, the wage-earning woman went from being the lower-class exception to being the unexceptional norm. The economic structure of the industrialized West thoroughly incorporated the presence of women's labor. (The same is now true of the global economy as a whole.) This largely unsung revolution of female paid labor provided the economic basis for a great many of the other revolutionary changes in sex and gender roles that took place in the twentieth century.

One of those other changes came under the banner of "human rights." In its simplest form, the philosophy of human rights holds that all human beings are equally deserving of opportunities to thrive and prosper, regardless of their social rank or sex. Progressives made it their business to address not only the horrors of poverty, disease, and various social ills like child labor and prostitution, but also violations of human rights like discrimination against women. Beginning in the late nineteenth century, organized feminism attacked bias against women in multiple arenas, leading to sweeping legal and attitudinal changes that permitted women to own and control their own property, instigate divorce, file lawsuits in their own names, and vote. Forward-thinking activists pushed for more and better public and private educational options for all and were especially vocal in regard to the need for education for girls and women, including sexuality and contraception education.

The working women of the early twentieth century lived in a very different world than their mothers and grandmothers. In many ways they themselves were a different breed: New Women. For these "thoroughly modern Millies," work meant leaving the house to earn a wage and socializing meant "going out." Dance halls, public parks, vaudeville houses, cinemas, restaurants, even beer gardens and nightclubs became the places where young people whose wages were not yet spoken for by spouses and children went to have fun. Music, fashion, art, and public mores all felt the impact of this new, largely young adult money and energy. Women rolled their stockings down and bobbed their long, high-maintenance hair. Skirts got shorter and clothing silhouettes leaner and more boyish. Corsets began to disappear in favor of elasticized girdles that allowed greater freedom of movement.

Perhaps most shocking of all, young women began to let it be known that they were both conscious of, and quite able to manipulate, their own sex appeal. Flappers and vamps visibly flaunted their sexuality on stage, on screen, and in the streets. As the film roles of silent-movie star Clara Bow made clear, being a desirable, sexually successful woman had nothing to do with being a traditionally "good" girl. Bow, also known as "The 'It' Girl," was often cast in the image of her working-class fans as a waitress or salesclerk. Success at love, these films told their audiences, had everything to do with good looks, urbanity, and daring.

A new game was afoot, and women and men alike were still trying to figure out what the rules were. The New Woman of the teens and twenties had not, despite all the enthusiastic press about her liberation, cast off the shackles of her sex and stepped unfettered into a brave new day where everything was possible. Rather, she had loosened a great many ties to old modes of living that no longer fit well, but had not yet established herself securely in something new. Sexuality was a much more visible and overt part of her life, from the films she saw to the clothes she wore to the dates she went on. Whether she personally kissed, necked, or petted or not, she wasn't likely to be ignorant of such practices. Her own feelings and desires only complicated things further. The New Woman's new sexuality was at least as much firewalk as pleasure cruise.

In theory women were still expected not to have sex before marriage. But with changes in gender roles, female independence, the new custom of going out, and new expectations of sexiness as part of female identity, "having sex"

had become a realm of many shades of gray. Even gynecology books acknowledged that wedding-night hymens were likely to have already been dilated by
probing fingers during hot and heavy petting, but refrained from qualifying
such acts as being definitively either "sex" or "not sex." The new economic and
social equations of sex and dating also meant that it was less clear what sex—
whatever *that* was—was supposed to mean to a relationship. Where exactly virginity fit into all of it was as difficult a question as all the others.

To many people, the new, overt sexiness of New Women promised not so
much freedom as havoc. Sexually active women have always been considered
troublesome, of course; one function virginity has served over the ages is to
control women's sexual activity and make it something that can be policed and
regulated. But as sexually self-willed women became more visible through
movies, theater, journalism, and novels, more and more people became nervous about what that might mean. People questioned whether the New Women
could still be trusted to fulfill their daughterly, wifely, and motherly roles. Seeing to it that they would became the subject of debate, research, and policy.

Part of this process involved the study of a strange new creature. Neither
child nor adult, this bizarre being was scarcely recognizable as properly
human. In 1904 psychologist G. Stanley Hall assayed a systematic description
of this troublesome changeling. *Adolescence: Its Psychology and Its Relations
to Physiology, Anthropology, Sociology, Sex, Crime, Religion, and Education*
was the opening salvo in the ongoing battle of Established Society versus the
Young Person.

Through Hall's eyes, the Young Person was a strange, volatile, contrary,
and vulnerable creature. When it came to female adolescents, much of that
vulnerability was specifically sexual. Anything that hinted at deviation from
the expected standards of premarital virginity, early marriage, and postmarital
monogamy was a cause for alarm. Not just psychologists but families, parents,
schools, friends, and religious organizations all placed their own types of pressure on young women to conform to older, more conservative sexual and behavioral standards—standards that were perceived as being under heavy attack.

The print media also had a large role to play in attempts to regulate the sex
lives of young people. A wide variety of articles and advice columns appeared in
magazines like *Mademoiselle*, *Nash's*, and *Women's Own*. Young people turned to
these publications not only to see what their peers were wearing, seeing, and

dancing to but also what they were thinking and how they were conducting their dating lives. The magazines attempted to strike a balance between the old and the new, simultaneously acknowledging the desirability of a certain amount of sexual freedom and insisting that it have strict limits. While dating was considered normative and kissing understood to be enjoyable, young women were also cautioned that "kisses, like other good things in life, are valued in proportion to their scarcity." Emily Post described the phenomenon in 1937 as "the same cheapening effect as that produced on merchandise which has through constant handling become faded and rumpled, smudged, or frayed and thrown out on the bargain counter in a marked-down lot." Peer pressure, enhanced by the messages disseminated in popular magazines, was another mode for ferocious grassroots enforcement of sexual expectations and limits.

Over the past century and a half, those expectations and limits have often been directly correlated to romance, emotional intensity, and perceived commitment to a relationship. Beginning around the mid-1800s, a particularly sentimental version of romantic love was held up as a relationship ideal for women. It was, as Joan Jacobs Brumberg points out, "a singularly important source of female identity," so much so that Stanley Hall enshrines it in his textbook on adolescence, adding the imprimatur of science to the notion that experience of romantic love was part and parcel of the adolescent female self. The presence of romantic love rapidly became a key factor in the equations that determined sexual boundaries for young women.

A promise of marriage has, across history, frequently been the price of admission for sexual access to a woman. But with the increased centrality of romantic emotion, the coin of the realm gradually became "true love." Established as the pinnacle of emotional experience—and often in a way that contrasted it negatively against marriage—being "in love" assumed extraordinary pride of place. Emotional intensity in a love relationship took on a marriagelike function in terms of representing commitment and the strength of a bond between two people, and it is still perceived in that light today. Currently, surveys show that about 80 to 90 percent of people who marry have some premarital sexual experience, and that well over half of them profess the belief that premarital sex is acceptable as long as it is in the context of a "committed" love relationship.

Just how many women had intercourse prior to marriage, during the early years of the twentieth century, is difficult to pinpoint. Sex-behavior studies dealing with that period are relatively few and far between, and their sample populations were often numerically limited, demographically skewed, or both, but the data we do have about women's premarital sex lives from the 1920s until the 1953 release of Kinsey's *Sexual Response in the Human Female* demonstrate a decided rising trend.

Katherine Bement Davis's 1929 *Factors in the Sex Life of Twenty Two Hundred Women* reported that only 8 percent of the women she surveyed who were married before World War I had had intercourse prior to marriage; a similar level, 12 percent, was noted in Stanford University psychologist Lewis Terman's *Psychological Factors in Marital Unhappiness* (1938) for those marrying prior to 1912. Contrast this with what Terman claimed for the women who married during and immediately after World War I: their premarital intercourse rate had, it seemed, jumped to 26 percent. New York physician G. V. Hamilton's *A Research in Marriage,* based on interviews with one hundred men and one hundred women conducted in 1928, showed a premarital sex rate of 35 percent. Dorothy Dunbar Bromley and Florence Haxton Britten's 1938 *Youth and Sex* looked at undergraduate university women and determined that somewhere between a quarter and a third of them had "indulged in the sex act."

Viewed in light of this upward trend, Kinsey's post–World War II revelations that of his female respondents, nearly 50 percent of those who married by age twenty-five and as many as 66 percent of those who married between the ages of twenty-six and thirty had lost their virginity before they married comes as no surprise at all. Premarital intercourse had been on the rise since the beginning of the century, and as the century progressed, it became increasingly obvious to the general public that for a rising plurality of women, virginity loss and marriage had become two separate events.

Progress in a Pill

People often refer to the period from the early 1960s through the early 1970s as "the sexual revolution," but as we have seen, this "revolution" did not appear out of nowhere. In truth, what historian of sexuality Hera Cook has characterized as "the long sexual revolution" began not with the Summer of Love but far earlier, and as Barbara Ehrenreich, Dierdre English, and other commentators have long noted, the revolution was primarily about women's sexuality, not men's.

A largely silent, but truly massive, part of this revolution consisted in the destabilization of the value placed on virginity. The development and availability of effective contraception has been and continues to be a major contributor to this destabilization.

Historically, women have been at the mercy of fate when it came to the question of whether and how often they would become pregnant, how many children they would bear, and even whether they would survive childbirth at all. The desperation and fear that even many married women felt in regard to sexual intercourse was a direct result of their inability to know whether or not a given episode of intercourse would mean another risky pregnancy. For unmarried women, of course, the prospect of pregnancy was all the more fraught. Although romantic and even sexual dating had become quite commonplace by the start of the World War II, sexual intercourse was still often reserved for an engagement or for marriage itself for the simple reason that women were justifiably terrified of ending up unwed mothers.

This was part of what lay behind the trend toward very youthful marriage during World War II and immediately after it. Youthful dating, with all its sexual intrigue, had become the norm, but the expectation that women would not become pregnant until they were married remained in full force. Although there were other forces in play as well, not least the emotional and demographic turmoil of a protracted world war, the upshot was that that brides were younger than they had been in some decades. Between 1940 and 1959, the percentage of women aged fourteen to seventeen who married had jumped by 33 percent in the United States, and by 1959 a quarter of first-time brides went to the altar prior to their nineteenth birthday. In the United Kingdom, a similar though less dramatic drop took place: between 1926 and 1930, most first-time brides were close to twenty-six years of age, but after that point the age went steadily down to hover at around twenty-three years of age by 1960. That marriage was taking place earlier by no means indicates that young people were marrying *instead* of having premarital sex—one British national survey revealed that 46 percent of women marrying in the 1950s did not marry as virgins—but rather that those who did have premarital sex were likely to marry soon after. This resurgence of early marriage led some people to believe that Jazz Age excesses had given way to a return to a more "traditional" prioritization of marriage and family, an interpretation that was extended as well to the 1950s' valorization of the happy space-age housewife. Such assumptions, however, proved premature.

Into this milieu it emerged that the biggest single obstacle to female sexual autonomy had, for all practical purposes, been overcome. For as long as we have records, women have attempted contraception, often at significant risk. Most contraceptives, historically, have been troublesome, difficult and expensive to obtain, unpleasant or even debilitating to use, and often dependent upon male cooperation. Adding insult to injury, many have been indifferently effective. Then the world changed: following several breakthroughs in the laboratory synthesis of hormones, the first contraceptive pills were released into the British and American markets between 1957 and 1960.

The birth control pill had been a dream of contraceptives activists since the beginning of their movement: Marie Stopes stated in 1928 that "the demand for a simple pill or drug" contraceptive would be unimaginably huge. She was correct. The Pill was originally available only to married women, yet by the mid-1960s, approximately a third of married American women and about 25 percent of younger working-class British couples used it. The percentages only rose from there.

The Pill's reliability and the fact that it was mess-free and convenient helped make it popular, but those were not the only reasons it was embraced so quickly by so many. For the first time in history, women could separate sex and pregnancy both literally and symbolically. The Pill did not have to be taken at the time one had sex. The Pill also did not directly involve the genitals. Contraception could happen entirely behind the scenes and on a woman's own initiative.

This unprecedented control was, as Lara Marks points out, not without ironic drawbacks. "By diminishing the risk of pregnancy, the oral contraceptive undermined the powerful psychological weapon women had previously possessed to deny sexual intercourse. After all, men could now argue that as there was no risk in having intercourse why should they not do so. Within this context the pill changed expectations about sexual intercourse. Now sexual intercourse was much higher on the agenda for some couples than other forms of sexual activity, such as heavy petting, which had been one way of avoiding pregnancy."

This insight provides some perspective on the popular perception of a link between the introduction of the Pill and the sexual revolution of the late 1960s

and early 1970s. While there is no question that the Summer of Love and related events came rather rapidly on the heels of the introduction of the Pill,
there is no evidence that suggests a cause-and-effect relationship between the
two. The Pill certainly revolutionized contraception and made it possible for
women to develop, for the first time, a concept of female heterosexuality that
concerned itself more with pleasure than with the prospect of pregnancy. But
as historians like Elizabeth Siegel Watkins accurately note, "In the 1960s and
early 1970s, demographers focused on the contraceptive habits of *married*
women to document the *contraceptive* revolution, while sociologists surveyed
the sexual attitudes and practices of *unmarried* women to study the *sexual* revolution. Journalists combined the two contemporaneous changes and developed the lasting image of the Pill as the symbol of the sexual revolution;
scientists and the public accepted and promoted this interpretation of the pill"
[emphases in the original].

The Day Virginity Died?

As Gloria Steinem, then a young journalist writing in the pages of *Esquire*
magazine, wrote in 1962, "The pill is obviously important to the sexual and the
contraceptive revolutions, but it is not the opening bombshell of either one."
Indeed, large percentages of unmarried women had for decades, as we have
seen, been having sex without it. The firestorm of sexual politics that took
place in the wake of the Pill was not caused by the Pill so much as catalyzed
around it.

In a time of intense, emotional, and self-consciously political challenge and
tumult, sexual politics was only one of the many issues on which the rebellious
and radical sought wholesale change. Second-wave feminism, the birth of the
gay and lesbian liberation movement, the idea of free love, and experimenta-
tion with family and household structures among young adults all contributed
to a dramatic, chaotic expansion of sexual politics and possibility.

Somewhere in the midst of it all, the pendulum of the ideology of virginity
took a hard swing to the left. Increasingly, there was a sensibility that female
virginity had finally been stripped of its mystic value and could now be regarded as essentially identical to male virginity, more an event than an attribute. It separated the mature and the immature, but not necessarily in the same

way that it traditionally had been understood to do: to many it was now seen as the difference between being "liberated" and being "hung up." To actually be a virgin betrayed one as repressed. *The Sensuous Man,* a popular 1971 guide to the new sexual culture of swinging singles and recreational sex, characterized virginity as "woman's most hideous ailment."

"Liberated" people were supposed to have gotten beyond feeling inhibited in regard to sexual appetite and pleasure. Along the way, more and more women began to insist that female sexual pleasure was just as important as male sexual pleasure. Rather than using romantic commitment and marriage as their sole yardsticks of a successful interpersonal life, some men and women took to gauging personal success on the basis of sexual experience. Intrepid explorers of the new "liberated" ethos experimented with sex independent of marriage or even romantic relationships, with thousands of men and women engaging in what was called "free love" but is more accurately described as merely relatively unfettered sex.

Despite the doomsday predictions of some pundits, this unprecedented and unabashed wantonness failed to cause the end of the world or even the downfall of civilization as we know it. Evolving egalitarian philosophies of sexuality and gender, however, have indeed transformed the way we civilize our sexual impulses, and this very much includes the way we think about virginity. Since the 1960s, the practice of placing social and economic value on virginity has often been dismissed out of hand as an artifact of an obsolete mode of patriarchy, a now-irrelevant throwback to an ignorant time. As such, the idea has appeared to many to have no legitimate place in a sexually liberated, nonsexist culture. "Virginity" could only be useful as a value-neutral term that distinguished between those who had experienced partnered sex and those who had not yet done so.

This way of thinking about virginity had its predictable critics among social conservatives, to be sure. But it also had its detractors among liberals and radicals. Lesbian feminists, notably including Marilyn Frye, took issue with the heterosexual bias inherent in the fashionable denigration of virginity as a social status. A virgin, Frye argued, was a woman who owed nothing to men, whatever her sexual history. Virginity, she argued, was still powerful, but only if it were understood in what she purported was its original meaning of feminine autonomy. (There is no real sense in either Greek or Latin that the words *parthenos* or *virgo* necessarily indicated anything of the sort when applied to human beings; as we have seen, they were primarily used to describe young unmarried women and girls.) Frye was in turn criticized by other lesbian feminists, who sought to rehabilitate the term "virgin" differently, applying it only to lesbians who were, as writer Rita Mae Brown quipped, "penis-pure and proud."

Such radical deconstructions and redefinitions contributed to the general instability of the idea of virginity. This instability has in turn enhanced the sense that virginity must be going the way of the button-hook and the Victrola. Reports of its demise are, of course, exceedingly premature: we are all still born virgins. As a point of social history, however, the anxiety over vanishing virginity is more defensible. If the course of the twentieth century is anything to go by, the ideology of virginity as a stand-in for specifically female virtue and human worth is indeed making its leisurely way to the egress. It seems clear that we are in the midst of a paradigm shift where virginity is concerned, one that neither began nor ended with the sexual revolution, but constitutes a broader, longer revolution all its own.

Pop Goes the Virgin

One of the better ways to gain some perspective on this shift is to look at where, when, and how virgins and virginity show up in popular culture. The virginity-related pop culture of the twentieth century could easily fill volumes, but zeroing in on a quartet of programs—the films *The Rocky Horror Picture Show* and *Little Darlings* and the internationally popular American television shows *Beverly Hills 90210* and *Buffy the Vampire Slayer*—lets us see some of what has been happening to virginity since the "revolutionary" 1960s, including our increasing tendency, as a culture, to reflect upon virginity itself.

Attracting a cult following from the earliest days of its existence as a stage musical in 1973 London (it ultimately ran for nearly three thousand performances), Richard O'Brien's *The Rocky Horror Show* became *The Rocky Horror Picture Show* in 1975 when it was made into a film version starring Susan Sarandon and Tim Curry. A send-up of horror and science-fiction movie clichés of the 1950s and 1960s, *Rocky Horror* is also a campy, overblown dissertation on the culture clashes of the sexual revolution. In it, the thoroughly virginal and comically repressed couple Brad Majors (Barry Bostwick) and Janet

Weiss (Susan Sarandon) become engaged following the wedding of friends, but while driving home from the wedding they become lost in a forest. It is a dark and stormy night, so naturally enough by the conventions of the B-movies *Rocky* exists to lampoon, they end up at the doors of the creepy Gothic castle of the outrageous hypersexed transvestite mad scientist, Dr. Frank N. Furter (Tim Curry).

In the course of things, both Brad and Janet are debauched by Frank, whose mottos are "give yourself over to absolute pleasure" and "don't dream it, be it," but Brad and Janet react very differently to their experiences of sex. Brad remains uptight, tense, and defensive of the conservative morals he espoused at the start of the film, while Janet embodies the virgin-to-slut cliché. She ends up having an illicit tryst with Rocky (Peter Hinwood), Dr. Frank N. Furter's muscle-bound, golden-haired "Frankenstein's monster." In the song "Touch-a Touch-a Touch Me," Janet sings to Rocky about having been the kind of girl who had "only ever kissed before" and of having been afraid of the consequences of petting, but then promptly announces, by way of inviting him to bed her, that everything changed when she lost her virginity. "I've tasted blood and I want more," she sings, echoed by two female household servants who voyeurize the whole thing via closed-circuit television, chanting "More! More! More!"

By the end of the film, Janet has been transformed into a joyous libertine who sings that she feels "released" and that her "mind has been expanded." In a parallel stanza within the same song, though, Brad sings "Help me, Mommy / I'll be good, you'll see / take this dream away." Only in the last minutes of the film does Brad cave in to Dr. Frank N. Furter's magical zone of sexual excess. While Dr. Frank N. Furter is ultimately killed by his own extraterrestrial fellows because his "lifestyle's too extreme," Brad and Janet survive. Clad in corsets, fishnet stockings, and stiletto-heeled patent leather pumps, they are left, their virginities long gone and their sensibilities entirely transformed, to scrabble their way out of the wreckage of Dr. Frank N. Furter's destroyed mansion.

As important as virginity and virginity loss are to *Rocky Horror*, it is not too surprising that its extensive audience subculture has adopted the motif. In most of the places where the movie airs on a regular basis—usually on a weekend night at midnight, accompanied by the costumed acting, singing, dancing, and assorted audience participation of contingents of devoted fans who have

seen the film dozens or even hundreds of times—first-timer "virgins" are singled out for special treatment. Though the specifics vary widely, *RHPS* "virgins" might be made to wear name tags advertising their virgin status, have
lipsticked *V*s put on their cheeks and foreheads, be goaded to participate in
suggestive pantomime, or just be paraded before the more experienced members of the audience before the film runs and they thus join the gleeful crowd
who will initiate the next week's crop of "virgins."

A very different sort of virginity-related peer pressure forms the subject of
director Ronald Maxwell's 1980 *Little Darlings*. Set at a sleepaway summer
camp for teenaged girls, this film pits a posh daughter of the old-money set,
Ferris (Tatum O'Neal), against the tough, streetwise Angel (Kristy McNichol),
who hails from a working-class single-parent home. The predictable storms of
adolescent bitchiness and put-downs among the various teen campers eventually lead to an insidiously competitive conversation about virginity. Although
most of the girls are lying through their teeth, all but two members of the
cabin claim that they are sexually experienced. The only ones to admit to virginity are Ferris and Angel. A wager is promptly lodged as to which of the two
girls will manage to lose her virginity first that summer.

Making loss of virginity into a matter for deadly earnest wagering is of
course nothing new in the annals of fiction; French writer and military officer
Pierre Ambroise Choderlos de Laclos's 1782 *Les liaisons dangereuses* (converted to the screen on more than one occasion) provides a classic, vicious example of such a bet. What makes *Little Darlings* so remarkable is that the bet
involves two teenaged girls, and that the virginities they are scheming to lose
are their own. In this movie we see lost virginity not just as an emblem of
adulthood but of *cool*: the young women who lie about having lost their virginities do so because they are desperately afraid of being socially unappealing to their peers. It is an extraordinary snapshot of what virginity implied
and entailed to women who were of an age to literally be daughters of the sexual revolution.

Although the film industry's interest in virginity has often been limited to
boys-will-be-boys raunchfests (*Porky's* [1982], *Losin' It* [1983], and *The Last
American Virgin* [1982], etc.), some comedies—*Animal House* (1978) is one
example—have managed to get in some cogent digs at conservative virginity
ideology along with their quotient of titty jokes. There have also been occasional serious treatments. Spike Lee's 1988 *School Daze* and John Hughes's

1985 *The Breakfast Club* both explored virginity as a socially and emotionally complex issue among young adults, both films providing a harsh look at the relationship between virginity and social acceptance.

Since the 1970s, television has also engaged with virginity narratives. The majority of television virginity plots tend to be neat single-episode packages aimed at high-school-aged viewers, in which characters of a similar age range go from confronting the possibility of virginity loss to dealing with the aftermath in a single swift half-hour installment. This is, at least in terms of age range, a relatively accurate reflection of reality: American age at virginity loss has hovered around the sixteen- to-eighteen-year-old range since the 1970s. Aside from the matter of age, what *Slate* television critic Kate Aurthur has called the "Very Special Virginity episode" has had consistent conventions over the thirty years that virginity has been a subject of television programming. Among them is the repeated contention that virginity loss always has consequences.

A fine case in point was provided by the extraordinarily long-lived prime-time soap opera *Beverly Hills 90210*, which ran from 1990 to 2000. Originally the saga of a Minnesotan family who relocates to Beverly Hills, the show centered around the family's twin high-school-aged children, Brandon and Brenda, as they came of age in the milieu of one of the United States' wealthiest communities. True to form for a teen-centric series drama, there was a virginity-loss narrative beginning in the very first season. Although it took most of the first season to do it, Brenda (Shannen Doherty), the daughter of the central family, lost her virginity to the Porsche-driving bad boy Dylan (Luke Perry). Brenda and Dylan's sexual liaison was foreshadowed very early in that year's story line, but Brenda, frightened by the possibility of sexually transmitted disease, postponed the act until the season's penultimate episode. This left an entire juicy episode of consequences, in this case a pregnancy scare and the breakup of Brenda and Dylan's relationship. The season thus ended, leaving fans to wait two months for the news that Brenda was not in fact pregnant.

Of the numerous deflorations that took place during *90210*'s ten seasons, the one that garnered the largest number of column inches in the press was that of the "good Catholic girl" character Donna, played by Tori Spelling, actress daughter of *90210*'s producer. Donna's virginity, an open topic of discussion among the core characters of the show from the beginning, lasted very nearly as long as the show itself. Although Donna was at the core of the cast from the first season and began a romantic relationship with the character David in the second season, the course of what ultimately turned out to be true love (or at least a Hollywood approximation of it) ran nowhere near close to smooth. Quite exceptionally, given the crazed rutting to which *90210*'s characters seemed so prone, Donna hung on to her virginity until her last year of college, the show's seventh year. When she finally did have sex with David, it took place offscreen, and while there were mild consequences—she had to break the news to her Catholic mother—there was no punishment. Ultimately, and anticlimactically, the Donna and David characters married.

What viewers and critics made of Donna's lengthy virginity—lengthy by Hollywood standards, anyway, although hardly so by a real-world metric— varied a great deal. Heralded by some as evidence of a newfound (and, it was implied, long overdue) return to traditional sexual mores among young people, others found Donna's perennial discussions and displays of virginity infuriating and heavy-handed. In terms of its historical moment, Donna's much-discussed virginity was both and neither.

Brenda and Donna both, simultaneously, reflected meaningful trends in the sexual culture of the era of *90210*. By the mid-1980s, approximately half of unmarried women between the ages of fifteen and nineteen were what the researchers euphemistically call "sexually active," meaning in most cases that they had identified themselves as having engaged in partnered sex at least once, à la Brenda.* And as in Brenda's case, the real issue wasn't whether one was or wasn't a virgin, but whether the consequences of sexual activity endangered one's own chances of middle-class success. Sexually transmitted diseases and,

---

*One of the numerous problems of the sexological research is that types of sexual activity are not always delineated separately in surveys. Where a survey presents figures on numbers of people who are "sexually active," there is often no concrete way to tell exactly what kind of activity that represents. The common assumption of many readers of such surveys is that "sexual activity" means "penis-in-vagina intercourse," but this assumption is not necessarily warranted. Additionally, being "sexually active" in terms of having a history of partnered sexual activity does not mean that a consistent or ongoing amount of sexual activity exists, as in fact it does not for most young people. The reader of sexual statistics does well to read "sexually active" as meaning only "has ever engaged in some form of partnered sex" in any report which does not define its terms more specifically.

particularly, unplanned pregnancies among women "old enough to know better" are often seen as revealing a lack of critical discipline. Brenda's pregnancy scare was thus a cautionary tale, while Donna succeeded in negotiating premarital sex "correctly."

In *Buffy the Vampire Slayer*, another long-running teen drama series (spring 1997–summer 2003), *Buffy* creator Joss Whedon addressed virginity from yet another perspective: that of the personally and sexually empowered young woman. That young woman is Buffy Summers (Sarah Michelle Gellar), slightly ditzy California high school student by day, anointed slayer of vampires and other supernatural menaces by night. With the help of the mentor and father figure who is her "watcher," Giles (Anthony Stewart Head), and a small group of close-knit friends, Buffy becomes a gifted warrior whose job it is to combat the forces of evil that frequently appear in their small "hellmouth" town of Sunnydale.

Along the way, as is traditional for teenaged heroines, she falls passionately in love. But the man with whom she falls in love is a vampire, Angel (David Boreanaz), known as Angelus to his vampire friends. He is a curious creature, living under a gypsy curse that gave him back his soul and thus also his conscience and which is destined to remain with him until such unlikely time as the guilt-ridden creature experiences a moment of perfect happiness. At the start of the show, Angel is thus that very *rara avis*, a vampire-hating vampire who himself fights the forces of darkness. Over the first half of the show's second year, the romance between Buffy and Angel intensifies. Finally, in the first half of a two-part episode that falls squarely in the middle of the second season, Buffy's seventeenth birthday arrives and she gives in to the passion that has been building in her relationship with Angel. Buffy loses her virginity in a steamingly erotic, yet nongraphic, visual vignette that conveys, in its glowing skin tones and rich, draped fabrics, a mixture of intense romance and profound sensuality.

The consequences are not long in arriving. Buffy wakes up to find Angel gone, and it rapidly becomes clear that sex with Buffy was the occasion of perfect happiness required to break the curse that equipped Angel with a soul. The paradox is overblown, but it works: the sincerity of Buffy and Angel's emotions is proven by his turning, quite literally, into a demon. Having had Buffy in one metaphorical sense, Angel is now determined to have her in the other. Buffy's life (as well as those of her family and friends) is on the line as a soulless Angel seeks revenge for having been forced to endure the apparently emasculating constraints of having a soul. No garden-variety pregnancy scare for Buffy.

The entire second half of the second season follows Buffy's attempts to deal not only with the threat Angel poses but also with her cherished memories of the lover and relationship she lost. Although at first she does not realize what has happened, and begins to blame herself for Angel's sudden cruelty, she soon realizes that the change in Angel represents a far larger problem than post-coital betrayal. Buffy rapidly deduces that there are only two solutions to the problem Angel represents: find a way to reinstate the curse and restore Angel's soul, or kill him. Ultimately, with the help of her friends, she does both. With tears in her eyes, she tells Angel to close his eyes, kisses him one last time, and plunges her sword through his heart, sending Angel to hell.

Buffy's virginity story, otherworldly as it is, is at root not about sin and punishment, but about maturity in the face of adversity. Buffy's decision to lose her virginity to Angel has its consequences, but those consequences are not in themselves consequences of sex. Angel loses his soul as a consequence of the power of emotion, not merely of orgasm. Whedon places romantic love on a pedestal only to kick the pedestal out from under it. In the Whedonverse, even the most culturally impeccable romantic virginity narrative is not enough to turn a girl into a woman. To truly be her own mistress a young woman must be capable of much more than just sex. In the world of *Buffy the Vampire Slayer*—and in our world as well, Whedon implies—a woman's true value does not lie in her virginity, or her ability to be sexually loved. It lies in her ability to love, be loved, and simultaneously kick ass, take names, and do whatever needs to be done, no matter how difficult.

True Love Legislates

Of all the countries of the developed world, the United States is the only one that has to date created a federal agenda having specifically to do with the virginity of its citizens. Involving hundreds of millions of dollars in taxpayer funding, this agenda has proven hotly controversial. Intersecting in a number of ways with evangelical Christian and other socially conservative efforts to promote a resurgence of what advocates term "traditional values" or "family values"—although both terms are to some extent misnomers when viewed from historical or anthropological viewpoints—the focus of this governmental program is to establish virginity as the only appropriate sexual status for any never-married person.

The history of this agenda and its associated legislation is simple enough in outline. In 1981, during the first term of President Ronald Reagan, a program known as Title XX of the Public Health Service Act, the Adolescent Family Life Act, or AFLA, was sponsored by then-senator Jeremiah Denton, a Republican from Alabama (later joined by Massachusetts Democrat Edward Kennedy). The bill passed and was instituted under the aegis of the U.S. Office of Population Affairs. AFLA's mandate was to create programs to decrease pregnancy rates among unmarried minors (the age of legal majority in the United States is eighteen) specifically by promoting chastity and sexual self-restraint. The media quickly began to refer to AFLA as "The Chastity Act."

A successor to the 1978 Adolescent Pregnancy Program, the first federal program designed to prevent teenaged pregnancies, programs funded under AFLA were required to teach abstinence from sex—in other words virginity, since these programs were to be aimed at adolescents who were not yet sexually active—as the normative standard and best practice for preventing pregnancy and disease. Abstaining from sexual activity was also to be taught as a "secondary prevention measure" for teenagers who had already had sex and/or a past pregnancy. The terms of AFLA forbade grant money to be given to projects that encouraged, promoted, or advocated family planning services, including contraception or medical abortion.

Initially funded at $11 million, AFLA was a fairly small program by U.S. federal standards. In 1982, with $13.5 million at stake, five hundred research grants were proposed and sixty-two were granted. Many AFLA grant recipients had close ties to churches and religious organizations. Programs funded by AFLA soon came under fire for using explicitly religious language and concepts, and it was not long before the American Civil Liberties Union (ACLU) filed suit on the grounds that AFLA's activities violated the Establishment Clause of the U.S. Constitution—the principle of separation of church and state.

This suit, filed in 1983, went as far as the Supreme Court but was ultimately settled out of court in 1993. The settlement left AFLA standing and provided parameters within which the program and others like it would be permitted to function. AFLA marched on. With regular funding increases, AFLA has grown from an $11-million-a-year program at its outset to a $31-million-a-year program in fiscal year 2004.

In 1994, the year after AFLA's more questionable practices had been reined in by the courts, congressional representative John Doolittle, a Republican from California, sponsored a bill to amend the reauthorization of the Elementary and Secondary Education Act. The Doolittle Act, had it succeeded, would have sharply limited what sorts of material state and local school districts could include in their HIV-prevention curricula, a major venue for sexuality-related education in American public schools. But because the U.S. federal government is prohibited from dictating curriculum standards to public schools (U.S. public schools are administered at the state and municipal levels), the Doolittle Act proved unpassable.

Between the ACLU challenge to AFLA and the abortive Doolittle Act, however, proponents of what had by then come to be called "chastity education" had received a primer on what would and would not be found legally acceptable in terms of legislation on the subject. Explicitly religious language was unacceptable, and medical and scientific inaccuracy in the name of discouraging sex frowned upon. But the government's right to use taxpayer-funded programs to teach specific sexual ideologies and behaviors had gone entirely unchallenged. Furthermore, no laws existed to prevent the federal government from linking grant monies to specific educational content. They had only to make the states responsible for accepting or rejecting the funds, and with them, the designated content.

These lessons were put into practice in 1996 in the form of a rider attached to the Personal Responsibility and Work Opportunity Reconciliation Act. This Act, a major legislative goal of the Clinton administration, was a component of a gargantuan overhaul of the American social welfare system. During the final hours of debate on the Act, a sleepy little rider—a sort of add-on legislation that piggybacks on a larger piece of legislation and is passed if the "parent" bill is passed—was attached to it. This rider received no public debate and, in fact, no real notice at all.

The Act passed, and with it, the rider, known as Title V, Section 510(b). This, as it turned out, was a bill that allocated $50 million per year, for each of five years, to be offered to the states for the purpose of funding programs that promoted chastity. Administered by the federal Maternal and Child Health

Bureau of the Department of Human Services, Section 510(b) required that the states provide matching funds at a 3:4 state-to-federal ratio. Total funds per year for the initial five years were $437.5 million. Renewed under the George W. Bush administration after its initial five-year run ended, the funding has consistently increased: federal 510(b) funding for fiscal year 2005 was $273 million.

The way these funds may be used has been exactingly spelled out. Recipients of Section 510(b) money include programs at the state, local, and community levels, educational agencies, and individual school districts. Program content is dictated by a list of eight tenets, none of which may be contradicted. Some programs are additionally prohibited from raising private funds to supplement 510(b) programming with information considered contrary to the eight required messages.

What is to be taught under Section 510(b)? "Abstinence education," defined as "an educational or motivational program" that does the following:

a) has as its exclusive purpose teaching the social, psychological, and health gains to be realized by abstaining from sexual activity; b) teaches abstinence from sexual activity outside marriage as the expected standard for all school-age children; c) teaches that abstinence from sexual activity is the only certain way to avoid out-of-wedlock pregnancy, sexually transmitted diseases, and other associated health problems; d) teaches that a mutually faithful monogamous relationship in the context of marriage is the expected standard of sexual activity; e) teaches that sexual activity outside the context of marriage is likely to have harmful psychological and physical effects; f) teaches that bearing children out-of-wedlock is likely to have harmful consequences for the child, the child's parents, and society; g) teaches young people how to reject sexual advances and how alcohol and drug use increase vulnerability to sexual advances, and h) teaches the importance of attaining self-sufficiency before engaging in sexual activity.

These are almost exclusively ideological statements. Statements about the harmfulness of sexual activity or even unmarried childbearing are meaningless unless they involve very specific social contexts. Significant rates of unmarried sexual activity have been a constant throughout the twentieth century, yet somehow we continue on the whole not only to survive but to thrive, much of the developed world enjoying standards of living and civil freedoms of which our forebears could only dream. As for the perniciousness of unmarried parenthood, the statistics from many northern European countries, such as Denmark and Sweden, as well as Iceland, give the lie to doomsday scenarios. Approximately half of the babies born in Denmark and Sweden are born to unmarried adults, and in Iceland the ratio of births to unwed parents jumps to two-thirds,* yet in none of these countries has this led to social trauma, economic catastrophe, or even a general hue and cry among the clergy of these Protestant nations.

The other planks of the Section 510(b) agenda are similarly reactionary and shaky. The importance of self-sufficiency prior to sexual debut, for instance, is just another version of the economic argument that for millennia has been used to argue for female virginity prior to marriage. Ironically, part of the reason that economic self-sufficiency is indeed an asset for would-be parents in the United States is that there is little provision for public, subsidized health or child care. To state unequivocally that an individual woman's economic self-sufficiency is the primary factor in whether it is difficult for her to raise a child as a single parent is to put the cart well before the horse. Although a "mutually faithful monogamous relationship in the context of marriage," as promoted by the 510(b) legislation, may enhance the resources available for childrearing, as generations of women have painfully learned, it is hardly a guarantee.

A similarly ideological, historically shortsighted item of Section 510(b) is its emphasis on monogamy and marriage. While it is generally true that females have historically been expected to refrain from sex prior to marriage, it is also true that males have not. This "expected standard" must perforce be a relatively new invention, and one which arguably owes its existence to gender-egalitarian feminist theory. It also bears noting that if this is indeed a standard

---

*A growing trend in many northern European countries is for couples to cohabit, then marry following the birth of a child. In Sweden, for example, 70 percent of cohabiting couples who have a child marry within five years of the child's birth. Out-of-wedlock childbirth is not an accurate predictor of harm to parent, child, or society, and is not even an accurate predictor of a child's likelihood of being raised in a single-parent home.

expected by some minority of the American populace, it has demonstrably never been the standard *observed* by the vast majority.

Additionally troublesome from a historical and legislative perspective are the words "school-age" and "children." In the United States, public schooling now commonly lasts until age eighteen. But in thirty states, secondary education is only compulsory until a young person reaches the age of sixteen (in another nine states it is seventeen). Therefore, the age at which a young person may be considered school-age can vary considerably, and the end of the school-age period may or may not coincide with the transition to legal adulthood.

This is not the only reason it can be tricky to determine who should be considered an adult and who must be considered a child in America. The federal age of majority is eighteen years of age, but individual state laws make it possible for minors to legally drive cars, hold paying jobs, and in some cases be prosecuted as adults in criminal court.* With parental consent, depending on state law, it may be possible for minors to marry. At age seventeen, and again with parental consent, minors may join the U.S. military. At the same time, young people must be at least eighteen to vote or buy pornography, and twenty-one to buy or consume alcohol. Even if the question of who is a child is based completely on whether a young person has the legal authority to consent to sex, the age at which this is possible varies from state to state and from fifteen years of age to eighteen. While it would be silly to suggest that Americans are incapable of recognizing the difference between children and adults when dealing with individuals, American law often makes it a confusing task to differentiate between them in legislative terms. Section 510(b) is clearly using the most inclusive possible definition of "child," which is to say including all legal minors as children. But by doing so, Section 510(b) contradicts, in spirit, the letter of many extant state laws.

All these things are troubling. More troubling still, from a political perspective, is that American abstinence-only legislation has generated a top-down

---

*Vermont's state law permits children as young as ten to be prosecuted as adults under some circumstances. Other states permit at least some cases involving minors to be moved from juvenile to standard criminal court, but the minimum ages for these moves vary. Most commonly the age limits for moving a case are somewhere between fourteen and seventeen years of age, or up to four years younger than the age of majority.

ideological program that rests neither on the demands of extant law nor upon the wishes of American voters. Surveys repeatedly find that more than 90 percent of Americans support comprehensive sex education in the schools, and that upward of 80 percent of American adults believe that birth control and safer-sex information should be provided even to teenagers who are not yet sexually active. Abstinence education does not reflect an American popular mandate, but rather an unasked-for imposition of a moral agenda. This is unprecedented in American history and unique among the nations of the contemporary developed world.

It is also, in its public refusal to use the actual word "virginity," both canny and strange. The word "virginity" appears nowhere in American legislation that deals with the ideal of "abstinence from sexual activity outside marriage as the expected standard." One might well wonder why. It seems odd that, having described premarital virginity in detail, they would shy away from simply using the term. It is, after all, what they're talking about.

But it does not appear to be what they want to be *perceived* as talking about. Virginity has, for reasons both valid and not, gotten something of a bad reputation over the course of the twentieth century. In America particularly, a person who is a virgin is often seen as a rarity, perhaps an oddity, probably an unredeemable loser. No wonder AFLA, Section 510(b) programs, and abstinence educators alike seem to prefer to avoid it.

Abstinence, on the other hand, is associated with virtuous self-control. Critically, it offers the impression of choice. One *is* a virgin, but one *chooses* to abstain. Using the word "abstinence" in this context suggests the quintessentially American ideals of self-determination and choice. It verbally transforms compliance with government propaganda into a celebration of personal liberty.

Renaming virginity "abstinence" lifts it out of a web of unpleasant associations and makes it modern. Conveniently, it also sidesteps religious implications: Jesus's mother was not Abstinent Mary. Use of the word "abstinence" is also convenient in that it applies not only to those who have never had sex, but also to those who have already had sex but might be convinced not to do it again. Virginity, after all, is seen as perishable, a one-time-only affair. While the idea of "secondary virginity" is popular in some circles, it is also a problematic term for any number of reasons, not least that it appears to be an oxymoron. Abstinence, on the other hand, can be used in reference to anyone, because a person can abstain from something whether he or she has or hasn't tried it to begin with. Given that approximately 50 percent of American young people have participated in partnered sex by the time they leave high school, the utility of all-encompassing terminology is evident.

Many critics of abstinence-only education have claimed that the abstinence-education agenda is transparently religiously motivated. Indeed, there are numerous connections between the abstinence movement, individual Christians, and Christian denominations more generally. Many recipients of AFLA funding in the early 1980s were religious individuals or organizations who used the funding to help finance the development of abstinence curricula and teaching materials based on overtly religious principles. When Section 510(b) made the teaching of abstinence ideology a condition of granting its educational funding to states and community organizations, those curricula and materials stood poised to supply the market that Section 510(b) created.

An often-cited example is the controversial grade seven to nine curriculum *Sex Respect*. A joint production of Catholic sex educator Coleen Kelly Mast, whose other titles include *Love and Life: A Christian Sexual Morality Guide for Teens,* and an organization based in Glenview, Illinois, called the Committee on the Status of Women (founded by longtime archconservative Phyllis Schlafly), *Sex Respect* was funded in part by a $391,000 AFLA grant awarded in 1985. Creation of a similar curriculum intended for a high-school audience, *Facing Reality*, it was funded by a three-year, $300,000 AFLA grant awarded in 1990. Mast is now considered one of the leading experts on abstinence education. Her résumé includes having been one of four Americans chosen to participate in a 1996 conclave on "Education for Chastity" held by the Vatican. Mast's curricula, which have been lambasted by the press as well as by scientific organizations for their medical inaccuracies and for instances of racial and other bias, are used in over two thousand American public school districts.

Religion collides with federal funding in the production of abstinence-education materials in a very different way in the case of the program called Free Teens USA. A recipient of Section 510(b) funding, Free Teens USA is run by a group of individuals with strong ties to the Rev. Sun Myung Moon's controversial Unification Church. In 2003 reporter John Gorenfeld, writing for the online magazine *Salon*, divulged the results of his spelunking into federal files made accessible through the Freedom of Information Act. Free Teens administrators have headed statewide Unification Church branches, worked for Unification Church–owned companies, including the gun manufacturer

Kahr Arms, and worked as senior financial officers within the central Unification Church. The Unification Church claims no official ties to Free Teens, but this is often the case for Moon-affiliated front organizations. It must be said that Free Teens abstinence education conforms quite well with the Unification stance on sexuality, which holds that any sexual experience outside of marriage is an abomination, even to the point that the Reverend Moon has advocated (in 1992) that women who are sexually attacked should kill themselves rather than go through the "fall" of being raped.

Religion also plays a role in abstinence education through the secular adaptation of teaching methods and strategies devised for use in religious contexts. Beginning in the early 1990s, evangelical Christian ministries targeting adolescent and young-adult populations began to form groups and create programs specifically designed to deal with what they view as a cultural onslaught against sexual purity. The best known of these, and one of the oldest, is True Love Waits, run by LifeWay Christian Resources, an operation of the Southern Baptist Convention. In addition to producing and licensing a number of products, including sportswear, stickers, and jewelry, True Love Waits also offers a number of counseling, educational, and motivational programs.

True Love Waits' most distinctive offering by far, however, is the True Love Waits Commitment Card. This is a simple piece of paper, with space for a signature at the bottom, that reads: "My Commitment: Believing that true love waits, I make a commitment to God, myself, my family, my friends, my future mate, and my future children to a lifetime of purity including sexual abstinence from this day until the day I enter a biblical marriage relationship."

True Love Waits' pledge cards have proven popular, a staple of TLW's small community groups as well as massive regional rallies. A similar pledge-taking phenomenon called the Silver Ring Thing puts a fifteen-dollar silver ring on the pledge-taker's left ring finger (the same finger on which Americans traditionally wear their wedding rings) as an outwardly visible sign that one has taken the pledge. Approximately eighty other religious virginity-pledge groups, including the Unification Church's Pure Love Alliance, exist and have modified this pledge process for their own uses. So have numerous abstinence curricula intended for use in public schools. *Sex Respect* includes a version that reads "I, [the undersigned], promise to abstain from sex until my wedding night. I want to reserve my sexual powers to give life and love for my future spouse and marriage. I will respect my gift of sexuality by keeping my mind and thoughts pure as I prepare for my true love. I commit to grow in character to learn to live in love and freedom." Although this and other secularized versions omit references to God, the Bible, and other explicitly religious concepts, they do exude a sanctimonious odor.

To the young people signing these pledges, however, the language is often less important than whether or not their friends are signing up. Two researchers, Peter Bearman of Columbia University and Hannah Brückner of Yale, devoted themselves for several years to researching the effects—good, bad, and indifferent—of virginity pledging. Their findings, released in several reports beginning with the landmark 2001 "Promising the Future: Virginity Pledges and the Transition to First Intercourse," which was published in *The American Journal of Sociology*, determined that while virginity pledges did have some effect on the sexual behavior of those who made them, what mattered most was whether signing—and keeping—the pledge was considered "cool."

The more pledgers there were in a particular school, the more likely pledgers were to keep their pledges. But this was only true as long as the number of pledgers did not grow so large that being a virginity pledger stopped being an identifiable subculture. There was, Bearman and Brückner discovered, a specific point beyond which pledges were no longer likely to have an effect. When more than 30 percent of the students at a given school took abstinence pledges, the pledgers stopped delaying virginity loss. As the researchers put it, "The pledge identity is meaningful, consequently, only if it is a minority identity, a common situation for identity movements."

For those pledgers to whom the "pledge identity is meaningful," on the other hand, it appears that pledging does indeed delay sexual debut. Not, it must be said, for the entire period stipulated in the pledge, but for roughly eighteen months. As Bearman and Brückner put it, "There comes a phase chronologically where the pledgers catch up with nonpledgers."

While abstinence promoters view this figure as evidence of success, critics have interpreted it as a sign of failure. Other researchers looking at the same data—the National Longitudinal Study of Adolescent Health (AddHealth), the only federally run sexuality research to date that has included virginity pledge questions—like Harvard's Janet Rosenbaum, have found similarly high rates of pledge breaking. Rosenbaum's research, published in 2006, indicates that 52 percent of pledgers had sex within a year. More troublesome,

Rosenbaum's research suggests that teens are likely to lie about their sexual experience to "reconcile their memories with present beliefs," with 73 percent of those who had sex after pledging later denying that they made the pledge at all. Perhaps such cognitive dissonance is to blame, as Bearman and Brückner suggest, for pledgers being approximately one-third less likely than non-pledgers to use contraception when they first have sex.

What little research has been done on abstinence-education programs has yielded similarly indifferent evidence of their effectiveness. Neither AFLA nor Title V Section 510(b) requires that the programs they underwrite provide proof of their effectiveness. Some states, though, have taken such evaluations upon themselves. Success, on the whole, has been elusive. Many state reviews, such as those conducted in Arizona (June 2003) and Texas (2004), found that sexual behavior among young people who have been taught "abstinence" curricula have not differed substantially from what they had been when students were taught earlier "comprehensive" curricula. Some reviews, such as the independent study commissioned by the Minnesota Department of Health to study the effect of the state's "Education Now and Babies Later" (ENABL) program from 1998 to 2002, revealed that in some schools, sexual activity among abstinence program participants increased substantially. Where positive effects have been shown to come from abstinence programs, they have been most strongly associated with short-term outcomes (a finding that seems congruent with Bearman and Brückner's research) and younger students.

What will come of the American experiment in disseminating a federal virginity ideology is uncertain. Since the system and its ideological agenda were instated without public debate or referendum, it is inaccurate to say that the program was one that the American public chose. But because there is no means by which these federal provisions can be repealed by national ballot, they are not likely to be repealed at all unless through a successful Supreme Court challenge of their constitutionality. For purely economic reasons, states are unlikely to forgo the funds offered through Section 510(b), although many individual municipal school districts have either refused to accept Section 510(b) funds or have channeled them to programs outside of the schools.

The abstinence agenda has its vocal critics—California congressman Henry Waxman is a notable example—both inside and outside of the Washington Beltway. But it also has its very vocal champions, not least in the Bush White

House. The intensity of executive support for abstinence programs has made itself felt beyond AFLA and Section 510(b), sometimes in disturbing ways.

The Centers for Disease Control, the federal medical research organization responsible for addressing infectious and chronic diseases, had until 2002 been conducting research into "Programs That Work," sex-education curricula that had been proven through empirical review to effectively reduce risky sexual behaviors. Of the five they identified as effective, none were abstinence centered. Since 2002, however, the CDC has discontinued this research program and the program's findings have been removed from public view at the CDC's Web site. Other CDC statements praising contraception in a public-health context have also mysteriously vanished from the CDC's online offerings, leaving, instead, statements of presidential and other official support of abstinence programs. It seems reasonable to surmise that high-ranking opposition to anything other than the official virginity-until-marriage agenda has created something of a chilling effect on the CDC's ability to conduct and present scientific research on reproductive health issues.

Where all this will leave the United States remains to be seen. Attempts to export American-style abstinence ideology to other countries have had little real success thus far, despite attempts to tie it to American foreign aid funding. Among its brethren in the developed West, the American government stands alone with its official virginity policy, and the American people stand alone among other First World countries in having to figure out how to deal with it. Perhaps the only thing that is at all clear about this unprecedented legislation of virginity-flavored agitprop is that a politically powerful right wing, faced with the cumulative social change of the last century, has begun to panic in earnest. Reactionary, hyperbolic, and heavily dependent upon a specifically Christian model of sexual morality, the American federal attempt to resurrect—or, more accurately, manufacture—an "expected standard" of virginity until marriage may be best understood as a signal of nothing more than a deep-seated terror of change.

Epilogue: The Once and Future Virgin

> The stone butch has the dubious distinction of being possibly the only
> sexual identity defined almost solely in terms of what practices she
> does not engage in. Is there any other sexual identity, we might ask,
> defined by what a person will not do?
> —Judith Halberstam

EVERY TABOO, every law, and every rule serves at least two functions. On an immediate level they exist to control behavior, to keep people from doing things that their culture considers inappropriate, unethical, or wrong. But on a larger level, rules and taboos exist as representations of the abstract concepts that a culture depends upon to help make sense of human experience. A rule like "thou shalt not steal" enjoins people not to steal the belongings of others. But it also conveys the message that the concept of "private property" plays an important role in the culture. Additionally, it presumes that there is something of a consensus within the society about what "private property" is and what "stealing" is, and that the people who live within this culture are aware of these ideas and what they mean.

Such rules are never entirely complete on their own. When these abstracts become embodied as laws, much less actual events, they acquire context. Context brings variables. With variables come challenges about how these abstracts are understood and interpreted. If a man steals to keep himself from starving, is "stealing" still understood the same way? What if he steals because another man has threatened to kill him if he does not? Or if he steals from someone who has monopolized all of the available resources so that no one else can have any? What then? No single abstract, and no single rule, can adequately serve every moment.

The job of bridging the gap between an abstract principle and its real-world embodiment is complex and highly temporal. The gap can only be bridged in the moment, and only by individual human beings, inheritors of specific histories and denizens of particular times and places. The process of putting abstract concepts into practice thus inevitably reflects both historical and current surroundings, theories, philosophies, and mores.

As such, the process also reflects change. The abstract concepts themselves change slowest, real-world applications of these abstracts change fastest. The laws and rules, the mechanisms that shape and guide daily practice, change at a rate somewhere in between. All are artifacts of human culture, tools that we use to organize our lives, our families, our communities, our cities and countries and institutions. They exist in a constant, complex web of creation and destruction, growth and change.

The regulation and organization of sexual behavior is one of the most basic, and often one of the most volatile, arenas in which culture does its work. Virginity is one of an array of abstract concepts that human cultures have developed to impose some sense of order on the sexual behavior of their members. Not every human culture places a particular value on virginity, and not every culture that does value it values it the same way or to the same degree. Indeed, a given culture's treatment of virginity can change over time.

Nonetheless, making some distinction between virgins and nonvirgins is a common motif in human culture, and it makes pragmatic sense that this should be so. Potentially reproductive sexual activity is critical to a culture's ability to survive and thrive. Thus the onset of such activity in the lives of individual members of a society is meaningful: it is the moment in which they enter the lists in the battle for long-term survival of their people.

Everything else we talk about when we talk about virginity, from definitions to rituals to legislation to morality, proceeds from the awareness that sex *matters*. Sex has always mattered to us as humans, and it is likely that it always will. The ways in which it matters have become increasingly complex, but this is just a testament to our big brains and the complicated cultures we have developed by using them. The fundamental issue remains that sex is important stuff, in very real ways the stuff of life itself. This is why we have always cared, and probably always will care, about virginity.

What confuses us is when the framework supporting our regard for virginity undergoes renovation. This happened during the early years of the Christan era, when virginity, customarily a socioeconomic and familial concern, was suddenly also mobilized as a primary mode of individual sanctity. And it is happening now, as virginity is drifting away from a religious framework and what remains of its socioeconomic and kinship underpinnings and is becoming instead a way to organize experience and identity.

The concepts of individual autonomy and human rights egalitarianism are philosophical products of the Enlightenment that have been developing over the course of the last three hundred years. They have not only led to things like women's rights, the abolition of slavery and apartheid, and other advances in social equality; they have, in combination with a number of other factors, also revolutionized sex. Increasingly, sexuality is considered a realm of personal autonomy. Families, religious authorities, and governments once faced little opposition to the idea that they had a legitimate stake in people's sexual behavior. Now we are increasingly likely to believe that the primary legitimate stakeholder in an individual's sexual life is the individual him- or herself. Individual consent, informed and self-aware, has become the gold standard by which sexual activity exists in a person's life.

Egalitarian and empirical thinking have also combined to generate a philosophy of sexuality that views it as a broadly universal aspect of the human condition, its glories and pitfalls shared by everyone without regard to sex or gender. Men and women alike are recognized to experience sexual feelings ranging from aversion to desire and beyond. We have learned to use an essentially psychoanalytic model to articulate our perception that human beings experience their individual sexualities as an integral component of the self, something we call "sexual identity." These sexual identities have been observed to encompass not only the statistically (and culturally) dominant heterosexual mode, but also many others as well, notably including homo- and transsexuality. Sexuality, we currently believe, is a constant of which there are myriad possible manifestations.

As our culture digests and assimilates these and related ideals, the ways we think about virginity continue to change. Virginity is still a meaningful term, and the sexual status it indicates is still important. But its importance is increasingly private rather than public, personal rather than institutional or familial. The decision to begin a partnered sex life is now quite likely to be predicated on the internal realities of emotion, arousal, or curiosity. This is a far cry from the days when a woman's partnered sex life was most likely to begin because mandatory marriage had forced the issue.

How one understands and defines virginity has likewise become more centered around the individual. The concept that sexuality is the universal, and specific acts only manifestations of that universal, has begun to noticeably nudge penis-in-vagina intercourse out of its long-held position as the sex act of record. Among gay men and lesbians, but also increasingly among hetero- and bisexuals, oral sex, anal sex, and mutual masturbation are now often identified as being the things that turn virgins into no-longer-virgins. Still other people speak, sometimes jokingly but other times earnestly, in terms of having a virginity for each of the orifices that might be involved in a sexual activity, or for each type of sexual act they might engage in. There are a number of different ways to conceptualize "sexual debut," and many different perspectives from which the notion of a first time can be considered.

Others have begun to redefine virginity according to the sensibility that sexuality is lifelong and ongoing and that a shift from one sexual status to another—the acquisition of genuine carnal knowledge—takes time. Losing one's virginity, in this way of thinking, is not so much an individual physical event but rather a process encompassing the physical, emotional, intellectual, and psychological. We often see evidence of this thinking when people grope for ways to explain a sensation of developing awareness in terms of sex, mentioning, say, a first time that satisfied the technical requirements for the end of virginity, and then describing some later experience or experiences that made them feel as if they had "really understood what it was all about" or "finally felt like I knew what I was doing." This is not necessarily revisionism or doublethink. It is often an honest attempt to express a process of sexual development that takes significantly longer than any single episode of sex.

Virginity loss as developmental phase may seem an odd conceit on some levels, but on others, it makes perfect sense. Just as adolescence is understood to exist as a developmental bridge between childhood and adulthood, it is not difficult to conceive of a phase of sexual development that bridges sexual inexperience and a sexual status for which we do not have a customary term, but could perhaps be characterized as sexual virtuosity. In a culture that has come to value both egalitarianism and a developmental model of human identity, thinking of a period of sexual learning—a practicum, if you will—as a segment of a lifelong fabric of sexuality has an attractive neutrality, equally applicable to males and females, heterosexuals and nonheterosexuals, irrelevant of chronological age.

The current multiplicity of ways of thinking about virginity is revolutionary in many philosophical and ideological respects, especially insofar as it represents a historically unprecedented view of women as free agents. But conceptualizing multiple virginities, as this book repeatedly shows, is nothing particularly new. Modern thinking has not smashed a virginal monolith for the simple reason that there has never been a monolith there to smash.

The current welter of ways of thinking about virginity is, however, unusual. It spans an enormous range of perspectives and philosophies. Such a chaotic maelstrom of virginities has not existed since the early centuries of Christianity, when the evolving sexual ideologies of Christianity swirled, fought, and in some cases mingled with the social, economic, and ritual virginity ideologies of pagan, Gnostic, and Jewish cultures. The intervening centuries have given us all the time in the world to become set in our ways, to assume that the ways in which the Church-dominated West thought about sexuality and virginity were innate, natural, or the will of God. But now, as new paradigms encounter old ones and evolving ideologies rub shoulders with ones that have been around for millennia, many of the ironclad long-timers are showing rather a lot of rust. People may react to this with fear and loathing, with skepticism and analysis, or with eager enthusiasm, but few people, whether they are virgins or not, seem uninterested.

This is true not just within the developed West, the arena of the broad "Western culture" that has formed the stage for this exploration of virginity's history, but around the world. Thanks to technological innovations from airplanes to e-mail, the world is, as they say, becoming smaller. Disparate cultures make contact in any number of ways every day. In these encounters, the enormous economic and political power of the industrialized West lends a proportionately enormous cultural impact as well. When we travel, when we export goods, when we provide aid, when we fight wars on foreign soil, we take our culture with us. This includes our culture of sexuality.

Thus the sexuality paradigm shift taking place in the West is not limited to the West at all. But whether it is an unstoppable juggernaut dragging the globe behind it is also debatable. Other cultures have their own priorities, their own philosophies, and their own rationales for handling issues of sex, gender, and virginity, and they are not necessarily any too keen on dealing with sex-culture gate-crashers from foreign parts.

This often leads to conflict. Women's issues, and particularly issues pertaining to women's sexual and reproductive lives, are routinely pushed to the bottom of international political and social agendas. When action is taken on these difficult issues, the divergent demands of human-rights philosophy, global-aid outreach, and cultural integrity can make it difficult to know what should be done. In the ongoing crusades to stop female genital mutilation (FGM, also known as "female circumcision"), practiced in many places and particularly in the Islamic world, there is enormous tension between the desire to protect girls and women from being physically mutilated against their wills, and the knowledge that by so doing, the largely Western organizations responsible for addressing the issue may only succeed in being seen as forcing their own cultural priorities and sexual ideologies down the throats of those they seek to help. Attempts to address "honor crimes" (acts of violence, including mutilation or murder, committed upon women who have in some way been judged to have damaged the honor of their families, often through perceived or actual violations of their families' and cultures' expectations of their virginity) frequently face a similar fate. Although the United Nations finally filed a resolution condemning honor crimes in October 2004, it is likely that meaningful international confrontations on this issue will be a long time in coming if they ever materialize at all.

Virginity-related practices of violence against women are outrageous violations of human rights, but they are also complicated cultural problems. Neither FGM nor honor crimes are issues that can be easily addressed in isolation. They cannot even be addressed simply as matters of problematic ideologies of virginity, for both FGM and honor crimes encompass much more than just virginity.

No matter how desperate our desire to see such devastating violence against women ended, expecting other cultures to simply stop in their tracks and adopt Western cultural priorities when it comes to sexuality is unrealistic. In so profoundly volatile a territory as virginity, particularly, the paths to doing so are often steep and uncertain. Attempting to negotiate such paths in the darkness of presumption and ignorance only makes the process more difficult. Books like this one—although certainly not limited to this one—are a crucial element of change. Information about the full spectrum of virginity issues and their history, even the awareness that one can study it at all, that virginity *has* a history, is an indispensable weapon when dealing with a social principle that is most often asserted as an irreducible fact of nature.

Anthropologists and historians have made only rare attempts to study virginity, and their attempts provide only spotty coverage: even a survey-style book like this one only skims the surface for a small portion of the world. There is a great deal of information that has yet to be gathered and many books that have yet to be written about virginity. It is my fond hope that they will fill in the many gaps I have left in these pages—as well as the vast territories of virginal history and culture I could not even begin to approach in this limited treatment—and that this subject will become better and better understood.

Historical hindsight is a convenience, and in some ways it is a fiction. Books of history often leave the reader with the sense that history happens according to some grandiose plan. The sheer vastness of the historical record, all the millions of bits of data that no given historian can ever include, however, proves that for better or worse this is not true. Events do not happen the way they do in order for certain well-known outcomes to come to pass. They simply happen. The events that make it into the history books do so due to a complicated mix of initiative, inertia, and plain dumb luck. While it seems evident that Western culture is right now in the throes of substantial shifts in its virginity culture specifically and its sex and gender culture at large, it is impossible to say where those shifts will take us.

Having led this tour throughout the ages of virginity, in the end I find that I can only return to what I stated in the opening chapter. Virginity is an abstract, but an abstract so meaningful to the way we have organized our Western cultures that we have arranged lives around it, built it into our religions, our laws, our definitions of marriage, and our ways of organizing families, and woven it into our very concepts of identity and self. If nothing else, I feel I can say with certainty that no matter where our changing culture takes us, and no matter how our notions of virginity change, as long as sex is important in the slightest, virginity and virgins will continue to matter profoundly to us all.

1: Like a Virgin?

The language of ancient Greek virginity is one of the topics discussed in Giulia Sissa, *Greek Virginity*, Arthur Goldhammer, trans. (Cambridge, MA: Harvard University Press, 1990). Medieval scholars' approaches to virginity and chastity are discussed in many sources; two of the most approachable are Pierre Payer's *Sex and the Penitentials: The Development of a Sexual Code, 550–1150* (Toronto: University of Toronto Press, 1984) and *The Bridling of Desire: Views of Sex in the Later Middle Ages* (Toronto: University of Toronto Press, 1993).

The sexuality of children, rarely discussed in even the sexological literature, is more frequently taken up by anthropologists. The massive four-volume encyclopedia of known research on children's sexuality globally, Diederik F. Janssen, *Corpus "Growing Up Sexually"* (Berlin: Magnus Hirschfeld Archive for Sexology, 2002–2005), is constantly updated at http://www2.rz.huberlin.de/sexology/GESUND/ARCHIV/GUS/GUS_MAIN_INDEX.HTM.

On prenatal genital self-stimulation, Catherine Blackledge, *The Story of V : A Natural History of Female Sexuality* (New Brunswick, NJ: Rutgers University Press, 2004), provides a discussion.

On the Jungian concept of the presexual, see C. G. Jung, "The Transformation of Libido," in *Collected Works of C. G. Jung*, vol. 5, Read, Herbert, et al., eds. (New York: Pantheon Books, 1953).

Statistics in regard to age at marriage were derived from the following reports: U.S. Bureau of the Census, "U.S. Adults Postponing Marriage 2001," prepared by the United States Department of Commerce, Office of the Census and Office of National Statistics, United Kingdom's "Report 2001: Population Trends 111: Marriages: Age at Marriage by Sex and Previous Marital Status." Subsequent reports from the United States, the United Kingdom, and other countries in the developed West have indicated that later marriage as a trend is well established and continuing.

For detailed information on Roman Catholic consecrated virgins consult the United States Association of Consecrated Virgins. See the United States Association of Consecrated Virgins Web site, http://www.consecratedvirgins.org.

The effectiveness of virginity pledges is the subject of Peter Bearman and Hanna Brückner, "Promising the Future: Virginity Pledges as They Affect Transition to First Intercourse," *The American Journal of Sociology* 106 (Chicago: University of Chicago Press, January 2001).

A growing number of anecdotal and scientific studies examine the discrepancies between definitions of sexual abstinence, in regard to what counts as sexual activity, what kinds of sexual activities are definitive of the end of virginity, etc., including: Patricia Goodson, Sandy Suther, et al. "Defining Abstinence," *Journal of School Health* 73 no. 3 (March 2003); Kaiser Family Foundation and *Seventeen* magazine, *Sex Smarts: National Survey of Teens Virginity and the First Time*, Henry J. Kaiser Family Foundation, publication no. 3368 (October 2003); Stephanie A. Sanders and June Machover Reinisch, "Would You Say You 'Had Sex' If?," *Journal of the American Medical Association* 281 no. 3 (January 20, 1999): 275–277; M. A. Schuster, R. M. Bell, and D. E. Kanouse, "The Sexual Practices of Adolescent Virgins: Genital Sexual Activities of High School Students Who Have Never Had Vaginal Intercourse," *American Journal of Public Health* 86 no. 11 (1996): 1570–1576; and Israel M. Schwartz, "Sexual Activity Prior to Coital Initiation: A Comparison Between Males and Females," *Archives of Sexual Behavior* 28 no. 1 (1999): 63–69.

2: The Importance of Being Virgin

Information on the comparative sexual biology and sociology of a wide variety of animal species is presented in, among other sources: Blackledge, *The Story of V: Opening Pandora's Box* (London: Weidenfeld & Nicolson, 2003); Sarah Blaffer Hrdy, *Mother Nature: Natural Selection & the Female of the Species* (London: Chatto & Windus, 1999); William G. Eberhard, *Sexual Selection and Animal Genitalia* (Cambridge, MA: Harvard University Press, 1985); and Bettyann Kevles, *Females of the Species: Sex and Survival in the Animal Kingdom* (Cambridge, MA: Harvard University Press, 1986).

An entry-level discussion of the property/patriarchy theory of the origins of human awareness of virginity can be found in Timothy Taylor, *The Prehistory of Sex: Four Million Years of Human Sexual Culture* (New York: Bantam Books, 1996). Other discussions may be found in sources including: Shirley Ardener, "Defining Females: The Nature of Women in Society," *Cross-cultural Perspectives on Women* 4 (Providence, RI: Berg, 1993); Ottokar Nemecek, *Virginity: Pre-Nuptial Rites and Rituals* (New York: Philosophical Library, 1958); and Elisa Janine Sobo and Sandra Bell, eds., *Celibacy, Culture, and Society: The Anthropology of Sexual Abstinence* (Madison: University of Wisconsin Press, 2001).

Aline Rousselle comments at length on exposure and infanticide in the ancient world, among other topics, in *Porneia: On Desire and the Body in Antiquity*, Felicia Pheasant, trans. (London: Basil Blackwell Ltd., 1988).

The translation of Deuteronomy 22:13–21 featured in this chapter is my own. Thanks are due to Danya Ruttenberg for her assistance.

3: Hymenology

In C. Jenny, M. L. Kuhns and F. Arakawa, "Hymens in Newborn Female Infants," *Pediatrics* 80 (1987), the estimated frequency of congenital (i.e., from birth) absence of the hymen is given at less than 0.03 percent.

Speculations on the evolutionary purpose of the hymen may be found in, among other sources, Blackledge, *The Story of V: Opening Pandora's Box* (London: Weidenfeld & Nicolson, 2003), and Elaine Morgan, *The Aquatic Ape Hypothesis* (New York: Stein and Day, 1982).

The variability of hymenal shape, size, and dimension is discussed in numerous reports, including: Abby Berenson, "A Longitudinal Study of Hymenal Morphology in the First 3 Years of Life," *Pediatrics* 95 no. 4 (April 1995): 490–6; Berenson, "Appearance of the Hymen at Birth and One Year of Age: A Longitudinal Study," *Pediatrics* 91 no. 4 (April 1993): 820–5; Berenson, and James J. Grady, "A Longitudinal Study of Hymenal Development from 3 to 9 Years of Age," *The Journal of Pediatrics* 140 no. 5 (May 2002): 600–607; Berenson, et al., "Appearance of the Hymen in Prepubertal Girls," *Pediatrics* 89 no. 3 (March 1992): 387–94; and Astrid H. Heger, et al., "Appearance of the Genitalia in Girls Selected for Nonabuse: Review of Hymenal Morphology and Nonspecific Findings," *Journal of Pediatric and Adolescent Gynecology* 15 (2002): 27–35.

A relevant case study detailing the matrilineal genetic transmission of imperforate hymen is: J. R. Stelling, et al., "Dominant Transmission of Imperforate Hymen," *Fertility and Sterility* 74 no. 6 (2000): 1241–44.

Two articles discussing the possible sexual abuse etiology implicated in some cases of what may be diagnosed as imperforate hymen are C. D. Berkowitz, S. L. Elvik, and M. Logan, "A Simulated Acquired Imperforate Hymen Following the Genital Trauma of Sexual Abuse," *Clinical Pediatrics* 26 (1987): 307–9, and Anne S. Botash and Florence Jean-Louis, "Imperforate Hymen: Congenital or Acquired from Sexual Abuse?" *Pediatrics* 108 no. 3 (September 2001): 53 ff.

The most useful comparative study of published hymenal research to date is Heger, et al., "Appearance of the Genitalia in Girls Selected for Nonabuse." The relative frequencies of different hymenal presentations discussed in this chapter are derived from the tables presented throughout this article.

The criteria used to determine the different configurations and presentations is taken from the American Academy of Pediatrics, "Committee on Child Abuse and Neglect: Guidelines for the Evaluation of Sexual Abuse of Children," *Pediatrics* 103 vol. 1 (1999): 186–191.

The case report on the remarkable imperforate-hymen trifecta described in this chapter is from the medical literature Chao-Hsi Lee and Ching-Chung Liang, "Hymen Re-Formation after Hymenotomy Associated with Pregnancy," *Australia and New Zealand Journal of Gynecology* 42 no. 5 (November 2002): 559–560.

4: A Desperate and Conflicted Search

Among the recent sources that deal in detail with the history of virginity in the ancient and medieval medical literature are: Joan Cadden, *The Meanings of Sex Difference in the Middle*

Ages (Cambridge: Cambridge University Press, 1993); Monica Green, "Obstetrical and Gynecological Texts in Middle English," *Studies in the Age of Chaucer* 14 (1992): 53–88, and her book *The Trotula: A Medieval Compendium of Women's Medicine* (Philadelphia: University of Pennsylvania Press, 2001); Ann E. Hanson, "The Medical Writers' Woman," in *Before Sexuality*, David Halperin, ed. (Princeton: Princeton University Press, 1990); Helen King, "Bound to Bleed: Artemis and Greek Women," in *Images of Women in Antiquity*, Averil Cameron and Amelie Kuhrt, eds. (Detroit: Wayne State University Press, 1983): 109–27, and her "Producing Woman: Hippocratic Gynecology," in *Women in Ancient Societies: An Illusion of the Night*, L. J. Archer, et al., eds. (London: Macmillan, 1994): 102–14; Esther Lastique and Helen Lemay, "A Medieval Physician's Guide to Virginity," in *Sex in the Middle Ages: A Book of Essays*, Joyce E. Salisbury, ed. (New York: Garland Publishing, 1991); Marie H. Loughlin, *Hymeneutics: Interpreting Virginity on the Early Modern Stage* (Lewisburg, PA: Bucknell University Press, 1997); Rousselle, *Porneia: On Desire and the Body in Antiquity*, Felicia Pheasant, trans. (London: Basil Blackwell Ltd., 1988); and Sissa, *Greek Virginity*, Arthur Goldhammer, trans. (Cambridge, MA: Harvard University Press, 1990). Last but by far not least, the spectacular overview given in Kathleen Coyne Kelly's *Performing Virginity and Testing Chastity in the Middle Ages*, Routledge Research in Medieval Studies Series (New York: Routledge, 2000), should be singled out for applause.

Discussions of the value of various hymenal attributes can be found in several sources, including: Berenson, et al., "A Case-Control Study of Anatomic Changes Resulting from Sexual Abuse," *American Journal of Obstetrics and Gynecology* 182 (2000): 1043–45; Berenson, et al., "Use of Hymenal Measurements in the Diagnosis of Previous Penetration," *Pediatrics* 109 no. 2 (February 2002): 228–35; K. Edgardh and K. Ormstad, "The Adolescent Hymen," *Journal of Reproductive Medicine* 47 no. 9 (September 2002): 710–14; and D. M. Ingram, et al., "The Relationship between the Transverse Hymenal Orifice Diameter by the Separation Technique and Other Possible Markers of Sexual Abuse," *Child Abuse & Neglect* 25 (2001): 1090–120.

5: The Virgin and the Doctor

Sources that speak to the issue of speculum examination in historical context include: Susan Edwards, *Female Sexuality and the Law: A Study of Constructs of Female Sexuality as They Inform Statute and Legal Procedure* (Oxford: Martin Robertson, 1981); Toby Gelfand, *Professionalizing Modern Medicine: Paris Surgeons and Medical Science and Institutions* (Westport, CT: Greenwood Press, 1980); Ornella Moscucci, *The Science of Woman: Gynaecology and Gender in England, 1800–1929*, Series: Cambridge History of Medicine, Charles Webster and Charles Rosenberg, eds. (Cambridge: Cambridge University Press, 1990); James V. Ricci, *The Geneaology of Gynaecology* (Philadelphia: Blakiston, 1943); and Peter Skegg, *Law, Ethics, and Medicine: Studies in Medical Law* (Oxford: Oxford University Press 1984).

A particularly thoughtful and instructive analysis of the virgin-cure myth in an industrialized, Western twentieth-century context is Roger Davidson, " 'This Pernicious Delusion': Law, Medicine, and Child Sexual Abuse in Early Twentieth-Century Scotland," *Journal of the History of Sexuality* 10/1 (January 2001): 62–77.

On the problems of venereal disease generally and venereal disease in children specifically, see Wayland Debs Hand, *Magical Medicine: The Folkloric Component of Medicine in Folk Belief, Custom, and Ritual of the Peoples of Europe and America* (Berkeley: University of California Press, 1980), and Timothy Taylor, "Venereal Disease in Nineteenth-Century Children," *Journal of Psychohistory* 12/4 (Spring 1985): 431–63.

Among the many valuable sources on the current problems in regard to the virgin-cure myth in South Africa is Eileen Meier, "Child Rape in South Africa," *Pediatric Nursing* 28/5 (2002): 532–35. News coverage on the issue can also be illuminating, although it does not offer clinical perspective.

Helen King's monograph *The Disease of Virgins: Green Sickness, Chlorosis, and the Problems of Puberty* (New York: Routledge, 2004) is a gem in the history of the intersection of medicine and culture. For a shorter but still useful assessment, see Robert P. Hudson, "The Biography of Disease: Lessons from Chlorosis," *Bulletin of the History of Medicine* 51 (1977): 448–463.

The doggerel quoted at the end of this section is of anonymous authorship. It can be found as "A Cure for ye Greene Sicknesse," Bodleian Ms. Rawlinson poet. 172, fol. 2v.

Data on average hymenal dimensions can be found in many sources, including Berenson and Grady, "A Longitudinal Study of Hymenal Development from 3 to 9 Years of Age," *Journal of Pediatrics* 140 (2002): 600–607, and Susan Pokorny, "Configuration of the Prepubertal Hymen," *American Journal of Obstetrics and Gynecology* 157/4 part 1 (October 1987): 950–56.

The mainstream press is peppered with articles about hymen restoration surgeries and the medical ethics surrounding them. A representative pair consulted in the preparation of this book are Sue Yeon Choi, "Restoring Virginity: Hymen Repair Surgery Saves Lives at the Expense of Deception," *Issues: Berkeley Medical Journal* (Fall 1998), viewed at (http://www .ocf.berkeley.edu/~issues/fall98/hymenrep.html), and Susan Oh, "Just Like a Virgin?" *Maclean's* 113/24 (June 12, 2000): 44–46. A useful overview of the medical profession's own ethical discussion of the issue is A. Logmans, et al., "Should Doctors Reconstruct the Vaginal Introitus of Adolescent Girls to Mimic the Virginal State? Who Wants the Procedure and Why," *British Medical Journal* 316/7129 (February 7, 1998): 459–60.

6: The Blank Page

Queen's University Belfast anthropologist Paloma Gay-y-Blasco's work on Gitano virginity, *Gypsies in Madrid: Sex, Gender and the Performance of Identity* (Oxford: Berg, 1999), is exemplary and astonishing. Her two articles, "Gitano Understandings of Female Virginity: Sex and the Construction of Ethnic Difference," *Cambridge Anthropology* 17 no. 1 (1994), and the 1997 "A 'Different' Body? Desire and Virginity among Gitanos," *The Journal of the Royal Anthropological Society* 3 no. 3, provide more focused discussions of the specific beliefs and practices addressed at the beginning of this chapter.

The remarks made by a young woman who spoke of the assumptions of her peers in regard to her virginity, based on their feelings about the appearance of her buttocks and hips, are from Kristin Haglund, "Sexually Abstinent African American Adolescent Females' Descriptions of Abstinence," *Journal of Nursing Scholarship* 35 no. 3 (2003): 231–36. There are many other similar "visual diagnosis" issues mentioned throughout the medical and sociological literature on virginity, as well as in sexual folklore. Some of them are addressed from this angle in Mariamne Watley and Elissa Henken, *Did You Hear About the Girl Who . . . ?: Contemporary Legends, Folklore, and Human Sexuality* (New York: New York University Press, 2000).

Virginity tests can be found in an enormous number of medical texts written prior to the twentieth century and have been discussed at some length in the historical literature, including: Clarissa W. Atkinson, "Precious Balsam in a Fragile Glass: The Ideology of Virginity in the Later Middle Ages," *Journal of Family History* (Summer 1983): 131–43; Vern L. Bullough and James Brundage, eds., *The Problem of Impotence in Sexual Practices and the Medieval Church* (Buffalo, NY: Prometheus Books, 1982): 135–40; Tassie Gwilliam, "Female Fraud: Counterfeit Maidenheads in the Eighteenth Century," *Journal of the History of Sexuality* 6 no. 4 (1996): 518–48; Danielle Jacquart and Claude Thomasset, *Sexuality and Medicine in the Middle Ages*, Matthew Adamson, trans. (Princeton: Princeton University Press, 1988); Kelly, *Performing Virginity and Testing Chastity in the Middle Ages*, Routledge Research in Medieval Studies Series (New York: Routledge, 2000); King, *The Disease of Virgins: Green Sickness, Chlorosis, and the Problems of Puberty* (New York: Routledge, 2004); Lastique and Lemay, "A Medieval Physician's Guide to Virginity," in *Sex in the Middle Ages,* Joyce E. Salisbury, ed. (New York: Garland Publishing, 1991); Lemay, *Women's Secrets: A Translation of Pseudo-Albertus Magnus' De secretis mulierum with Commentaries*, SUNY Series in Medieval Studies, Paul Szarmach, ed. (Albany: State University of New York Press, 1992); Lemay, "The Stars and Human Sexuality: Some Medieval Scientific Views," *Isis* 71 (March 1980): 127–37; Hermann Moller, "Voice Change in Human Biological Development," *Journal of Interdisciplinary History* 16 no. 2 (Autumn 1985): 239–53; Jacqueline Murray, "The Origins and Role of 'Wise Women' in Causes for Annulment on the Grounds of Male Impotence," *Journal of Medieval History* 16 (1990): 235–49; Stephen Robertson, "Signs, Marks, and Private Parts: Doctors, Legal Discourses, and Evidence of Rape in the United States, 1823–1930," *Journal of the History of Sexuality* 9 no. 3 (1998): 345–88; Rousselle, *Porneia: On Desire and the Body in Antiquity*, Felicia Pheasant, trans. (London: Basil Blackwell Ltd., 1988); Joyce E. Salisbury, "Fruitful in Singleness," *Journal of Medieval History* 8 (1982).

Dr. Sara Paterson-Brown's informal research in regard to the percentages of women who report bleeding at the time of virginity loss was given in the context of: "Commentary: Education about the Hymen Is Needed," in the February 7, 1998, *British Medical Journal*, p. 341.

The American College of Obstetricians and Gynecologists' statement of its expectations of a physician's ability to diagnose a "normal" versus an "altered" hymen was made in the context of a technical bulletin on pediatric gynecology, *American College of Obstetricians and Gynecologists, Technical Bulletin No. 201: Pediatric Gynecologic Disorders* (Washington, D.C.: The College, 1995).

Dr. Abby Berenson's comments on the relative infrequency with which examiners find reliable genital evidence of sexual abuse can be found in Berenson, et al. "A Case-Control Study of Anatomic Changes Resulting from Sexual Abuse," American *Journal of Obstetric Gynecology* 182 (2000); Debarge, et al. "Examen médico-légal de l'hymen: Étude analytique de 384 dossiers d'expertises médico-légales pratiquées à l'occasion d'agressions sexuelles,"

Médecin Legale et Dommage Corporelle 6 no. 3 (1973): 298–300, provides a bit of independent (and much earlier) confirmation that the same sort of variability of findings is also true in regard to rape cases.

Additional reflections on the ability of the hymen to reflect specific sexual histories can be found in: S. J. Emans, et al., "Hymenal Findings in Adolescent Women: Impact of Tampon Use and Consensual Sexual Activity," *Journal of Pediatrics* 125 (1994); Felicity Goodyear-Smith and Tannis Laidlaw, "Can Tampon Use Cause Hymen Changes in Girls Who Have Not Had Sexual Intercourse? A Review of the Literature," *Forensic Science International* 94 nos. 1–2, (1998); and Edgardh and Ormstad, "The Adolescent Hymen," *Journal of Reproductive Medicine* 47 no. 9 (September 2002).

The *British Medical Journal* article dealing with practitioner education and beliefs about aspects of the hymen is in Emma Curtis and Camille San Lazaro, "Appearance of the Hymen in Adolescents Is Not Well Documented," *British Medical Journal* (February 27, 1999), 605.

The studies directed by Jan Paradise cited in this chapter are Paradise, et al., "Assessments of girl's genital findings and the likelihood of sexual abuse: agreement among physicians self-rated as skilled," *Archives of Pediatric and Adolescent Medicine* 151 no. 9 (1997): 883–91, and Paradise, et al. "Influence of History on Physicians' Interpretation of Girls' Genital Findings," *Pediatrics* 103 no. 5 part 1 (1999), 980–986.

The short story from which the title of this chapter was taken, and which is discussed at the chapter's end, is from Isak Dinesen, "The Blank Page," in *Last Tales* (New York: Random House, Inc., 1957): 99–106.

7: Opening Night

Among the numerous fine sources on marriage and marriage customs history are: Nancy F. Cott, *Public Vows: A History of Marriage and the Nation* (Cambridge, MA: Harvard University Press, 2003); Chrys Ingraham, *White Weddings: Romancing Heterosexuality in Popular Culture* (New York: Routledge, 1999); Wendy Leeds-Hurwitz, *Wedding as Text: Communicating Cultural Identities through Ritual* (Mahwah, NJ: Lawrence Erlbaum Associates, 2002); and George Ryley Scott, *Curious Customs of Sex & Marriage* (London: Senate, 1995).

The anthropological literature on the rite of passage begins properly with Arnold van Gennep, *The Rites of Passage*, Monika Vizedom and Gabrielle Caffe, trans. (Chicago: University of Chicago Press, 1975). A useful companion volume is Louise Carus Mahdi, Nancy Geyer Christopher, and Michael Meade, eds., *Crossroads: The Quest for Contemporary Rites of Passage* (Chicago: Open Court, 1996).

A variety of discussions of virginity-loss narratives can be found in: Françoise Barret-Ducroq, *Love in the Time of Victoria: Sexuality, Class, and Gender in Nineteenth-Century London*, John Howe, trans. (New York: Penguin Books, 1992); Karen Bouris, *The First Time: Women Speak Out About Losing Their Virginity* (Emeryville, CA: Conari Press, 1993); Louis Crozier, *Losing It: The Virginity Myth* (Washington, D.C.: Avocus Publishing, Inc., 1993); Ginger Frost, *Promises Broken: Courtship, Class, and Culture in Victorian England*, Victorian Literature and Culture Series, Herbert Tucker and Jerome McGann, series eds. (Charlottesville:

University Press of Virginia, 1995); Alice Schlegel, "The Social Criteria of Adulthood," *Human Development* 41 (1999): 323–25; and Sharon Thompson's *Going All The Way: Teenage Girls' Tales of Sex, Romance, and Pregnancy* (New York: Hill and Wang, 1996) and "Putting a Big Thing into a Little Hole: Teenage Girls' Accounts of Sexual Initiation," *The Journal of Sex Research* 27/3 (August 1990): 341–61.

Of the many statistical reviews of adolescent pregnancy and childbearing in the medical, socio-logical, and demographic literature, two helpful ones are Susheela Singh and Jacqueline Darroch, "Adolescent pregnancy and childbearing: levels and trends in developed coun-tries," *Family Planning Perspectives* 32/1 (2000): 14–23, and Stephanie Ventura, et al., "Trends in Pregnancy Rates for the United States, 1976–97: An Update," *National Vital Statistics Reports* 49/4 (2001): 1–10.

The single Western scholar who has done the most research on contemporary virginity loss is Vanderbilt University sociologist Laura M. Carpenter, whose book *Virginity Lost: An Inti-mate Portrait of First Sexual Experiences* was published by New York University Press in 2005. See also: Carpenter, "Gender and the Social Construction of Virginity Loss in the Contemporary United States," *Gender & Society* 16/3 (2002): 345–65; "The Ambiguity of 'Having Sex': The Subjective Experience of Virginity Loss in the United States," *The Jour-nal of Sex Research* 38/2 (2001): 127–39; "The First Time/ Das Erstes Mal: Approaches to Sexuality in U.S. and German Teen Magazines," *Youth & Society* 32/3 (2001): 31–61; and "From Girls Into Women: Scripts for Sexuality and Romance in *Seventeen* Magazine, 1974–1994," *The Journal of Sex Research* 35/2 (1998): 158–68.

On the related (but not identical) subjects of bridewealth and dowry, consult: Jack Goody and Stanley J. Tambiah, eds., *Bridewealth and Dowry*, Cambridge Papers in Social Anthropology no. 7 (Cambridge: Cambridge University Press, 1973); Karen Ericksen Paige, "Virginity Rituals and Chastity Control during Puberty: Cross-Cultural Patterns," in *Menarche: The Transition from Girl to Woman*, Sharon Golub, ed. (Lexington, KY: D.C. Heath, 1983): 155–74; Jane Schneider, "Of Vigilance and Virgins: Honor, Shame, and Access to Resources in Mediterranean Societies," *Ethnology* 10 (1971): 1–24; Lawrence Stone, *The Family, Sex, and Marriage in England 1500–1800* (New York: Harper and Row, 1977); and Randolph Trumbach, *The Rise of the Egalitarian Family* (New York: Academic Press, 1978).

In the literature about the specific relationship of virginity, dowry, status, and social manage-ment, Alice Schlegel's work deserves particular notice, specifically her "Status, Property, and the Value of Virginity," *American Ethnologist* 18 (1991): 719–34; "The Cultural Man-agement of Adolescent Sexuality," in *Sexual Nature Sexual Culture*, Paul R. Abramson and Steven D. Pinkerton, eds. (Chicago: University of Chicago Press, 1995): 177–94; and "The Chaste Adolescent" in *Celibacy, Culture, and Society: The Anthropology of Sexual Absti-nence*, Elisa J. Sobo and Sandra Bell, eds. (Madison: The University of Wisconsin Press, 2001): 87–103.

A selective roster of sources discussing reactions to virginity loss includes: Anonymous, *Aris-totle's Master-Piece; or, the Secrets of Generation Displayed in All the Parts Thereof* (London: For WB, 1695); Talmud, Tractate Ketubot, vol. 11, The Steinsaltz Edition (New York: Ran-dom House, 1996); Blackledge, *The Story of V: Opening Pandora's Box* (London: Weiden-feld & Nicolson, 2004); Ruth Bodden-Heidrich, et al., "What Does a Young Girl Experience in Her First Gynecological Examination? Study on the Relationship between

Anxiety and Pain," *Journal of Pediatric and Adolescent Gynecology* 13/3 (August, 2000): 139–42; Cowan, *The Science of a New Life* (New York: Cowan & Company, Publishers, 1880); Dickson, et al., "First Sexual Intercourse: Age, Coercion, and Later Regrets Reported by a Birth Cohort," *British Medical Journal* 316 (January 3, 1998): 29–33; Sigmund Freud, "The Taboo on Virginity," in *Sexuality and the Psychology of Love*, Philip Reiff, ed. (New York: Simon and Schuster, 1963); Goodyear-Smith and Laidlaw, "Can Tampon Use Cause Hymen Changes in Girls who Have Not Had Sexual Intercourse? A Review of the Literature," *Forensic Science International* 94 (1998): 148–53; Dannah Gresh, *And The Bride Wore White: Seven Secrets to Sexual Purity* (Chicago: Moody Publishers, 2002); Carol Groneman, *Nymphomania: A History* (New York: W. W. Norton, 2000); Deanna Holtzman and Nancy Kulish, "A Brief Communication on Defloration," *Psychoanalytic Quarterly* LXXII (2003): 477–82; Bronwen Lichtenstein, "Virginity Discourse in the AIDS Era: A Case Analysis of Sexual Initiation Aftershock," *National Women's Studies Association Journal* 12/2 (Summer 2000): 52–69; Marie Stopes, *Married Love: A New Contribution to the Solution of Sex Difficulties*, 19th ed. (New York: G. P. Putnam's Sons, 1931): 30; Thompson, *Going All The Way: Teenage Girls' Tales of Sex, Romance, and Pregnancy* and "Putting a Big Thing into a Little Hole: Teenage Girls' Accounts of Sexual Initiation"; D. L. Weis, "The Experience of Pain during Women's First Sexual Intercourse: Cultural Mythology about Female Sexual Initiation," *Archives of Sexual Behavior* 14/5 (1985): 421–38; and Daniel Wight, et al., "Extent of Regretted Sexual Intercourse among Young Teenagers in Scotland: A Cross Sectional Survey," *British Medical Journal* 320 (May 6, 2000): 1243–44.

8: *In a Certain Way Unbodily*, and 9: *Heaven and Earth*

Because these two chapters are so substantially preoccupied with the subject of Christianity and share a great deal of source material, I have chosen to combine the sources in order to avoid large numbers of duplicate listings across chapters.

Among the many worthwhile sources on pre-Christian antiquity are: Mary Beard, "The Sexual Status of Vestal Virgins," *Journal of Roman Studies* 70 (1980): 12–27; David Biale, *Eros and the Jews: From Biblical Israel to Contemporary America* (New York: Basic Books, 1992); Daniel Boyarin, *Carnal Israel: Reading Sex in Talmudic Culture* (Berkeley: University of California Press, 1995); Peter L. Brown, *The Body and Society: Men, Women, and Sexual Renunciation in Early Christianity* (New York: Columbia University Press, 1988); Henri Crouzel, *Origen: The Life and Thought of the First Great Theologian*, A. S. Worrall, trans. (San Francisco: Harper and Row, 1989); Judith Hallett, *Fathers and Daughters in Roman Society: Women and the Elite Family* (Princeton, NJ: Princeton University Press, 1984); Lesley Hazleton, *Mary: A Flesh-and-Blood Biography of the Virgin Mother* (New York: Bloomsbury, 2004); Mary R. Lefkowitz and Maureen B. Fant, *Women's Life in Greece & Rome: A Source Book in Translation*, 2nd ed. (Baltimore: Johns Hopkins University Press, 1992); Sarah Pomeroy, *Goddesses, Whores, Wives, and Slaves* (New York: Schocken, 1975); Aline Rousselle, *Porneia: On Desire and the Body in Antiquity*, Felicia Pheasant, trans. (New York: Barnes and Noble Books, 1988); and Sissa, *Greek Virginity*, Arthur Goldhammer, trans. (Cambridge, MA: Harvard University Press, 1990).

Analysis and critical close-readings regarding Christian antiquity may be found in: Kerstin Aspegren, *The Male Woman: A Feminine Ideal in the Early Church*, Renee Kieffer, ed. (Stockholm: Almqvist & Wiksell International, 1990); Augustine, *Holy Virginity in Marriage and Virginity: The Excellence of Marriage, Holy Virginity, The Excellence of Widowhood, Adulterous Marriages, Continence*, David G. Hunter, ed., Ray Kearney, trans.; *The Works of Saint Augustine: A Translation for the Twenty-first Century*, vol. I/9, Augustinian Heritage Institute (Hyde Park, NY: New City Press, 1999); Brown, *The Body and Society: Men, Women, and Sexual Renunciation in Early Christianity*; Elizabeth Castelli, "Virginity and Its Meaning for Women's Sexuality in Early Christianity," *Journal of Feminist Studies in Religion* 2 (1986): 61–88; Kate M.Cooper, *The Virgin and the Bride: Idealized Womanhood in Late Antiquity* (Cambridge, MA: Harvard University Press, 1996); Susanna Elm, *"Virgins of God": The Making of Asceticism in Late Antiquity* (Oxford: Clarendon Press, 1994); Roberta Gilchrist, *Gender and Material Culture: The Archaeology of Religious Women* (London: Routledge, 1994); Joyce N. Hillgarth, *The Conversion of Western Europe, 350–750* (Englewood Cliffs, NJ: Prentice-Hall, 1969); Stephanie Hollis, *Anglo-Saxon Women and the Church: Sharing a Common Fate* (Woodbridge: Boydell Press, 1992); Jean Laporte, *The Role of Women in Early Christianity*, Studies in Women and Religion 7 (New York: Edwin Mellen Press, 1982); Elisabeth Schüssler Fiorenza, *In Memory of Her: A Feminist Theological Reconstruction of Christian Origins* (New York: Crossroads, 1985); and Tertullian, *De Virginibus Velandis*, Corpus Scriptorum Ecclesiasticorum Latinorum 76, V. Bulhart, ed. (Vienna: Hölder-Pichler-Tempsky, 1957).

The history of monks and nuns is often specific and esoteric, but there also exist many approachable studies on medieval ecclesiasticism: John Bugge, *Virginitas: An Essay in the History of a Medieval Ideal*, International Archives of the History of Ideas no. 17 (The Hague: Martinus Nijhoff, 1975); David Herlihy, *Medieval Households* (Cambridge: Harvard University Press, 1985); Andrew Macleish, ed., *The Medieval Monastery* (St. Cloud, MN: North Star Press, 1988); Penelope D. Johnson, *Equal in Monastic Profession: Religious Women in Medieval France* (Chicago: University of Chicago Press, 1991); Friedrich Kempf, Hans-Georg Beck, and Josef Andreas Jungmann. *The Church in the Age of Feudalism* (New York: Seabury Press, 1980); Henrietta Leyser, *Hermits and the New Monasticism: A Study of Religious Communities in Western Europe, 1000–1150* (New York: St. Martin's, 1984); Joan Morris, *The Lady Was a Bishop: The History of Women with Clerical Ordination and the Jurisdiction of Bishops* (New York: MacMillan, 1973); Elizabeth Alvilda Petroff, ed., *Medieval Women's Visionary Literature* (New York: Oxford University Press, 1986); Eileen Power, *Medieval English Nunneries, 1275–1535* (Cambridge: Cambridge University Press, 1922); Suzanne Fonay Wemple, *Women in Frankish Society: Marriage and the Cloister, 500–900* (Philadelphia: University of Pennsylvania Press, 1981); Donald Weinstein and Rudolph M. Bell, *Saints and Society: The Two Worlds of Western Christendom, 1000–1700* (Chicago: University of Chicago Press, 1982); and Ulrike Weithaus, ed., *Maps of Flesh and Light: The Religious Experience of Medieval Women Mystics* (Syracuse: Syracuse University Press, 1993).

These chapters owe a particular debt to the exemplary work of historian of women's monasticism JoAnn McNamara. Her work includes: *A New Song: Celibate Women in the First Three Christian Centuries* (New York: Haworth Press, 1983) and *Sisters in Arms: Catholic Nuns through Two Millennia* (Cambridge, MA: Harvard University Press, 1996).

On the specifically sexual aspects of medieval religion, see: Brundage, *Law, Sex, and Christian Society in Medieval Europe* (Chicago: University of Chicago Press, 1987); Bullough and Brundage, eds., *Sexual Practices and the Medieval Church* (Buffalo, NY: Prometheus Books, 1982); Graciela Daichman, *Wayward Nuns in Medieval Literature* (Syracuse, NY: Syracuse University Press, 1986); Dyan Elliott, *Spiritual Marriage: Sexual Abstinence in Medieval Wedlock* (Princeton, NJ: Princeton University Press, 1993); and Guido Ruggiero, *The Boundaries of Eros: Sex, Crime, and Sexuality in Renaissance Venice* (New York: Oxford University Press, 1985).

On the virgin martyrs: Peter Brown, *The Cult of the Saints: Its Rise and Function in Latin Christianity* (Chicago: University of Chicago Press, 1981); Hippolyte Delehaye, *The Legends of the Saints: An Introduction to Hagiography*, V. M. Crawford, trans. (Notre Dame, IN: University of Notre Dame Press, 1961); Mand Burnett McInerney, *Eloquent Virgins: From Thecla to Joan of Arc* (New York: Palgrave Macmillan, 2003); Karen A. Winstead, *Virgin Martyrs: Legends of Sainthood in Late Medieval England* (Ithaca, NY: Cornell University Press, 1997), and *Chaste Passions: Medieval English Virgin Martyr Legends* (Ithaca, NY: Cornell University Press, 2000); Jocelyn Wogan-Browne's "Saints' Lives and the Female Reader," *Forum for Modern Language Studies* 27 (1991): 314–32.

On Mary and the *Protoevangelion*: Biale, *Eros and the Jews: From Biblical Israel to Contemporary America*; Boyarin, *Carnal Israel: Reading Sex in Talmudic Culture*; Howard Eilberg-Schwartz, ed., *People of the Body: Jews and Judaism from an Embodied Perspective*, SUNY Series, The Body in Culture, History, and Religion (Albany: SUNY Press, 1992); J. K. Elliott, ed., *The Apocryphal New Testament: A Collection of Apocryphal Christian Literature in English Translation* (Oxford: Clarendon Press, 1993); Beverly Roberts Gaventa, *Mary: Glimpses of the Mother of Jesus* (Columbia: University of South Carolina Press, 1995); Ronald F. Hock, *The Infancy Gospels of James and Thomas: Introduction, Greek Text, English Translation, and Notes*, Scholars Bible (Santa Rosa, CA: Polebridge Press, 1995); Mary Foskett, *A Virgin Conceived: Mary and Classical Representations of Virginity* (Bloomington: Indiana University Press, 2002); Jacob Neusner, *The Mishnah: A New Translation* (New Haven, CT: Yale University Press, 1988); Jaroslav Pelikan, *Mary through the Centuries: Her Place in the History of Culture* (New Haven, CT: Yale University Press, 1996); Jane Schaberg, *The Illegitimacy of Jesus: A Feminist Theological Interpretation of the Infancy Narratives* (San Francisco: Harper & Row, 1987); and Maria Warner, *Alone of All Her Sex: The Myth and Cult of the Virgin Mary* (New York: Vintage Books, 1983).

Biographical sources dealing with the life and crimes of Countess Erzsébet Báthory are reasonably common, but worthwhile ones are rare. Two that are reasonably reliable and accessible are Raymond McNally's *Dracula Was a Woman: In Search of the Blood Countess of Transylvania* (New York: McGraw-Hill, 1983) and Tony Thorne's *Countess Dracula: The Life and Times of the Blood Countess, Elisabeth Bathory* (London: Bloomsbury, 1997).

The three major sources on the *jus primae noctis* and its heritage are Alain Boureau, *The Lord's First Night: The Myth of the Droit de Cuissage*, Lydia G. Cochrane, trans. (Chicago: University of Chicago Press, 1998); Eleanor Palermo Litvack, *Le Droit du Seigneur in European and American Literature from the Seventeenth through the Twentieth Century* (Birmingham, AL: Summa Publications, Inc., 1984); and Jörg Wettlaufer, *Das Herrenrecht der ersten Nacht:*

Hochzeit, Herrschaft und Heiratszins im Mittlealter und in der frühen Neuzeit, Campus Historische Studien Band 27 (Frankfurt: Campus Verlag, 1999).

10: To Go Where No Man Has Gone Before

The body of literature concerning Queen Elizabeth I is enormous. The sources used for this book tend to be ones that concentrate heavily or exclusively on issues regarding the role of sexuality in the queen's life and rule and include: Susan Doran, *Monarchy and Matrimony: The Courtships of Elizabeth I* (New York: Routledge, 1996); Susan Doran and Thomas S. Freeman, eds., *The Myth of Elizabeth* (New York: Palgrave Macmillan, 2003); Helen Hackett, *Virgin Mother, Maiden Queen: Elizabeth I and the Cult of the Virgin Mary* (Basingstoke, UK: Macmillan, 1995); Christopher Hibbert, *The Virgin Queen: The Personal History of Elizabeth I* (New York: Viking, 1990); John N. King, "Queen Elizabeth I: Representations of the Virgin Queen," *Renaissance Quarterly* 43/1 (Spring 1990): 30–74; Carole Levin, *The Heart and Stomach of a King: Elizabeth I and the Politics of Sex and Power* (Philadelphia: University of Pennsylvania Press, 1994); John Rogers, "The Enclosure of Virginity: The Poetics of Sexual Abstinence in the English Revolution," in *Enclosure Acts: Sexuality, Property, and Culture in Early Modern England*, Richard Burt and John Michael Archer, eds. (Ithaca, NY: Cornell University Press, 1994); Kathryn Schwarz, "The Wrong Question: Thinking Through Virginity," *differences* 13/2 (Summer 2002); and Julia M. Walker, *The Elizabeth Icon, 1603–2003* (New York : Palgrave Macmillian, 2004.)

On sex, gender, religion, and economics in the early modern era, see: Susan Cahn, *Industry of Devotion: The Transformation of Women's Work in England, 1500–1660* (New York: Columbia University Press, 1987); Natalie Zemon Davis and Arlette Farge, eds., *A History of Women in the West*, vol. III, *Renaissance and Enlightenment Paradoxes* (Cambridge, MA: The Belknap Press of Harvard University Press, 1993); Philip Greven, *The Protestant Temperament: Patterns of Child-Rearing, Religious Experience, and the Self in Early America* (New York: Knopf, 1977); R. Marie Griffith, *Born Again Bodies: Flesh and Spirit in American Christianity* (Berkeley: University of California Press, 2004); Bridget Hill, *Women Alone: Spinsters in England 1660–1850* (New Haven, CT: Yale University Press, 2001); Theodora Jankowski, *Pure Resistance: Queer Virginity in Early Modern English Drama* (Philadelphia: University of Pennsylvania Press, 2000); Susan C. Karant-Nunn and Merry E. Weisner-Hanks, *Luther on Women: A Sourcebook* (New York: Cambridge University Press, 2003); Beth Kreitzer, *Reforming Mary: Changing Images of the Virgin Mary in Lutheran Sermons of the Sixteenth Century* (Oxford: Oxford University Press, 2004); Alister E. McGrath and Darren C. Marks, eds., *The Blackwell Companion to Protestantism* (Malden, MA: Blackwell Publishers, 2004); Donald K. McKim, *The Cambridge Companion to Martin Luther* (New York: Cambridge University Press, 2003); Peter Marshall, *Reformation England, 1480–1642* (London: Arnold, 2003); and Mark A. Noll, *America's God: From Jonathan Edwards to Abraham Lincoln* (New York: Oxford University Press, 2002).

The long and contentious history of the exploration and settlement of the Americas is chronicled not only in the work of historians but also in writings by those who were on the ground at the time. Among the sources that informed the North American sections of this chapter are: Robert Beverley, *The History and Present State of Virginia* (Chapel Hill: University of North Carolina Press, 1947); Gordon Brotherston, *Image of the New World: The American Continent Portrayed in Native Texts* (London: Thames and Hudson, 1979); Cornelia Hughes Dayton, *Women Before the Bar: Gender, Law and Society in Connecticut, 1639–1789* (Chapel Hill: University of North Caronlina Press, 1995); David Flaherty, "Law and the Enforcement of Morals in Early America," in *Perspectives in American History*, vol. 5, Donald Fleming and Bernard Bailyn, eds. (Cambridge, MA: Harvard University Press, 1971); Peter Charles Hoffer, *Law and People in Colonial America* (Baltimore: Johns Hopkins University Press, 1992); Lyle Koehler, *A Search for Power: The "Weaker Sex" in Seventeenth-Century New England* (Urbana: University of Illinois Press, 1980); Annette Kolodny, *The Lay of the Land: Metaphor as Experience and History in American Life and Letters* (Chapel Hill: University of North Carolina Press, 1975); John Lawson, *A New voyage to Carolina, containing the exact description and Natural History of that Country, together with the present state thereof and a Journal of a Thousand Miles Travel'd thro; several Nations of Indians, Giving a particular Account of their Customs, Manners, etc.* (Chapel Hill: University of North Carolina Press, 1967); Merril D. Smith, ed., *Sex and Sexuality in Early America* (New York: New York University Press, 1998); Thomas Morton, *New English Canaan* (New York: Arno Press, 1972); John Murrin, "Magistrates, Sinners and a Precarious Law" and "Liberty: Trial by Jury in Seventeenth-Century New England," in *Saints and Revolutionaries: Essays on Early American History*, Hall, et al., eds. (New York: W. W. Norton, 1984); Kirkpatrick Sale, *The Conquest of Paradise: Christopher Columbus and the Columbian Legacy* (New York: Penguin, 1991); Roger Thompson, *Sex in Middlesex: Popular Mores in a Massachusetts County, 1649–1699* (Amherst: University of Massachusetts Press, 1986); and Laurel Thatcher Ulrich, *Good Wives: Image and Reality in the Lives of Women in Northern New England, 1650–1750* (New York: Oxford University Press, 1980).

11: The Erotic Virgin

Some individual pornographic sources for this chapter are listed by title within the chapter. The others are both legion and much too ephemeral to bother listing them here.

On pornography and sexually explicit writings, and specifically that of the eighteenth and nineteenth centuries, see: Helen Lefkowitz Horowitz, *Rereading Sex: Battles over Sexual Knowledge and Suppression in Nineteenth-Century America* (New York: Alfred A. Knopf, 2002); Walter Kendrick, *The Secret Museum: Pornography in Modern Culture* (Berkeley: University of California Press, 1996); Julie Peakman, *Mighty Lewd Books: The Development of Pornography in Eighteenth-century England* (London: Palgrave Macmillan, 2003); Ronald Pearsall, *The Worm in the Bud: The World of Victorian Sexuality* (New York: Penguin Books, 1983); Ellen Bayuk Rosenman, *Unauthorized Pleasures: Accounts of Victorian Erotic Experience* (Ithaca: Cornell University Press, 2003); Lisa Z. Sigel, *Governing Pleasures: Pornography and Social Change in England, 1815–1914* (New Brunswick, NJ: Rutgers University Press, 2002).

The history of English and American sexuality-related philanthropic and legislative reform, as well as historical attitudes concerning sexuality and gender generally, are detailed in:

Barret-Ducroq, *Love in the Time of Victoria: Sexuality and Desire Among Working-Class Men and Women in Nineteenth-Century London*, John Howe, trans. (New York: Penguin, 1991); Lucy Bland, *Banishing the Beast: Sexuality and the Early Feminists* (New York: The New Press, 1995); John D'Emilio and Estelle Freedman, *Intimate Matters: A History of Sexuality in America* (New York: Harper & Row, 1988); Peter Gay, *Education of the Senses*, vol. I, *The Bourgeois Experience: Victoria to Freud* (New York: Oxford University Press, 1984); Linda Hirshman and Jane Larson, *Hard Bargains: The Politics of Sex* (New York: Oxford University Press, 1998); Michael Mason, *The Making of Victorian Sexuality* (New York: Oxford University Press, 1994); Michelle Oberman, "Turning Girls into Women: Re-Evaluating Modern Statutory Rape Law," *Journal of Criminal Law and Criminology* 85 (1994): 15, 31–36; Roy Porter and Lesley A. Hall, *The Facts of Life: The Creation of Sexual Knowledge in Britain, 1650–1950* (New Haven, CT: Yale University Press, 1995); Cynthia Eagle Russett, *Sexual Science: The Victorian Construction of Womanhood* (Cambridge, MA: Harvard University Press, 1989); Christine Stansell, *City of Women: Sex and Class in New York, 1789–1860* (New York: Knopf, 1986); and Judith Walkowitz, *City of Dreadful Delight: Narratives of Sexual Danger in Late-Victorian London* (London: Virago, 1992).

A selection of worthwhile works on the history and definition of childhood, as well as the roles of the family, the community, and the state in the lives of children, include: David Archard, *Children: Rights and Childhood* (London: Routledge, 1993); Phillippe Aries, *Centuries of Childhood*, Robert Baldick, trans. (New York: Vintage, 1962); Marjorie Heins, *Not in Front of the Children: "Indecency," Censorship, and the Innocence of Youth* (New York: Hill and Wang, 2001); Anne Higonnet, *Pictures of Innocence: The History and Crisis of Ideal Childhood* (London: Thames and Hudson, 1998); Linda A. Pollock, *Forgotten Children: Parent-Child Relations from 1500 to 1900* (Cambridge: Cambridge University Press, 1983); C. John Somerville, *The Rise and Fall of Childhood* (Beverly Hills, CA: Sage, 1982); and Lawrence Stone, *The Family, Sex, and Marriage in England, 1500–1800* (Harmondsworth, U.K.: Penguin, 1977).

12: The Day Virginity Died?

On the rise of scientific gynecology and sexology, including various examples of the rise itself, see: Bullough, *Science in the Bedroom: A History of Sex Research* (New York: Basic Books, 1994); Oliver Butterfield, *Sex Life in Marriage* (New York: Emerson Books, Inc., 1940); Alan Hunt, "The Great Masturbation Panic and the Discourses of Moral Regulation in Nineteenth and Early Twentieth-Century Britain," *Journal of the History of Sexuality* 8/4 (1998): 575–615; Alfred Kinsey, Wardell Pomeroy, and Clyde Martin, *Sexual Behavior in the Human Male* (Philadelphia: W. B. Saunders Company, 1948); Kinsey, et al., *Sexual Behavior in the Human Female* (Philadelphia: W. B. Saunders Company, 1953); Franziska Lamott, "Virginität als Fetisch: Kulturelle Codierung und rechtliche Normierung der Jungfräulichkeit um die Jarhrhundertwende," *Tel Aviver Jahrbuch für Deutsche Geschichte* (1992): 153–70; Ferdinand Lundberg and Marynia Farnham, *Modern Woman: The Lost Sex* (New York: Harper & Brothers Publishers, 1947); Heldi Rimke and Alan Hunt, "From Sinners to Degenerates: The Medicalization of Morality in the Nineteenth Century," *History of the*

Human Sciences 15/1 (2002): 59–88; Robertson, "Signs, Marks, and Private Parts: Doctors, Legal Discourses, and Evidence of Rape in the United States, 1823–1930," *Journal of the History of Sexuality* 8/3 (1998): 345–88; and Theodor van de Velde, *Ideal Marriage: Its Physiology and Technique,* Stella Browne, trans. (New York: Random House, 1930).

The rise of the "new woman" resulted in a great deal of writing, both historical and otherwise. The following sources are specifically relevant to the sexual and sex-political sides of women's rights and female emancipation: Beth L. Bailey, *From Front Porch to Back Seat: Courtship in Twentieth-Century America* (Baltimore: Johns Hopkins University Press, 1998); Joan Jacobs Brumberg, *The Body Project: An Intimate History of American Girls* (New York: Random House, 1997); and " 'Ruined' Girls: Changing Community Responses to Illegitimacy in Upstate New York, 1890–1920," *Journal of Social History* 18 (Winter 1984): 247–72; Dickinson, "Bicycling for Women from the Standpoint of the Gynecologist," *American Journal of Obstetrics* 21 (1895): 25; Ellen Garvey, "Reframing the Bicycle: Advertising-Supported Magazines and Scorching Women," *American Quarterly* 47/1 (March 1995): 66–101; Christina Simmons, "Women's Power in Sex Radical Challenges to Marriage in the Early-Twentieth-Century United States," *Feminist Studies* 29/1 (Spring 2003): 169–98; Penny Tinker, "Cause for Concern: Young Women and Leisure, 1930–1950," *Women's History Review* 12/2 (2003): 233–59.

Three excellent discussions of the history of contraceptives are: Hera Cook, *The Long Sexual Revolution: English Women, Sex, and Contraception 1800–1975* (Oxford: Oxford University Press, 2004); Lara V. Marks, *Sexual Chemistry: A History of the Contraceptive Pill* (New Haven, CT: Yale University Press, 2001); and Elizabeth Siegel Watkins, *On The Pill: A Social History of Oral Contraceptives 1950–1970* (Baltimore: Johns Hopkins University Press, 1998).

The so-called sexual revolution of the 1960s and 1970s spawned its own supply of commentators and historians. The following works are useful, informative, and, most important, reliable: David Allyn, *Make Love, Not War: The Sexual Revolution, an Unfettered History* (Boston: Little, Brown, 2000); Bullough and Bullough, *Sexual Attitudes: Myths and Realities* (Amherst, NY: Prometheus Books, 1995); David Buss, et al., "International Preferences in Selecting Mates: A Study of 37 Cultures," *Journal of Cross-Cultural Psychology* 21/1 (March 1990): 5–47; D'Emilio and Freedman, *Intimate Matters: A History of Sexuality in America*; Jane Gerhard, *Desiring Revolution: Second-Wave Feminism and the Rewriting of American Sexual Thought, 1920–1982* (New York: Columbia University Press, 2001); Paula Kamen, *Her Way: Young Women Remake the Sexual Revolution* (New York: New York University Press, 2000); and Judith A. Levine, *Harmful to Minors: The Perils of Protecting Children from Sex* (Minneapolis: University of Minnesota Press, 2002).

The ongoing controversies over abstinence education and related legislation in the United States continue to generate literature, of which this is a highly limited sample: Bearman and Brückner, "After the Promise: The STD Consequences of Adolescent Virginity Pledges," *Journal of Adolescent Health* 36/4 (April 2005): 271–78; Bearman and Brückner, "Promising the Future: Virginity Pledges and First Intercourse," *The American Journal of Sociology* 106/4 (January 2001): 859–912; Ted Carter, *Evaluation Report for the Kansas Abstinence Education Program* (Topeka: Kansas Department of Health and Environment, November 2004); Centers for Disease Control, *Youth Risk Behavior Surveillance Survey* (2001); Lisa

J. Crockett, C. Raymond Bingham, et al., "Timing of First Sexual Intercourse: The Role of Social Control, Social Learning, and Problem Behavior," *Journal of Youth and Adolescence* 25/1 (1996): 89–111; J.F. deGaston, L. Jensen, and S. Weed, "A Closer Look at Adolescent Sexual Activity," *Journal of Youth and Adolescence* 24/6 (1995): 465–79; Patricia Goodson, et al., *Abstinence Education Evaluation Phase 5: Technical Report* (College Station: Texas A&M University, Department of Health & Kinesiology, 2004); Marjorie Heins, "Sex, Lies, and Politics: Congress Is Poised to Reauthorize Fearmongering 'Abstinence-Only' Sex Ed," *The Nation* 272/18 (May 7, 2001); Kaiser Family Foundation, *Issue Update: Sex Education in the U.S.: Policy and Politics* (March 2002); Kaiser Family Foundation and *Seventeen* magazine, *SexSmarts: National Survey of Teens: Virginity and the First Time*, 2003; Kaiser Family Foundation and *YM* magazine, *The Kaiser Family Foundation and YM Magazine 1998 National Survey of Teens* (1998); Douglas Kirby, "Do Abstinence-Only Programs Delay the Initiation of Sex Among Young People and Reduce Teen Pregnancy?" (Washington, D.C.: The National Campaign to Prevent Teen Pregnancy, October 2002); Kirby, "Emerging Answers" (Washington, D.C.: The National Campaign to Prevent Teen Pregnancy, 2001); Jonathan D. Klein and the Committee on Adolescence, American Academy of Pediatrics, "Adolescent Pregnancy: Current Trends and Issues," *Pediatrics* 116 no. 1 (July 1, 2005): 281–86; R. Mayer and L. Kantor, "1995–1996 Trends in Opposition to Comprehensive Sexuality Education in Public Schools in the United States," *SIECUS Report* 24/1 (1996); Josh McDowell, *Why True Love Waits: The Definitive Book on How to Help Your Kids Resist Sexual Pressure* (Wheaton, IL: Tyndale House Publishers, 2002); Karen Kay Perrin and Sharon Bernecki DeJoy, "Abstinence-Only Education: How We Got Here and Where We're Going," *Journal of Public Health Policy* 24/3–4 (2004): 445–59; Robert E. Rector, "The Effectiveness of Abstinence Education Programs in Reducing Sexual Activity Among Youth," Backgrounder no. 1533 (Washington, D.C.: The Heritage Foundation, April 2002); Lisa Remez, "Oral Sex Among Adolescents: Is it Sex or Is It Abstinence," *Family Planning Perspectives* 32/6 (November/December 2000); Edward Smith, Jacinda Dariotis, and Susan Potter, *Evaluation of the Pennsylvania Abstinence Education and Related Services Initiative: 1998–2002* (Philadelphia: Maternal and Child Health Bureau of Family Health, Pennsylvania Department of Health, January 2003); Adam Sonfield and Rachel Benson Gold, "States' Implementation of the Section 510 Abstinence Education Program, FY 1999," *Family Planning Perspectives* 33 (2001): 166–71; and Jackie West, "(Not) Talking About Sex: Youth, Identity, and Sexuality," *The Sociological Review* (1999): 525–47.

ACKNOWLEDGMENTS

I owe a huge debt of gratitude to the friends and colleagues who read and critiqued chapter drafts, passed on bits of virgin lore, pointed me to sources, advised me in their academic specialties, helped me with translations, hung out with me while I watched several seasons of *Buffy the Vampire Slayer*, and generally helped me stay sane throughout this long and frequently maddening project. Thanks are due to many, but in particular I wish to acknowledge the contributions of Rahne Alexander, S. Bear Bergman, Heather Corinna, Dr. Leigh Ann Craig, Melissa Fox, Roxane Gay, Dr. Lesley A. Hall, Laura Waters Jackson, Dr. Helen King, Dr. Kathleen Kennedy, Keridwen Luis, Dr. Sarah Monette, Moira Russell, Danya Ruttenberg, and Elizabeth Merrill Tamny. I must also thank the interns who assisted me at various points during this project, Kristen Simpson, Judy Berman, Kate McGill, and the incomparable Beverly Rivero. Additionally, I am grateful to Philip Cronenwett of the Massachusetts Institute of Technology Dibner Library, Harry Finley of the Museum of Menstruation, Erin Clements Rushing of the Smithsonian Institution Libraries, and Bettina Smith of the Folger Shakespeare Library for their expert referrals and aid. My deep appreciation also goes to those by whose efforts my work became the book you hold in your hands: Colin Dickerman, Lindsay Sagnette, and Greg Villepique of Bloomsbury USA, and especially Christopher Schelling. Any errors or inaccuracies that remain in this book are mine alone.

My deep thanks also go to a handful of fellow virginologists, on whose exemplary historical, archival, and medical work I have drawn heavily throughout these pages and without which I would have been unable to write this book. They include Abby Berenson, Peter Brown, John Bugge, Laura Carpenter, Theodora Jankowski, Kathleen Coyne Kelly, Helen King, Helen Rodnite Lemay, Marie Loughlin, JoAnn McNamara, Aline Rousselle, and Giulia Sissa.

The Institute for Teaching and Research on Women at Towson University, Towson, Maryland, and its director, Dr. Karen Dugger, welcomed me as Scholar of the Institute during 2004–2005. This book owes a great deal to ITROW's kind patronage of this independent scholar, and for providing that "room of one's own" for a critical period of time.

Also to be thanked are Johns Hopkins University's Program for the Study of Women and Gender, the Johns Hopkins Department of Philosophy, the Department of History at Virginia Commonwealth University, the University of Delaware, and West Virginia University, all of which at various times in my research and writing process provided me with welcome opportunities to get out of my solitary office and present some of this material to living, breathing, interactive audiences.

The various libraries of the Johns Hopkins University and the Library of Congress, the places where I did the bulk of the research for this book, were perhaps my most important institutional benefactors of all. The existence of grand libraries like these is a credit to our species.

Lastly, I must publicly thank Malcolm Gin for his impeccable tolerance of my long hours and ever-expanding collection of research materials, for distracting me as needed with *Star Trek*, *The Thin Man* movies, and Katamari Damacy, and, last but very much not least, for a decade (and counting!) of loving partnership.

INDEX

A NOTE ON THE AUTHOR

Hanne Blank is a writer, historian, and public speaker whose activities have taken her from university lecture halls to the pages of *Penthouse*. An independent scholar, she has served in various capacities at several institutions of higher learning, most recently as the 2004–2005 Scholar of the Institute for Teaching and Research on Women, Towson University, Maryland. A former professional classical musician, she lives in Baltimore.